# Learning Salesforce Visual Workflow and Process Builder

## Second Edition

Click your way to automating various business processes using Salesforce Visual Workflow and Process Builder

**Rakesh Gupta**

BIRMINGHAM - MUMBAI

# Learning Salesforce Visual Workflow and Process Builder

## *Second Edition*

Copyright © 2017 Packt Publishing

All rights reserved. No part of this book may be reproduced, stored in a retrieval system, or transmitted in any form or by any means, without the prior written permission of the publisher, except in the case of brief quotations embedded in critical articles or reviews.

Every effort has been made in the preparation of this book to ensure the accuracy of the information presented. However, the information contained in this book is sold without warranty, either express or implied. Neither the author, nor Packt Publishing, and its dealers and distributors will be held liable for any damages caused or alleged to be caused directly or indirectly by this book.

Packt Publishing has endeavored to provide trademark information about all of the companies and products mentioned in this book by the appropriate use of capitals. However, Packt Publishing cannot guarantee the accuracy of this information.

First published: April 2015

Second edition: May 2017

Production reference: 1120517

Published by Packt Publishing Ltd.
Livery Place
35 Livery Street
Birmingham
B3 2PB, UK.
ISBN 978-1-78728-499-9

www.packtpub.com

# Credits

**Author**
Rakesh Gupta

**Reviewers**
Chris Edwards
Jeff May

**Commissioning Editor**
Aaron Lazar

**Acquisition Editor**
Chaitanya Nair

**Content Development Editor**
Kinnari Sanghvi

**Technical Editor**
Vivek Pala

**Copy Editor**
Stuti Srivastava

**Project Coordinator**
Vaidehi Sawant

**Proofreader**
Safis Editing

**Indexer**
Francy Puthiry

**Graphics**
Abhinash Sahu

**Production Coordinator**
Arvindkumar Gupta

# Foreword

One of the undeniable trends of the 21st century has been "data is king". Our ability to collect and store data is reaching new heights every year. In 2000, companies knew who their customers were and how to contact them by phone, fax, or e-mail. In 2015, we have the technology to not only know who our customers are, but what each customer is doing with our products. Customers can submit feedback and help with requests with the click of a button, and there are "service needed" alerts built into products and equipment in nearly all industries. The "Internet of Things" allows a level of data collection that far exceeds our ability to review and respond.

Successful businesses know that the only thing worse than not knowing what your customers and products need is knowing but not doing anything about it. Data interpretation and response are just as important as collection and analysis. One of the most effective ways to ensure an appropriate and timely response is to let our business technology systems react to the data using the same business rules we would apply if we had the time to review the data ourselves.

This book, *Learning Salesforce Visual Workflow and Process Builder, Second Edition*, teaches Salesforce administrators how to use the business process automation features available in Salesforce to do just that—detect and react to data as it's being collected by your employees, your customers, and your products. These powerful tools can be confgured by admins (no development teams and custom coding needed), maintained by admins, and be quickly modified to meet the ongoing needs of your business.

Salesforce, a leading global business technology platform, knows that the key to their customers' success is the ability to understand and interact with data. With three releases each year, Salesforce consistently adds and enhances features that help maximize the value of each piece of data and customer contact. The Spring '15 release was no exception. Enhancements to Visual Flow and the introduction of the powerful new Process Builder put even complex business process automation into the hands of non-programming system administrators.

The author, Rakesh Gupta, is a long-time veteran of the IT industry and has been part of the evolution, from raw data collection to information analysis. His previous books explain how to collect and share data using the Salesforce platform and also how to report and analyze that data. With this book, Rakesh adds another key piece to the data–to-information cycle: data interpretation and response.

Using the techniques explained in this book, Salesforce administrators will be able to provide truly responsive business processes to their operational teams—putting data in the right format, in front of the right people, and at the right time—all without developing custom code.

**Jeff May**

Salesforce MVP and Partner @ Miss The Iceberg

# About the Author

**Rakesh Gupta** is a graduate of SRM University, Chennai, with a degree in information technology. He previously worked at iGate Computer Systems Limited (now part of Capgemini). He is a three-time Salesforce MVP, evangelist, Salesforce trainer, blogger, and works as a Salesforce solution architect. He has been working on the Salesforce.com platform for over 6 years. He is from Katihar, Bihar, and lives in Alpharetta, USA. He is the co-author of *Developing Applications with Salesforce Chatter* and *Salesforce.com Customization Handbook*, both by Packt. He is the author of *Learning Salesforce Visual Workflow* and *Mastering Salesforce CRM Administration*, also by Packt. He is also a technical reviewer of *Learning Force.com Application Development* and *Mastering Application Development with Force.com*, Packt Publishing.

He's best known as an automation champion in the Salesforce ecosystem, as he has written over 110 articles on Visual Workflow and Process Builder to show how someone can use them to minimize code usage. He is one of the biggest Visual Workflow and Process Builder experts in the industry. He has trained more than 600 professionals around the globe and conducted corporate trainings. He currently holds nine certifications in Salesforce. He works on all the aspects of Salesforce and is an expert in data migration, process automation, configuration, customization, and integration. He is the leader of the Navi Mumbai and Nashik Salesforce developer user groups in India. He is also the initiator of the Mumbai Salesforce user group, and the initiator of the biweekly online webinar Automation Hour (`automationhour.com`). He is very passionate about Force.com and shares information through various channels, including the Salesforce Success Community and his blog at `https://automationchampion.com/`.

You can follow him on Twitter at `@rakeshistom` and `@automationchamp`.

*First and foremost, I would like to thank my parents, Kedar Nath Gupta and Madhuri Gupta, and my sister, Sarika Gupta, for having patience with me for taking yet another challenge, which decreases the amount of time I can spend with them. They have been my inspiration and motivation for continuing to improve my knowledge and move my career forward. I would like to thank Packt Publishing for giving me this opportunity to share my knowledge via this book. I would also like to thank my friend Meenakshi Kalra for helping me while I was writing this book. A special thanks to all my well-wishers and friends. I would like to especially thank Jeff May (Salesforce MVP) and Chris Edwards (Salesforce MVP); without you, this book would never find its way to the Web. At the end, I'm grateful to every member of Salesforce Ohana--hope you will find this book useful!*

# About the Reviewer

Chris Edwards is a Salesforce MVP, user group leader, writer, and holder of 12 Salesforce certifications, including Application Architect. He has been working on the Salesforce platform for 7 years as an administrator, consultant, and architect, and is currently using cloud solutions to connect people to cures through his work as a Solution Architect in the healthcare industry with Mavens (www.mavens.com).

*Uncountable thanks, as ever, to my (much) better half, Natalie, who makes me feel lucky to be alive--in the sense that she's forever leaving sharp knives blade-up in the dishwasher but hasn't succeeded in mortally wounding me quite yet.*

# www.PacktPub.com

For support files and downloads related to your book, please visit www.PacktPub.com.

Did you know that Packt offers eBook versions of every book published, with PDF and ePub files available? You can upgrade to the eBook version at www.PacktPub.com and as a print book customer, you are entitled to a discount on the eBook copy. Get in touch with us at service@packtpub.com for more details.

At www.PacktPub.com, you can also read a collection of free technical articles, sign up for a range of free newsletters and receive exclusive discounts and offers on Packt books and eBooks.

https://www.packtpub.com/mapt

Get the most in-demand software skills with Mapt. Mapt gives you full access to all Packt books and video courses, as well as industry-leading tools to help you plan your personal development and advance your career.

## Why subscribe?

- Fully searchable across every book published by Packt
- Copy and paste, print, and bookmark content
- On demand and accessible via a web browser

# Customer Feedback

Thanks for purchasing this Packt book. At Packt, quality is at the heart of our editorial process. To help us improve, please leave us an honest review on this book's Amazon page at https://goo.gl/97OEal.

If you'd like to join our team of regular reviewers, you can e-mail us at customerreviews@packtpub.com. We award our regular reviewers with free eBooks and videos in exchange for their valuable feedback. Help us be relentless in improving our products!

# Table of Contents

# Preface

We wrote this book for Salesforce developers, administrators, customers, and partners to get started with Salesforce Flow and Process Builder. This book will act as both a reference for the administrator and a configuration guide for the newbie customer who want to develop an application in Salesforce without code, using Process Builder and Flow.

This book covers all the possible features of Salesforce Flow and Process Builder. We have taken the hands-on approach with real-time scenarios so that you can get a complete overview of these topics. At the end of every chapter, you will find key points and exercises for practice. Salesforce CRM is a service by Salesforce.com, which is commercial, but all the material in this book is developed using the developer edition.

## What this book covers

Chapter 1, *Getting Started with Visual Workflow*, starts with basic knowledge of Salesforce Visual Workflow. We will then pick a few business examples and see how to use Flow instead of Apex code to solve them, and we'll the discuss the benefits of using Salesforce Visual Workflow. You will also get an overview of the Flow canvas and its elements.

Chapter 2, *Creating Flows through Point and Click*, introduces you to the various variables available in Flow, and then proceeds toward the designing of Flow using the **Screen**, **Wait**, **Assignment**, and **Decision** elements.

Chapter 3, *Manipulating Records in Visual Workflow*, talks about constant and Text template in Flow and then takes you toward the manipulation of data using **Record** elements. We will see how to send an e-mail from Flow. We will also cover various ways to access the Flow.

Chapter 4, *Debugging and New Ways to Call a Flow*, serves as the climax of the book, where you will learn how to debug and launch a Flow. We will cover various ways to set the Flow variable using the Visualforce Pages and apex.

Chapter 5, *Developing Applications with Process Builder*, helps you get a complete understanding of the Process Builder designer and all the actions available inside it.

Chapter 6, *Building Efficient and Performance Optimized Processes*, helps you understand Process Builder and its concepts, such as how to use Custom Metadata Types, Custom Permissions, and Custom Labels with Process Builder. We will also cover some key concepts, such as using multiple groups of actions and how to call an Apex class from Process Builder.

Chapter 7, *Building Applications without Code*, starts by introducing you to the various ways to deepen the Flow. We will also cover key elements such as Login Flow using the **Wait** element in the Flow. We will also cover how you can use custom settings in the Flow and create a scheduled job that will run on a daily basis.

Chapter 8, *Enabling Flows to Work with Lightning Experience*, explains how you can use new or existing Flows to work with Salesforce Lightning Experience.

# What you need for this book

Visual Workflow is available in Enterprise, Performance, Unlimited, and Developer Editions. The requirements are as follows:

- Windows Internet Explorer versions 8 through 11 (6 and 7 are not supported), Google Chrome, or Mozilla Firefox
- Adobe Flash Player Version 10.1 and later, the minimum version required to run the Cloud Flow Designer is 10.0
- A minimum browser resolution of 1024 x 768

# Who this book is for

This book is intended for those who want to use Flow to automate their business requirements by click, not code. Whether you are new to Salesforce or you are a seasoned expert, you will be able to master both Flow and Process Builder. Since Salesforce maintains an incredibly user-friendly interface, no previous experience in computer coding or programming is required. The things that you do require are your brain, your computer with a modern web browser, a free Salesforce developer org, and just basic knowledge of Salesforce.

# Conventions

In this book, you will find a number of text styles that distinguish between different kinds of information. Here are some examples of these styles and an explanation of their meaning.

Code words in text, database table names, folder names, filenames, file extensions, pathnames, dummy URLs, user input, and Twitter handles are shown as follows: "The next lines of code read the link and assign it to the `BeautifulSoup` function."

A block of code is set as follows:

```
<style type="text/css">
.FlowDate {
  color: Blue;
  font-family: Courier New;
}
</style>
```

**New terms** and **important words** are shown in bold. Words that you see on the screen, for example, in menus or dialog boxes, appear in the text like this: "The next task is to add a new custom button on the campaign page layout. Navigate to **Setup** | **Build** | **Customize** | **Campaigns** | **Page Layouts**, and click on the **Edit** link."

Warnings or important notes appear in a box like this.

Tips and tricks appear like this.

# Reader feedback

Feedback from our readers is always welcome. Let us know what you think about this book-what you liked or disliked. Reader feedback is important for us as it helps us develop titles that you will really get the most out of.

To send us general feedback, simply e-mail `feedback@packtpub.com`, and mention the book's title in the subject of your message.

If there is a topic that you have expertise in and you are interested in either writing or contributing to a book, see our author guide at `www.packtpub.com/authors`.

# Customer support

Now that you are the proud owner of a Packt book, we have a number of things to help you to get the most from your purchase.

# Downloading the example code

You can download the example code files for this book from your account at http://www.packtpub.com. If you purchased this book elsewhere, you can visit http://www.packtpub.com/support and register to have the files e-mailed directly to you.

You can download the code files by following these steps:

1. Log in or register to our website using your e-mail address and password.
2. Hover the mouse pointer on the **SUPPORT** tab at the top.
3. Click on **Code Downloads & Errata**.
4. Enter the name of the book in the **Search** box.
5. Select the book for which you're looking to download the code files.
6. Choose from the drop-down menu where you purchased this book from.
7. Click on **Code Download**.

Once the file is downloaded, please make sure that you unzip or extract the folder using the latest version of:

- WinRAR / 7-Zip for Windows
- Zipeg / iZip / UnRarX for Mac
- 7-Zip / PeaZip for Linux

The code bundle for the book is also hosted on GitHub at https://github.com/PacktPublishing/Learning-Salesforce-Visual-Workflow-and-Process-Builder. We also have other code bundles from our rich catalog of books and videos available at https://github.com/PacktPublishing/. Check them out!

# Errata

Although we have taken every care to ensure the accuracy of our content, mistakes do happen. If you find a mistake in one of our books-maybe a mistake in the text or the code-we would be grateful if you could report this to us. By doing so, you can save other readers from frustration and help us improve subsequent versions of this book. If you find any errata, please report them by visiting http://www.packtpub.com/submit-errata, selecting your book, clicking on the **Errata Submission Form** link, and entering the details of your errata. Once your errata are verified, your submission will be accepted and the errata will be uploaded to our website or added to any list of existing errata under the Errata section of that title.

To view the previously submitted errata, go to https://www.packtpub.com/books/content/support and enter the name of the book in the search field. The required information will appear under the **Errata** section.

# Piracy

Piracy of copyrighted material on the Internet is an ongoing problem across all media. At Packt, we take the protection of our copyright and licenses very seriously. If you come across any illegal copies of our works in any form on the Internet, please provide us with the location address or website name immediately so that we can pursue a remedy.

Please contact us at copyright@packtpub.com with a link to the suspected pirated material.

We appreciate your help in protecting our authors and our ability to bring you valuable content.

# Questions

If you have a problem with any aspect of this book, you can contact us at questions@packtpub.com, and we will do our best to address the problem.

# 1
# Getting Started with Visual Workflow

This chapter starts with an overview of Visual Workflow (also called **Flow**) and its benefits, which take the discussion forward to the various business requirements where we can use Flow. We will discuss various business problems and how we can develop an application without using code to solve them. By the end of this chapter, you will have learned various ways to invoke a Flow and the fundamentals of Visual Workflow.

In the next few chapters, you will be briefed about various concepts related to Visual Workflow and learn numerous ways to create point-and-click solutions without using code. We will also see different ways to streamline our sales process and automate our business process using a Flow. In the last few chapters, we will go through how to automatically launch a Flow using Process Builder, how to create reusable processes using Process Builder, and how to enable Visual Workflows to work with Lightning Experience.

We will cover the following topics in this chapter:

- Business problems
- The benefits of Visual Workflow
- System requirements for using Visual Workflow
- An overview of the Visual Workflow life cycle
- An overview of the Cloud Flow Designer
- An overview of Visual Workflow building blocks
- The various ways to invoke a Flow
- Visual Workflow outcome behavior

Visual Workflow is a drag and drop interface that allows you to automate business processes by creating applications using clicks not code. Using Visual Workflow, we can create, update, edit, and delete records as well as send e-mail, submit records for approval, post to chatter, and take user input in Salesforce and then make those Flows available to the business users or systems. Visual Workflow can execute business processes, interact with the database, invoke `Apex` classes (an Apex class implements the `Process.Plugin` interface), and create a series of screens to take user input in order to collect and update data in Salesforce; Flows can also be built with no user interface to allow them to be run from automated processes.

# Business problems

As a Salesforce administrator or developer, you may get business requirements from businesses to streamline the processes. Many of them are achievable using **out-of-the-box (OOB)** concepts, and for others, we have to use Apex or Visualforce pages. Visual Workflow gives us another method that will let us implement many business processes without needing custom coding. A few examples are discussed in the following sections.

# Business use case 1

Sara Bareilles is working as a Vice President, Sales, in a company named Universal Containers. She wants to auto-close all the open opportunities with the **Closed Lost** stage, when an account `out of business` field (that is, custom field) is checked.

There are several ways to solve the business requirement; these are mentioned in the following sections.

# Solution 1 - using an Apex trigger

Because this requirement means that many child records (opportunities) need to be updated when a parent record (`Account`) is edited, we can't achieve the preceding business requirement using the Workflow rule. The next possibility is to use an Apex trigger. Generally, a developer writes an Apex trigger on the `Account` object to update all the open opportunities when an account's custom field, `out of business`, gets updated to `True`. The following is the sample code:

```
trigger UpdateRelatedOpportunites on Account (after update) {
  for (Account AccountToUpdate : trigger.new)
    {
        If (AccountToUpdate.Out_Of_Business__c==True)
        {
        // Your logic;
        }
    }
}
```

In addition, you'll need a test class and then use a change set, Force.com IDE or Force.com Migration Tool, to deploy the trigger and test classes to production. This also means that any change to the business logic will require more development work.

# Solution 2 - a combination of Visual Workflow and Process Builder

Another way to achieve the same business requirement is to use a combination of Visual Workflow and Process Builder. Here is the description of the next screenshot:

- **Section highlighted as 1**: In this, a sample Flow updates all the open Opportunity stages to Closed-Lost related to an account that is marked as out of business.
- **Section highlighted as 2**: This is the process on the **Account** object; it will always fire whenever an account record gets created or updated.

The following screenshot represents solutions for a similar business scenario by using Visual Workflow and Process Builder:

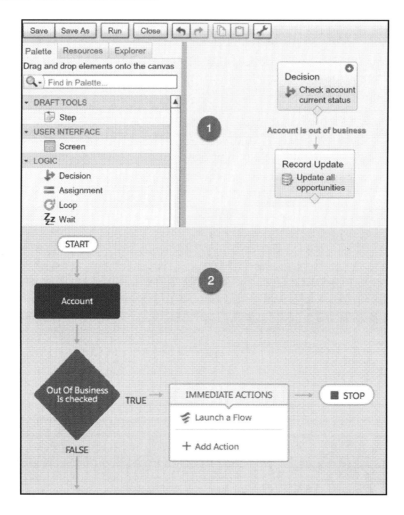

Process Builder is one of the ways to automate complex business requirements using click not code, similar to the Workflow rule and Visual Workflow. The benefit of using this approach is that you can easily follow the Salesforce best practice to create one process per object and use Visual Workflow to manage logic for multiple business requirements. We will discuss this in Chapter 5, *Developing Applications with Process Builder*, and Chapter 7, *Building Applications without Code.*

# Solution 3- using Process Builder

Another way to achieve the same business requirement is to use a process created on Process Builder. Here is the description of the next screenshot:

- A process on the **Account** object, which will fire when the out of business checkbox is checked
- Then the **Update Records** action will be fired, and it will update all the open Opportunity stages to the Closed-Lost stage related to an account which is marked as out of business

The following screenshot represents solutions for a similar business scenario using Process Builder:

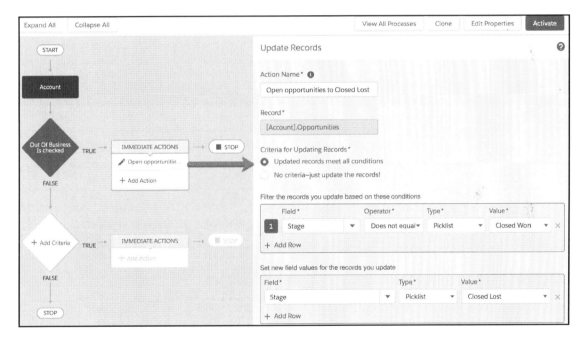

Process Builder allows you to automate complex business processes using click not code.

# Business use case 2

Robby Williams is working as a customer success manager in Universal Containers. He wants to send a reminder e-mail on a weekly basis to all the users who don't have a profile picture on Chatter.

Again, there are plenty of ways to solve this requirement. Some of the ways are as follows.

# Solution 1 - using Apex

We can't achieve this goal by the Workflow rule. For this, we have to write an Apex class that implements the `Schedulable` interface for the class and then use **Schedule Apex** to run it on a regular basis. The following is the code for this Apex class:

```
global class SendChatterEmail implements Schedulable
{
    global SendChatterEmail (){
      // Batch Constructor
    }

    // Start Method
    global Database.QueryLocator start(){
      /* Use SOQL query to get the records you want to operate upon
      select Id, fullPhotoUrl from User where isactive = true AND
FullPhotoUrl like '%photo/005%'*/
    }

    // Execute Logic
    global void execute(){
      // perform the operation

    }

    global void finish(){
      // Logic which we want to execute at finish
    }
}
```

# Solution 2 - a combination of Visual Workflow and Process Builder

An alternative way to accomplish the same business requirement is to use a combination of Visual Workflow and Process Builder. Here is the description of the next screenshot:

- **Section highlighted as 1**: This represents a Flow to send e-mail alerts to all users who do not have profile pictures on Chatter
- **Section highlighted as 2**: This represents the **Flows** action from Process Builder on a custom object (reminder notification) to trigger our Flow

The following screenshot represents the solution for business scenario 2 using Visual Workflow and Process Builder:

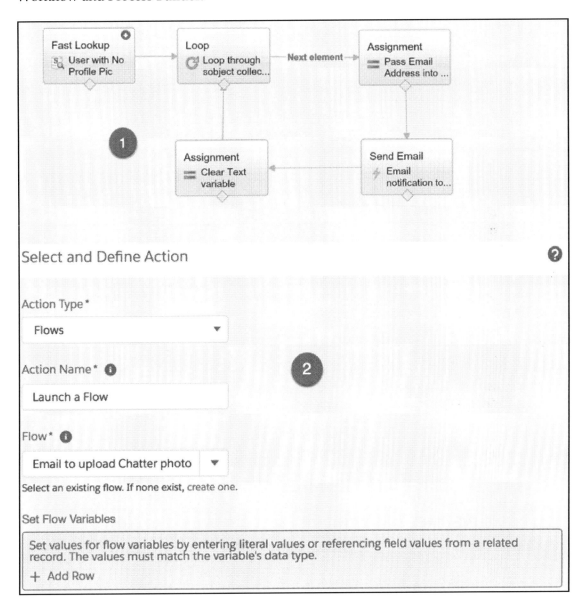

# The benefits of Visual Workflow

There are certain benefits of using Visual Workflow. They are as follows:

- It allows you to create an automated business process using clicks not code.
- Visual Workflow does not require coding, and even if you do not know Apex code, you can still develop business processes.
- Using screens, fields, and choices, you can implement complex business processes to make sure that your users are entering data in the right format.
- Through Visual Workflow, you can manipulate data for certain objects that are not available for the Workflow rule or Process Builder. For example, when a "contact role" is created or updated as primary for an opportunity, then create a new task.
- It allows you to auto submit records for approval.
- It allows you to apply assignment rules on leads or cases that are created by API calls.
- You can post messages on Chatter. For example, if the Opportunity status is changed to Closed-Won, post a message on the Chatter group.
- It allows you to embed the Flow into the Visualforce page, and you can expose it for unauthenticated access using the `Force.com` site.
- Once you embed your Flow into the Visualforce page, it allows you to use HTML, CSS, JavaScript, and other Visualforce components.
- It can be easily maintained by non-developers.
- Since it is not code, you don't need to write test classes.
- You can make changes directly to your production organization, just like other configuration changes.
- Every time unhandled processes fail or an error occurs in the Flow, the author will get an e-mail from Salesforce with the error details.
- Using the debug log, you can debug your Flow. Visual Workflow also has a built-in debugging tool. To open the debug window, press *Ctrl + Shift + M* (on PC) or *command + shift + M* (on Mac).
- It allows you to invoke the Apex class that implements the `Process.Plugin` interface.

# System requirements for using Visual Workflow

Visual Workflow is available in Lightning Enterprise, Lightning Unlimited, and Developer Editions. You can access Flow on any platform. The requirements are as follows:

- Windows Internet Explorer versions 8 through 11 (6 and 7 are not supported), Google Chrome, or Mozilla Firefox.
- Adobe Flash Player Version 10.1 and later. The minimum version required to run the Cloud Flow Designer is 10.0.
- A minimum browser resolution of 1024 x 768.

# An overview of the Visual Workflow lifecycle

The Cloud Flow Designer is a tool to create Flows, configure screens, and define business logic for your Flows without writing a single line of code. Visual Workflow has three different parts, which are as follows:

- **Design**: This allows you to create the Flows using the Flow Designer, which has a drag and drop user interface that allows you to draw the Flow structure and configure how it runs, without writing a single line of code.
- **Administration**: Once you have created a Flow, you can manage it, edit its properties, activate, deactivate, delete, save as a new version or new Flow, or run it as well.
- **Runtime**: A Flow user can run the active Flow from a custom button, link, Visualforce page, or directly from the Flow URL. If it is **Autolaunch Flow**, then systems can run active Flows through Process Builder or an Apex class.

# An overview of the Cloud Flow Designer

The Cloud Flow Designer is a tool that allows you to implement business requirements by constructing Flows (without any code); this is a way to collect, update, edit, and create data in Salesforce. The Cloud Flow Designer user interface has different functional parts as shown in the following screenshot:

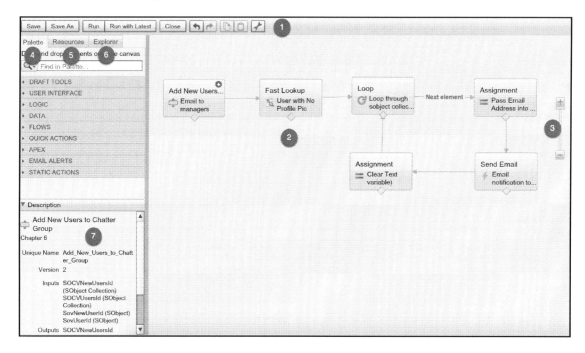

These functional parts are as follows:

1. **The button bar**: You can use **Save**, **Save As**, **Run**, **Run with Latest**, **Close**, undo, and redo changes to run or view properties of your Flow buttons available in the button bar. The status indicator marked in the red rectangle on the right-hand side of the bar shows the status (**Active** or **Inactive**) of your Flow:
   - **Save**: Use this option to save/quick save your Flow.
   - **Save As**: If you want to clone the Flow you are working on or save as a new version, then use this option.
   - **Run**: This runs the most recent version of the Flow you are working in. If the Flow comprises subflow elements, then each subflow refers to the active version of its referenced Flow. If the referenced Flow has no active version, then the subflow element runs the latest version of its referenced Flow.

- **Run with Latest**: This button will only appear if you are working in a Flow that contains a subflow element.
- **Close**: If you are working on a Flow and want to close it, then use this button. If Flow is not saved and you clicked on the **Close** button, then it will return to the Flow list page or else you will be redirected to the Flow detail page.
- **Undo** or **Redo**: Use these to undo or redo recent activities on the canvas.

- **Flow Properties**: Click on the screw driver 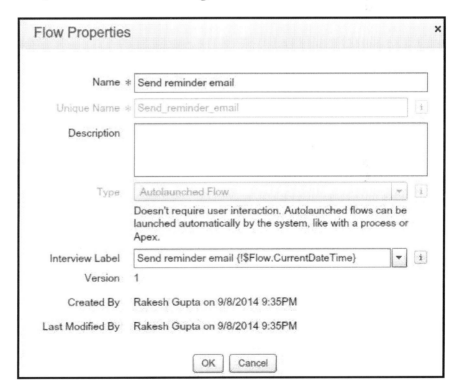 icon to see information related to your Flow, such as **Name**, **Unique Name**, **Description**, its type (**Autolaunched Flow** or **Flow**), **Interview Label**, **Version**, and created and modified dates. Salesforce allows you to change **Name**, **Description**, and **Interview Label** of your Flow at any time, as shown in the following screenshot:

- The **Interview** label helps us differentiate between the interviews of the same Flow when an interview is paused.

2. **The Flow canvas**: You can use this area to design your Flow. To edit any element in the main canvas, double-click on it.
3. **The zoom control:** This is a slider that helps you to zoom in and out of the canvas so that you can focus on particular areas. This feature is also combined with the search options on the **Explorer** tab, so it will highlight results on the canvas tab:

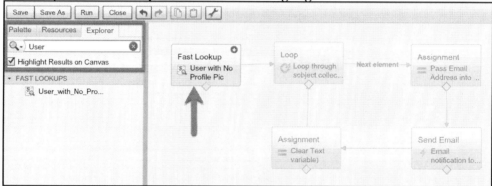

4. **Palette**: This is the area where you can find all the element types available for your Flow. You have to drag and drop elements from the palette onto the canvas to use it. To see the element description/properties in the **Description** panel (7), click on an element in the palette. Once you have created new elements, they will appear in the **Explorer** tab. The **Palette** tab also has a search field to quickly find what you need.
5. **Resources**: The **Resources** tab allows you to create new resources for your Flow, for example, variables, formulas, and templates. Once you have created new resources, they will appear in the **Explorer** tab. To create new resources, double-click on it.
6. **Explorer**: The **Explorer** tab contains all the elements and resources added to the Flow. Double-click on the items from the list to edit them and click to view their details and usage in the **Description** panel (7).
7. **Description**: The **Description** panel shows the item's description when you view an item in the **Palette** or **Resources** tab. It has two subtabs, as follows:

- **Properties**: This shows the information, such as **Unique Name**, **Description**, **Data Type**, **Input/Output Type**, and **Default Value** for the element or resource you have selected:

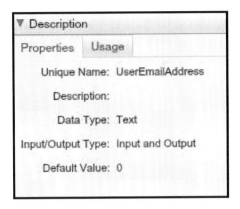

- **Usage**: This lists the elements where the selected item is used:

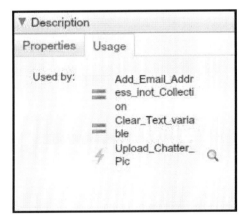

In Chapter 2, *Creating Flow through Point and Click*, we will start using the elements, variables, and concepts that you learned here.

# An overview of the building blocks of Visual Workflow

Flow has three major building blocks known as **Element**, **Connector**, and **Resource**. With the help of these blocks, you can easily develop Flows.

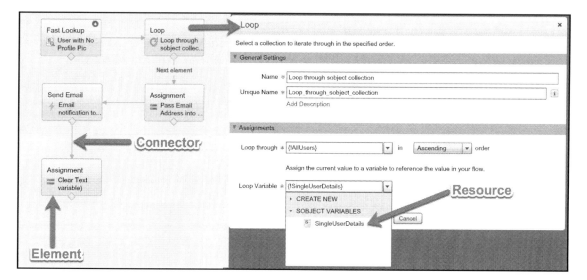

The **Element** block represents an action that Flow can use to display or collect information from the Flow user, create or update records, delete records, or loop logic. The **Element** block is used to manipulate the data. The **Connector** block is used to establish the path between the elements. A **Resource** block is used to hold the data that you can reference in your Flow.

## Flow elements

Flow elements represent actions that Flow can execute such as **Record Update, Record Lookup, Fast Lookup, Loop, Screen**, and **Decision**. This is used to read, write, or delete data. Using the element (**Screen**), you can also display data and capture input from users. Use the **Palette** tab to drag and drop new elements onto your canvas. Once you add elements, it will be available on the canvas and **Explorer** tabs.

There are several types of elements available under the **Palette** tab. They are as follows:

| Flow element | Description |
| --- | --- |
| Step | You can use this as a placeholder while designing your Flow. Later, you can convert **Step** elements into **Screen** elements. |
| Screen | This will display a screen to the user who is running the Flow. The **Screen** element contains input or output fields. The **Screen** element is mainly used to take input from users or display guided information. |
| Decision | This is used to evaluate conditions to determine which Flow path to take. |
| Assignment | This is used to set or change values of variables, collection variables, SObject variables, and SObject collection variables. |
| Loop | This iterates through an SObject collection variable and assigns an item's value to an SObject variable. |
| Wait | If you want your Flow to wait for one or more defined events to occur, then use this element. |
| Record Create | This is used to create one record using the field values that you specify separately. You can assign these values from Flow resources such as variables, SObject variable, and the screen fields. |
| Record Update | This is used to update records using the field values that you specify separately. You can assign these values from Flow resources such as variables, SObject Variable, and the screen fields. |
| Record Lookup | This is used to extract one record that meets the filter criteria you specify, and then assign the record's field values to separate, individual Flow variables or individual fields on SObject variables. |
| Record Delete | This is used to delete records from Salesforce that meet the filter criteria you specify in your Flow. |
| Fast Create | This is used to create records using the fields' value from an SObject collection variable or to create one record using the field's value from an SObject variable. |
| Fast Update | This is used to update records using the field's value from an SObject collection variable or to update one record using the field's value from an SObject variable. |
| Fast Lookup | This is used to extract records to assign their field values to an SObject collection variable or query one record to assign its field values to an SObject variable. |
| Fast Delete | This is used to delete records using the ID value from an SObject collection variable or to delete one record by using the ID value from an SObject variable. |
| Apex Plug-in | This is used to call an Apex class that implements the `Process.Plugin` interface. If you used the tag property in the `PluginDescribeResult` class, the Apex class appears under a customized section. Otherwise, it appears under the **APEX PLUG-INS** section. |
| Subflow | This is used to invoke another Flow in the organization. |
| Quick action | This calls an object-specific or global action, such as `NewTask` and `LogACall`. |
| E-mail Alerts | This is used to send an e-mail using a Workflow e-mail alert to specify e-mail template and recipients. |
| Post to Chatter | Using this element, you can post a message to the feed for a specific record, user, or Chatter group. |
| Send Email | This is used to send an e-mail using Flow with the specific subject, body, and recipients. |
| Submit for Approval | This is used to auto submit one record for approval. |

From `Chapter 2`, *Creating Flow through Point and Click*, we will start using these elements.

# Flow resources

Resources are used to hold the data that you can refer in your Flow. The **Explorer** tab displays the resources that you added to the Flow. To create new resources, double-click on this tab. Global constants and system variables are automatically provided by the system. There are several types of resources available under the **Resource** tab. They are as follows:

| Flow resource | Description |
| --- | --- |
| **Variable** | This is used to store a value that can be updated as the Flow is executed. It can be referenced throughout the Flow and can be used as the value of a field in a record. |
| **Global variable** | These are system-provided variables that can be referenced as resources, such as an organization ID (`{!$Organization.Id}`) or running user ID (`{!$User.Id}`). Visual Workflow global variables are only available in flow formulae. |
| **Collection variable** | This is used to store values with a single data type. You can use a collection variable as a container in the Flow to store and reference multiple values at once. |
| **SObject Variable** | This is used to store a record for a specified object. Use an SObject variable as a container in the Flow to store, update, and reference field values for a record. |
| **SObject Collection Variable** | This is used to store multiple records for a specified object. Use an SObject collection variable as a container in the Flow to store, update, and reference field values for multiple records. |
| **Constant** | This is used to store a fixed value. |
| **Formula** | This is used to calculate a value from other resources in the Flow. |
| **Text templates** | This is used to store formatted text with merge fields that refer to resources. |
| **Choice** | This represents an individual value that can be used in a variety of screen fields. |
| **Dynamic record choice** | This looks up data from an object's record and dynamically generates a set of choices for screen fields at runtime. When referenced as a resource, a dynamic choice value is determined by the most recent user selection of a choice within the generated set. For example, display all contacts from an account if a user entered a valid account ID. |
| **Element** | Any element that you add to the Flow is available as a resource with the visited operator in outcome criteria. An element is considered to be visited if the element has already been executed in the Flow interview. |
| **Global constant** | This is used to store fixed system-provided values, such as `EmptyString`, `true`, and `false`, that can be assigned as the values of Flow resources. |
| **Outcome** | For the **Decision** element you have added to the Flow, its outcomes are available as Boolean resources. If an outcome path has already been executed in the Flow interview, the resource's value is `true`. |
| **Picklist values** | These are system-provided values that are available as resources only in **Assignment** and **Decision** elements when selecting values for or to compare against picklist fields in SObject variables and SObject collection variables. |
| **Picklist Choice** | This is used to store picklist or multi-select picklist values, those are generated from standard or custom object picklist or multi-select picklist field. |
| **Screen field** | This is the field that you add to the Flow is available as a resource. |
| **System variable** | These are system-provided values that can be referenced as resources, such as `{!$Flow.CurrentDate}`, `{!$Flow.CurrentDateTime}`, and `{!$Flow.FaultMessage}`. |

| Wait element | **Wait element** events are always available as Boolean resources. If an event's waiting conditions are met, the resource's value is `true`. If the event has no waiting conditions set, the resource's value is always `true`. |
|---|---|

From `Chapter 2`, *Creating Flow through Point and Click*, we will start using these resources.

# Flow connectors

A connector is used to establish the path between the Flow elements. A connector looks like an arrow that points from one element to another. There are several types of connectors available. They are as follows:

| Label | Sample | Description |
|---|---|---|
| Unlabeled | | This is used to identify which element to execute next. |
| Decision outcome name | Remove | This is used to identify which element to execute when the criteria of a decision outcome are met. |
| Wait event name | 10 days after Close | This is used to identify which element to execute when an event that's defined in a wait element occurs. |
| Fault | FAULT | This is used to identify which element to execute if the previous element results in an error. |
| Next element | Next element | This is used to identify the first element to execute for each iteration of a loop element. |
| End of loop | End of loop | This is used to identify which element to execute after a loop element finishes iterating through a collection. |

From `Chapter 2`, *Creating Flow through Point and Click*, we will start using these connectors.

# The various ways to invoke a Flow

As soon as you are done with Flow development, the next task is to configure Flow access for business users, so they can use it. There are various ways through which you can invoke/launch your Flows. They are as follows:

- The Flow URL
- From another Flow (as a Subflow)
- A custom button or URL
- The web or Visualforce tab
- A combination of the Visualforce page and the `Force.com` site or customer portal and partner portal
- The Login Flow
- The Visualforce page
- Inline Visualforce page
- Salesforce1 navigation menu
- From a Chatter Action
- Embedding a Flow in Lightning Record page
- Embedding a Flow in Lightning App page
- Embedding a Flow in Lightning Home page
- Embedding a Flow in Lightning for Outlook
- Process Builder
- The Apex `start()` method
- Apex Trigger
- The Invocable Action resource in the Force.com REST API

# Visual Workflow outcome behavior

Lightning Experience is a new generation productive user interface designed to help your sales team to close more deals and sell quicker and smarter. With the **Spring'16** release, Salesforce announced the Lightning edition of Sales and Service cloud. Lightning editions are a completely reimagined packaging of Sales and Service Cloud to offer additional functionality to their customers and increased productivity with a relatively small increase in cost. It might be possible that you have enabled Lightning Experience in your organization or are planning to enable it in the near future.

We now have two different outcome screen for flow, as mentioned here:

- Salesforce classic outcome for Flows
- Lightning Runtime for Flows

Lightning runtime for Flows allows you to create two column flows and embed a Flow in a third-party application, such as Microsoft Outlook. In `chapter 8`, *Enabling Flows to Work with Lightning Experience*, you will be briefed about the differences between these two outcome screens. We will also discuss what modifications you have to do in order to use your existing flows in Lightning Experience.

# Creating an Admin playground account

To get started with the topics in this book and practice them on your own, it is recommended you have access to a Salesforce Developer account. Using the Salesforce production instance is not essential for practicing. You can use the Salesforce Sandbox or Admin playground to practice the examples covered in this book.

If you currently do not have your own Admin playground, you can create a new Salesforce Admin playground. The Salesforce Admin playground is completely free and can be used to practice newly learned concepts, but you cannot use this for commercial purposes.

To create a Salesforce Admin playground, perform the following steps:

1. Visit `https://developer.salesforce.com/promotions/orgs/admin-playground`.

2. This will open a sign-up page for your free Admin playground account; it will display the following screen:

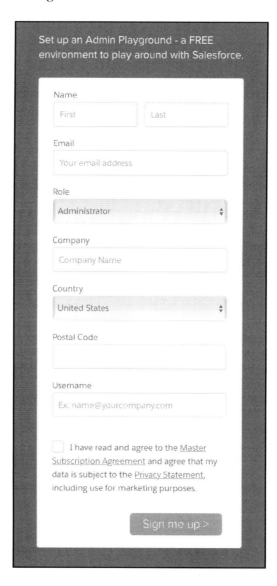

3. Fill in the form and accept the master subscription agreement.

4. Click on the **Sign me up >** button.

 The Salesforce login ID (username) must be unique and in the form of an e-mail ID.

Once you register for the admin playground, Salesforce.com will send you the login details on the e-mail ID you provided during registration. By following the instructions in the e-mail, you will be ready to get started with Salesforce.

# Logging in to Salesforce.com

Here, we will continue by logging in to `Salesforce.com`:

- If you are logging into the Salesforce production or admin playground, go to `http://login.salesforce.com`
- If you are logging into a Salesforce Sandbox instance, then go to `http://test.salesforce.com`
- Once the login screen loads, provide your username and password
- Salesforce may ask you to enter a verification code depending upon the organization's security and settings
- After verification, you will be allowed to access Salesforce; and the next time you log in, Salesforce will not ask for the verification code

A new admin playground will be launched in Lightning Experience; ensure that you switch back to Salesforce Classic using the switcher, as shown in the following screenshot:

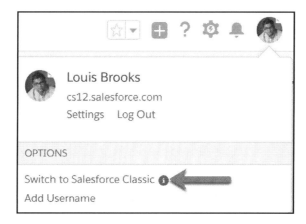

In Salesforce Classic, navigate to the Flow canvas by navigating to **Setup** | **Build** | **Create** | **Workflow & Approvals** | **Flows** and clicking on the **New Flow** button.

# Summary

In this chapter, we covered various concepts related to Visual Workflow. We started with the business scenario where you can use Visual Workflow and followed with the benefits of using Flow. We also covered the requirements for Visual Workflow. Then, we moved forward and discussed the life cycle of the Flow development and gave you an overview of Cloud Flow Designer. Finally, we discussed various ways through which you can invoke your Flow and get the idea of Flows Lightning Experience outcome behavior. We have also discussed how to create a free admin playground. In the next chapter, we will go through variables, element creation concepts, and we will also cover how to design your Flow.

# 2
# Creating Flow through Point and Click

In the previous chapter, we gave you an overview of Visual Workflow. We discussed the benefits of using Visual Workflow and the system requirements for it. You learned various ways to invoke the Flow. In this chapter, you will see how easily you can create user interaction screens without Visualforce and complex process automation without Apex. This chapter mainly focuses on the design of Visual Workflow using various components. The following topics will be covered in this chapter:

- Creating the building blocks of the Flow:
    - Creating a variable
    - Creating a Collection variable
    - Creating an SObject variable
    - Creating an SObject Collection variable

- Allowing users to pause Flows
- Designing the Flow: In this topic, we will cover:
    - Displaying the logged-in user ID
    - Real estate commission calculator
    - Displaying feedback forms based on conditions
    - Displaying related records based on search functionality

Till the `Chapter 4`, *Debugging and New Ways to Call a Flow*, we will use the Salesforce Classic user interface to display Visual Workflow output. In this book, we have dedicated `Chapter 8`, *Enabling Flows to Work with Lightning Experience*, to discuss Lightning Experience for Visual Workflow.

# Creating the building blocks of Flow

In Chapter 1, *Getting Started with Visual Workflow*, we discussed the building blocks of Flow; for example, Flow elements, Flow resources, and Flow connectors. Before going ahead, you will first learn to create variables in Flow, and then we will discuss the other building blocks in upcoming chapters. The few building blocks we are going to discuss here are as follows:

- Creating a variable
- Creating a collection variable
- Creating an SObject Variable
- Creating an SObject Collection Variable

## Creating a variable

A variable is used to store a value. You can use the variable throughout your Flow; for example, while creating a record, performing an update, or with delete operations.

Here is business scenario: Robby Williams is working as a system administrator for Universal Containers. Currently, he is developing a Visual Workflow and wants to create a variable to store customer names.

To create a variable in your Flow, follow these instructions:

1. Navigate to **Setup** | **Build** | **Create** | **Workflow & Approvals** | **Flows**.
2. Click on the **New Flow** button; it will open the Flow canvas for you.

 If you are using Flow for the first time, then it will pop up a welcome page. On the bottom of the page, you can see the **Don't Show Again** checkbox. If you want the Flow page to load faster, then select this checkbox.

3. Navigate to the **Resources** tab and double-click on the **Variable** option that is available under the **CREATE NEW** section, as shown in the following screenshot:

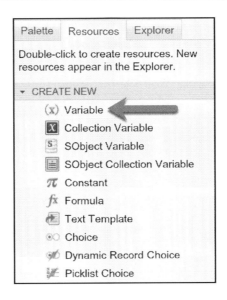

This will open a window for you, where you have to enter the following details:

- **Unique Name**: Enter a unique name. The name must begin with a letter, and use only alphanumeric characters and underscores. Uniqueness applies only to elements within the current Flow. In this case, enter `VarTCustomerName`.

- **Description**: Write some meaningful text so other developers/administrators can easily understand why this variable has been created. When you select the **Variable** in the **Explorer** tab, then this description appears in the **Description** pane.

- **Data Type**: This determines which types of value a variable can store. Select the data type of **Text**. The following are the available data types for a variable:

  - **Text**: This is used to store any combination of letters and numbers.
  - **Number**: This is used to store any numbers.
  - **Currency**: This is used to store currency.
  - **Date**: This is used to store the date.
  - **DateTime**: This is used to store the date with the time.
  - **Boolean**: This is used to store either true or false.
  - **Picklist**: This is used to store picklist values. It supports the `ISPICKVAL()` function in Flow formulas.

- **Picklist (Multi-select)**: This is used to store multi-select picklist values.
- **Scale**: This is only available when the data type is set to **Number** or **Currency**. **Scale** is the number of digits to the right of the decimal point.
- **Input/Output Type**: This defines whether a variable is available within the Flow or can also be accessed outside the Flow. The different input/output types are as follows:
  - **Private**: This variable can be allocated and used only within the Flow.
  - **Input Only**: This allows you to set a variable at the start of the Flow using Visualforce controllers, URL parameters, or subflow inputs.
  - **Output Only**: This means that you can access a variable's value from Visualforce controllers and other Flows.
  - **Input and Output**: This means that you can set a variable's value at the start and access its value outside the Flow. In our case, select **Input and Output**.
  - **Default Value**: This allows you to set a default value for the variable. You can either manually enter the value or use the drop-down list to assign the value of a Flow resource as the default. In our case, select **{!$GlobalConstant.EmptyString}** available under **GLOBAL CONSTANT**. This will look like the following screenshot:

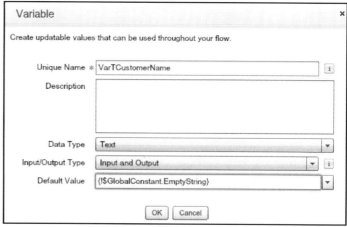

4. Once you are done, click on the **OK** button.

 For best practice, in this book we will be using `VarT` as the prefix for the **Text** variable, `VarN` for **Number**, `VarC` for **Currency**, `VarD` for **Date**, `VarDT` for **DateTime**, and `VarB` for the **Boolean** variable type.

# Creating a collection variable

Collection variables are used to store multiple values of similar data types; for example, a group of e-mail addresses. Once you have populated a collection variable with values, you can use it throughout the Flow.

Here is a business Scenario: Helina Jolly is working as a system administrator for Universal Containers. Currently, she is developing a Visual Workflow and wants to create a variable to store customers' e-mail addresses to send out an e-mail to them.

To create a collection variable in your Flow, follow these instructions:

1. Navigate to **Setup** | **Build** | **Create** | **Workflow & Approvals** | **Flows**.
2. Click on the **New Flow** button; it will open the Flow canvas for you.
3. Then navigate to the **Resources** tab and double-click on **Collection Variable**, which is available under the **CREATE NEW** section. It will open a window for you, where you have to enter the following details:
   - **Unique Name**: Enter the unique name. The name must begin with a letter, and use only alphanumeric characters and underscores. Uniqueness applies only to elements within the current Flow. In this case, enter `CovEmailAddress`.
   - **Description**: Write some meaningful text so other developers/administrators can easily understand why this Collection variable was created. When you select a collection variable in the **Explorer** tab, then the description appears in the **Description** pane.

- **Data Type**: This determines which types of value variables can be stored. Select the data type of **Text**. The available data types for variables are as follows:
    - **Text**: This is used to store any combination of letters and numbers.
    - **Number**: This is used to store any numbers.
    - **Currency**: This is used to store currency.
    - **Date**: This is used to store the date.
    - **DateTime**: This is used to store the date with the time.
    - **Boolean**: This is used to store either true or false.
    - **Picklist**: This is used to store a picklist value. It supports the `ISPICKVAL()` function in flow formulas.
    - **Picklist (multi-select)**: This is used to store multi-select picklist values.
- **Input/Output Type**: This defines whether a variable is available within the Flow or can also be accessed outside the Flow. Different input/output types are as follows:
    - **Private**: This variable can be allocated and used only within the Flow.
    - **Input Only**: This allows you to set a variable at the start of the Flow using Visualforce controllers, URL parameters, or subflow inputs.
    - **Output Only**: This means that you can access a variable's value from Visualforce controllers and other Flows.
    - **Input and Output**: This means that you can set a variable's value at the start and access its value outside the Flow.

This will look like the following screenshot:

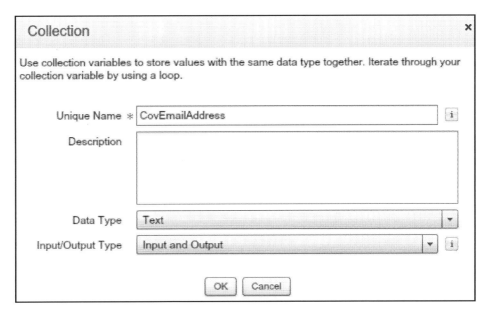

4. Once you are done, click on the **OK** button.

 For best practice, in this book we will use Cov as the prefix for a Collection Variable.

# Adding values to a collection variable

You can't refer to your collection variable either in the **Record Lookup** or **Fast Lookup** element to populate it with values. The following are a few ways through which you can populate values in your collection variable:

- **Screen fields**: Using an **Assignment** element, this allows you to populate values for a collection variable by referring to **Screen** fields such as **Choice**, input, or output field values. You can also populate values for a collection variable by referring to values stored in a variable using an **Assignment** element.

- **Variable**: This also allows you to populate values for a collection variable by referring to values stored in a variable using an **Assignment** element.
- **SObject Variable**: Using an **Assignment** element, this allows you to populate values for a collection variable by referring to one SObject Variable field value.
- **SObject Collection Variable**: To assign SObject Collection Variable field values to a collection variable, you have to use a **Loop** element. Within the **Loop** element, using an **Assignment** element, you can populate values for collection variables by referring to the **Loop** variable's stored field values.

In `Chapter 3`, *Manipulating Records in Visual Workflow*, you will learn how to populate values for a collection variable.

# Creating an SObject Variable

Here is a business scenario: Robby Williams is working as a system administrator for Universal Containers. Currently, he is developing a Visual Workflow and wants to create a variable to store the **Account** record field's values.

An SObject Variable is used to hold the field values for a record of a particular object. You can use an SObject Variable as a container in the Flow to store, update, and reference field values for a record. To create an SObject Variable in your Flow, follow these instructions:

1. Navigate to **Setup** | **Build** | **Create** | **Workflow & Approvals** | **Flows**.
2. Click on the **New Flow** button; it will open the Flow canvas for you.
3. Then navigate to the **Resources** tab and double-click on **SObject Variable**, which is available under the **CREATE NEW** section.
4. This will open a window where you have to enter **Unique Name**, **Description**, **Input/Output Type**, and **Object Type**. In this scenario, select the **Account** object from the drop-down list, as shown in the following screenshot:

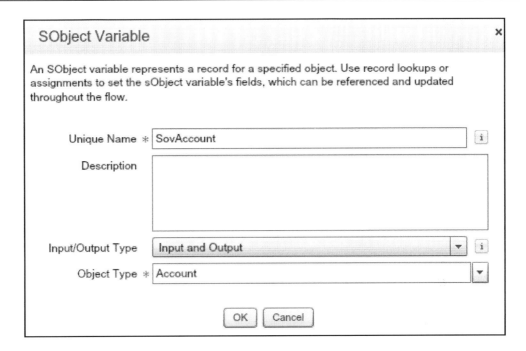

5. Once you are done, click on the **OK** button.

 For best practice, in this book we will use Sov as the prefix for an SObject Variable.

# Creating an SObject Collection Variable

An SObject Collection Variable is used to store multiple records for a particular object. You can use an SObject Collection Variable as a container in the Flow to store, update, and reference field values for records. For example, if you want to store the account name, billing, and shipping details for 10 accounts; you can use an SObject Collection Variable. In a similar fashion to an SObject variable, you can create an SObject Collection Variable.

For best practice, in this book we will use SOCV as the prefix for an SObject Collection Variable.

You can use an SObject Collection Variable with fast elements to store, update, create, and delete records in bulk.

# Allowing users to pause Flows

You can allow your users to pause a Flow interview that they can't finish at that time by customizing your organization's process automation settings. A Flow interview is nothing but a running instance of a Flow. For example, a customer support agent can pause a Flow interview when they don't have the complete information for their customer. Perform the following steps to enable pause Flow options in your Salesforce organization:

1. Navigate to **Setup** | **Build** | **Create** | **Workflow & Approvals** | **Process Automation Settings.**
2. Select **Let Users Pause Flows.**
3. Once you are done, click on the **Save** button.

If you pause a Flow interview, the data that was entered by you into the screen gets saved with the interview. So, when you resume later, you can use the data you entered, as long as the values are valid. Users can access paused interviews from the following locations:

- The **Paused Flow Interviews** component on their home tab page layout
- The **Paused Flow Interview** on the Salesforce1 navigation menu

The following screenshot displays the details of a Paused Flow interview on the Salesforce1 mobile application:

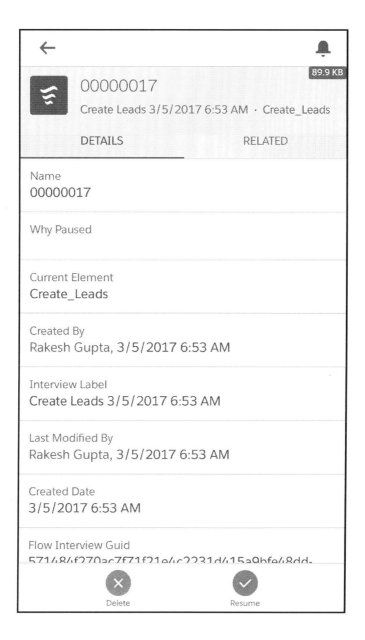

Only the user who paused the Flow or an administrator can resume or delete a paused interview. If it is tried to resume a Flow interview tries and the interview's owner is inactive, the interview fails, and the Flow owner receives a Flow fault e-mail with details of what happened and how to fix it.

> Screen elements don't automatically display the Pause button once the **Let Users Pause Flows** option is enabled. If you want your users to be able to pause at a given screen, select the **Show Pause** button when you configure that screen.

# Designing the Flow

Now, we will discuss how to use these building blocks to design the Flow using a few recipes. It is recommended that you have access to a Salesforce Developer account. Using the Salesforce production instance is not essential for practicing. You can use the Salesforce Sandbox or Developer account to practice the examples covered in this book.

## Hands on 1 - displaying a logged-in user ID

Let's start with an example: Sara Bareilles is working as a system administrator in Universal Containers. She wants to develop a Flow to display logged-in user IDs on a **Screen** element. To develop the Flow, follow these instructions:

1. Navigate to **Setup** | **Build** | **Create** | **Workflow & Approvals** | **Flows**.
2. Click on the **New Flow** button; it will open the Flow canvas for you.
3. Navigate to the **Resources** tab, double-click on **Formula** available under the **CREATE NEW** section, and create a formula as shown in the following screenshot:

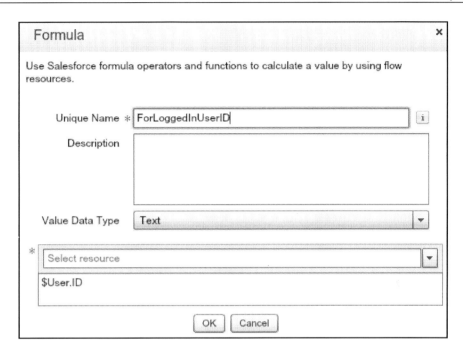

For best practice, in this book we will use `For` as the prefix for **Formula**. In the preceding formula, we have used user global variables. For the complete list of global variables, visit `http://www.salesforce.com/docs/developer/pages/Content/pages _variables_global.htm`.

4. Click on the **OK** button and then navigate to the **Palette** tab.

# Creating a Screen element

We will now add a **Screen** element (it is used to take the input from a user or display the data) to the Flow by following these instructions:

1. Drag and drop the **Screen** element onto the canvas; it will open a **Screen** element window. Navigate to the **General Info** tab, where you have to enter the following details:
   - **Name**: This helps you to find the element on the canvas. In this case, enter `Display LoggedIn User ID`.

- **Unique Name**: This will be auto-populated based on the name.
- **Description**: This is where we enter some text to let other developers/administrators easily understand why this **Screen** element was created. When you select the **Screen** element in the **Explorer** tab, then the description appears in the description pane.
- **Navigation Options**: This section allows you to specify the screen navigation options; for example, the behavior of the **next, previous,** and **finish** buttons at runtime. It also allows you to define the pause button's behavior and the pause message.
- **Help Text**: This allows you to define the help text, which can be seen by Flow users when they click on **Help** for this form; it will look as shown in the following screenshot:

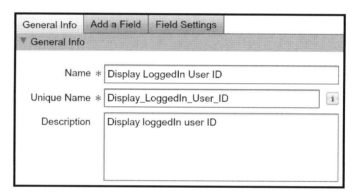

2. The next step is to add the **Formula** field into a screen element.

## Adding fields to the Screen element

To add fields to the **Screen** element, follow these instructions:

1. Navigate to the **Add a Field** tab, which is available under the **Screen** element. Double-click on **Display Text**, which is available under the **OUTPUTS** section.

2. On the **Screen** overlays preview pane, click on the **Display Text** field to configure its settings by entering a unique name. In this case, enter `LoggedInUserID` in the **Unique Name** field; to display text from the dropdown, select **FORMULAS**, which we created in step 3 of the *Hands on- displaying a logged-in user ID* section:

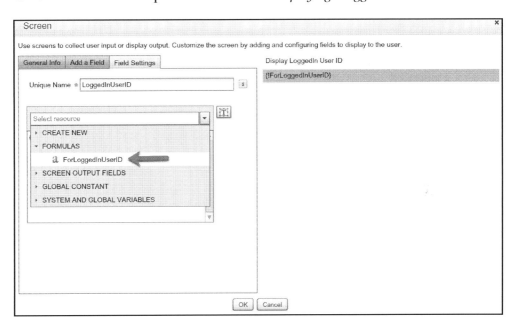

3. Once you are done, click on the **OK** button.

# Removing fields from the Screen element

To remove a field from the **Screen** element, perform the following steps:

1. On the Flow canvas, double-click on the **Screen** element from which you want to remove the field.

2. Point your mouse pointer to the field and click on the trash icon, as shown in the following screenshot:

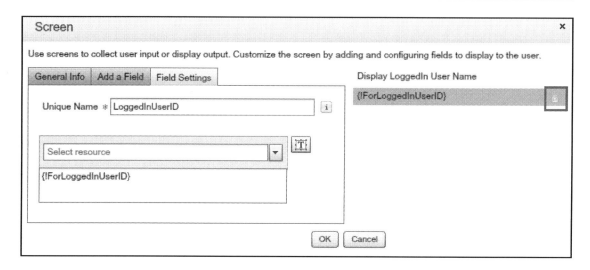

3. Click on the **OK** button to save the changes.

# Setting the Start element in a Flow

Navigate to the element that you want to use as the first screen in your Flow, hover over it, and click on  to set it as the Start element. In our case, select the **Screen** element, **Display LoggedIn User ID**, as the Start element; the Flow will look as shown in the following screenshot:

If your Flow doesn't contain a Start element, you won't able to see the **Active** button on the Flow detail page.

# Saving a Flow

Once you are done with the Flow development, the next task is to save the Flow. To do this, click on the **Save** button available in the top-left corner of the Flow canvas; you will see a window pop up, which is where you have to enter the following details to save your Flow:

1. **Name**: Enter the name for the Flow or Flow version. In this case, enter `Display LoggedIn UserID` as the name. The Flow name appears in the Flow management page and the Flow detail page; it also appears at the runtime user interface.

2. **Unique Name**: This will be auto-populated based on the name.

3. **Description**: Enter the description for the Flow or Flow version. This description is displayed in the list of Flows to help you understand what the Flow does.

4. **Type**: This is the type for the Flow or Flow version. The type will appear in the Flow detail and Flow management page. The following are the different types of Flow:

   - **Flow**: To execute this type of Flow, it requires human interaction because it may contain one or more screens, steps, choices, or dynamic choices. Flows don't support **Wait** elements.

   - **Autolaunched Flow**: This type of Flow doesn't require human interaction to start. It doesn't support screens, steps, choices, or dynamic choices. It can be launched through a Process Builder action, inline Visualforce page, or Apex code.

   - **User Provisioning Flow**: This provisions users for third-party services. A user provisioning Flow can only be implemented by associating it with a connected app when running the user-provisioning wizard. It also provisions users for third-party services. Contact the support at `http://www.salesforce.com/` to enable this for your organization.

   - **Workflow**: This is a running instance of a process created in the Process Builder. We are not allowed to create such Flows.

   In this case, select **Flow** as the **Type.**

5. **Interview Label**: This displays a label for the Flow interview. An interview is a running instance of a Flow. A label appears in paused and waiting for interviews on the Flow management page. You can pause the interview from the home tab and also pause the interview items in Salesforce1.

The following screenshot displays all the details:

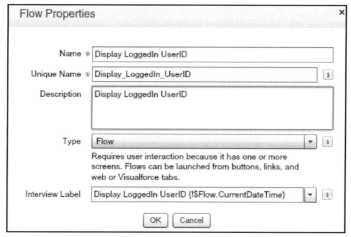

6. Once you are done, click on the **OK** button.

# Running a Flow

To test a Visual Workflow, click on the **Run** button, which is available in the top-left corner, and you can check the following output:

Once you are done with testing, click on the **Close** button to close the Flow canvas. The **Run** button allows a system administrator to test the Flow without activating it so that they can verify the Flow's outcomes and modify it if necessary.

# Hands on 2 - real estate commission calculator

Let's start with an example: Robby Williams is working as a system administrator for Universal Containers. He wants to develop an application using Flow to calculate the commission for real-estate brokers. What he wants, on the very first screen, is to allow real-estate agents to enter the property's value and commission in percentage, and, on the next screen, to display the commission amount. He also wants to make sure that the property value is always greater than 10,000. To develop the Flow, follow these instructions:

1. Navigate to **Setup** | **Build** | **Create** | **Workflow & Approvals** | **Flows**.
2. Click on the **New Flow** button; it will open the Flow canvas.
3. Then navigate to the **Palette** tab, and drag and drop the **Screen** element onto the canvas; it will open a **Screen** element window.
4. In the **Name** field, enter `Real estate commission calculator`; you can also add a description. Under the **Navigation Options** section, select **Don't show Previous button** (we don't want to allow users to go back to the previous screen) from the dropdown, check the **Show Pause button** checkbox, and enter a pause message. A **Paused Message** window will appear when the user pauses the interview of this Flow. It will look as shown in the following screenshot:

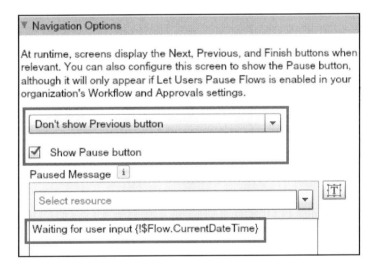

 If you pause the interview, the data that you have entered into the fields on screen gets saved with the interview. So, when you resume later, you can use the data you entered, as long as the values were valid.

5. If you want to format the pause message, then click on 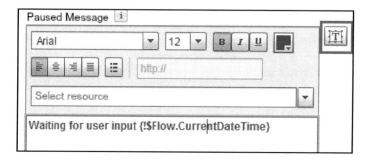; it will open the rich text editor. The rich text editor saves the content in an HTML format:

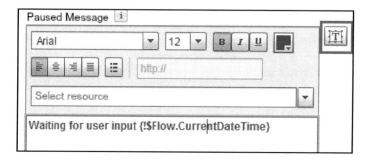

6. Once you are done, click on the **OK** button.

7. The next task is to add fields to the screen. On the **Screen** element, navigate to the **Add a Field** tab and double-click on the **Currency** field, which is available under the **INPUTS** section, to add it on to the **Screen** element, as shown in the following screenshot:

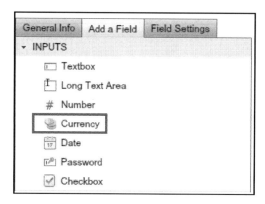

8. On the **Screen** overlays preview pane, click on the **Currency** field to configure its settings by entering **Label**, **Unique Name**, **Input Type**, **Default Value**, and **Scale** (enter 0), and select the **Required** checkbox under the **General Info** section, as shown in the following screenshot:

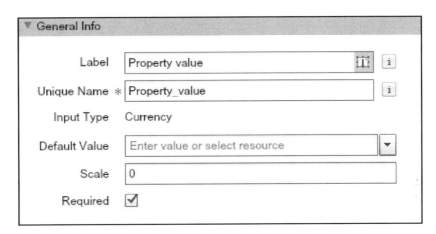

9. To make sure that the user always enters a property value greater than 10,000, we have to add a validation rule for it. To do this, navigate to the **Input Validation** section and select the **Validate** checkbox, then it will open the formula editor where you can write a validation rule for this field. It also allows you to configure error messages for the validation rule. It will display the error message when the formula evaluates to false.

 In Flow, if the formula statement evaluates as true, the input is valid. If the formula statement evaluates as false, the error message is displayed to the user. It means that this is the reverse of a validation rule in Salesforce, where the error message is displayed when the validation rule is TRUE.

The Validation rule allows you to use a standard formula composition in a formula resource, and you can also use it to validate user input in a **Screen** element. However, a Flow formula doesn't support all functions. A Flow formula can't contain more than 3,000 characters.

The formulas that are not supported by Flow as of the **Spring'17** release are GETRECORDIDS, IMAGE, INCLUDE, ISCHANGED, ISNEW, ISPICKVAL, PARENTGROUPVAL, PREVGROUPVAL, PRIORVALUE, REQUIRE SCRIPT, and VLOOKUP. If you use these functions in your formula, it will always return *null*. A validation rule for the currency field will look as shown in the following screenshot:

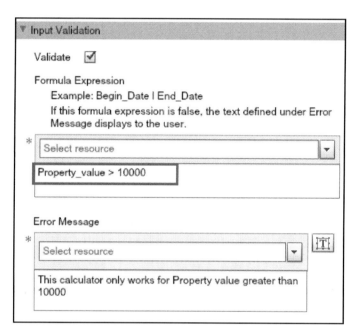

10. On the Screen, add a **Number** field to allow users to enter Commission in Percentage ( %), as shown in the following screenshot:

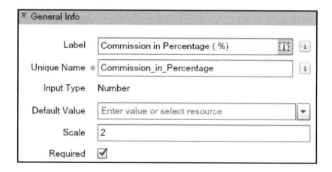

11. The next step is to add a validation rule to this input field:
    1. Add a validation rule so that the user will always enter a commission in percentage greater than zero. To achieve this, use the formula `Commission_in_Percentage > 0.00`.
    2. You can also configure the help text for the screen under the **Help Text** section of the **Screen** element.
12. Click on the **OK** button, which is available on the **Screen** element, to close the Screen element and return to the canvas.
13. To calculate the commission amount, we have to create a formula. To do that, navigate to the **Resources** tab and double-click on **Formula**, which is available under the **CREATE NEW** section, and create a formula as shown in the following screenshot:

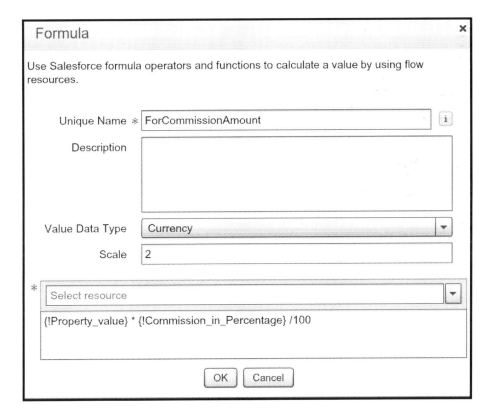

14. Add `{!Property_value}` and `{!Commission_in_Percentage}` to the screen input fields that we created in steps 7 and 10. Once you are done, click on the **OK** button.

15. The next task is to display the commission amount on the screen. For this, drag and drop the **Screen** element from **Palette** to the canvas. It will open a **Screen** element window where you have to enter `Display Commission amount` in the **Name** field; you can also add a description. Under the **Navigation Options** section, select **Don't show Previous button** from the drop-down.

16. Now navigate to the **Add a Field** tab, which is available under the **Screen** element, and double-click on **Display Text**, which is available under the **OUTPUTS** section.

17. In the **Screen** overlays preview pane, click on the **Display Text** field to configure the commission amount's settings by entering the **Unique Name**; to display text from the drop-down, select the formula that we created in step 12. It will look as shown in the following screenshot:

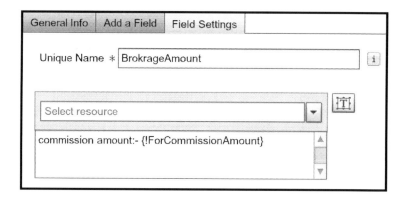

18. Once done, click on the **OK** button available in the **Screen** element.

# Connecting the Flow elements

So far, we have created two screens: one to get the inputs from users and another to show the commission amount. Our next task is to connect both the elements, so Flow will be able to decide the order of execution of the elements at runtime.

To do this, in the source element, find the node at the bottom and drag it to the target element; it prompts you to select which outcome you want to assign to the path in the case of a **Decision** or **Loop** element, as shown in the preceding screenshot. Also, set the **Screen** element **Real estate commission calculator** as the Start element, as shown in the following screenshot:

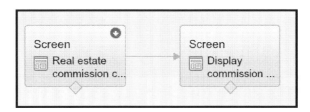

The next task is to save your Flow; to do this, you need to perform the following steps:

1. Click on the **Save** button, which is available in the top-left corner of the Flow canvas, and enter in the `Real estate commission calculator` values for **Name**, **Unique Name**, **Description**, and **Interview Label**, and select **Type** as the **Flow**. To test this Flow, click on the **Run** button, and enter the amounts in the **Property value** and **Commission in Percentage ( %)** fields, as shown in the following screenshot:

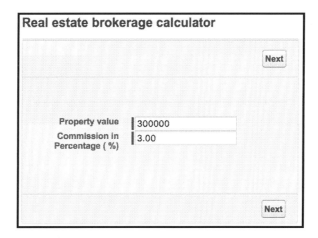

2. Click on the **Next** button; it will display the commission amount on another screen:

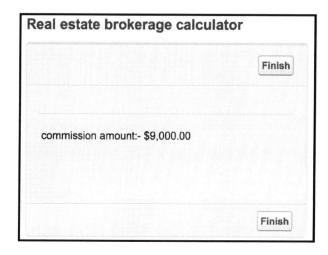

3. Finally, click on the **Finish** button; it will redirect you to the first screen.

# Hands on 3 - displaying a feedback form based on conditions

Let's start with an example: Sara Bareilles is working as a system administrator for Universal Containers. She has received a requirement from her customer success manager to develop a feedback form (containing name, e-mail address, and a rating radio button). Her manager wants to display feedback only when the user's age is greater than 18, and he also wants to expose this visual Flow for unauthenticated access (to people who are not Salesforce users).

To develop this Flow, it's necessary that we first ask for the age as user input, then use the **Decision** element to check the age; if the age is greater than 18, it will display a feedback form or a sorry message. To develop the Flow, follow these instructions:

1. Navigate to **Setup** | **Build** | **Create** | **Workflow & Approvals** | **Flows**.
2. Click on the **New Flow** button; it will open the Flow canvas.
3. Then navigate to the **Palette** tab, and drag and drop the **Screen** element on to the canvas; it will open a **Screen** element window.
4. Enter the **Name** field as `Enter your age`; you can also add description. Under the **Navigation Options** section, select **Don't show Previous button** from the drop-down. Optionally, you can add **Help Text** as well.
5. The next task is to add a **Date** field onto the screen to allow your users to enter their date of birth. On the **Screen** element, navigate to the **Add a Field** tab and double-click on the **Date** field, which is available under **INPUTS**, to add it to the screen. In the **Screen** overlays preview pane, click on the **Date** field to configure its settings by filling out the **Label**, **Unique Name**, and **Default Value** fields, and selecting the **Required** checkbox under the **General Info** section, as shown in the following screenshot:

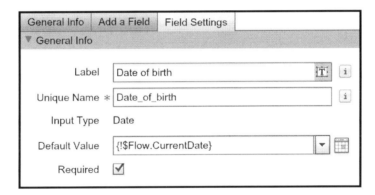

6. Also, add a validation rule so the user can't enter a future date. To achieve this, use the `Date_of_birth < Today()` formula.
7. Now, we will create a formula field to calculate the age from the date of birth field. To create a formula, navigate to the **Resources** tab and double-click on **Formula**, which is available under the **CREATE NEW** section, and create a formula as shown in the following screenshot:

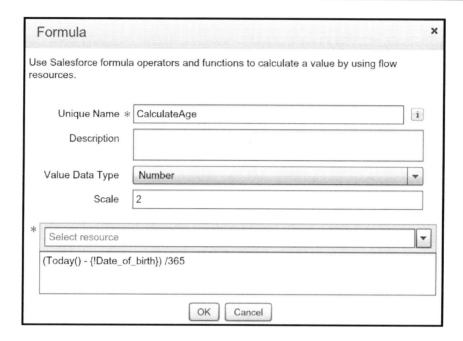

Here, {!Date_of_birth} is the screen input element that we have created in step 5.

8.  Once you are done, click on the **OK** button.
9.  Now we will use the **Decision** element to check the age.

## Adding a Decision element

To add a **Decision** element, follow these instructions:

1.  Drag and drop the **Decision** element onto the Flow canvas.
2.  Enter the **Name** and **Unique Name** in the details window. Optionally, you can also add a description for the **Decision** element.
3.  Now we will set up the conditions for the outcome. It also allows you to create new resources from the **Resource** or **Value** drop-down lists. In this case, it will look like this:

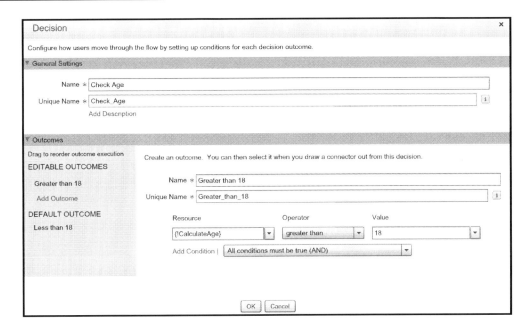

Now we will define the path for the **Decision** element:

> 1. If you want to add multiple conditions, then use **Add Condition**. It also allows you to define your own logic when the outcome contains more than one condition.
> 2. Also add a **DEFAULT OUTCOME** to identify the Flow's path when none of the outcome's conditions are met. In our case, **Less than 18** is the default outcome, as shown in the preceding screenshot.

4. Once you are done, click on the **OK** button.

5. The next task is to add two screens: one to display the sorry message and another for the feedback form. First, we will create a screen to display the sorry message. For this, drag and drop the **Screen** element onto the canvas; this will open a **Screen** element window where you have to enter `Display sorry message` in the **Name** field; you can also add a description. Under the **Navigation Options** section, select **Don't show Previous button** from the drop-down.

6. Now navigate to the **Add a Field** tab, which is available under the **Screen** element. Double-click on **Display Text**, which is available under the **OUTPUTS** section.

7. In the **Screen** overlays preview pane, click on the **Display Text** field to configure its settings by entering a unique name; to display text, enter the message you want to display. It will look like the following screenshot:

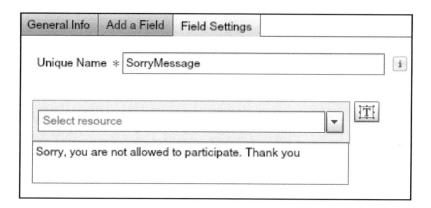

8. Once you are done, click on the **OK** button.

9. Now we will add one more screen to display the feedback form. For this, drag and drop the **Screen** element onto the canvas; it will open a **Screen** element window. Enter `Feedback form` in the **Name** field; you can also add a description. Under the **Navigation Options** section, select **Don't show Previous button** from the drop-down. Optionally, you can add **Help Text** as well.

10. The next step is to add three fields (**Name**, **Email Address**, and **Rating**) onto the screen element to create a feedback form. To do this, follow these instructions:

11. Navigate to the **Add a Field** tab, which is available under the **Screen** element. Double-click on **Textbox**, which is available under the **INPUTS** section. In the **Screen** overlays preview pane, click on the **Textbox** field to configure its settings by entering **Label**, **Unique Name**, and **Default Value**, and also by selecting the **Required** checkbox, as shown in the following screenshot:

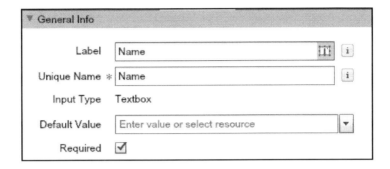

12. In a similar manner, add one more field for the e-mail address.

# Adding a choice to a Flow

Now we are going to add the third field; that is, **Rating**. To add a **Choice** element, follow these instructions:

1. For rating, we will use the **Radio Buttons** field. Double-click on the **Radio Buttons** field, which is available under the **CHOICES** section. In the **Screen** overlays preview pane, click on the **Radio Buttons** field to configure its settings by entering **Label**, **Unique Name**, **Value Data Type**, the **Required** checkbox, and **Default Value**, as shown in the following screenshot:

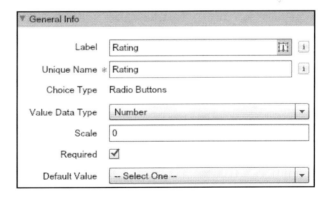

2. Under the **Choice Settings** section, create a new choice by expanding the **CREATE NEW** list and then clicking on **Choice**, as shown in the following screenshot:

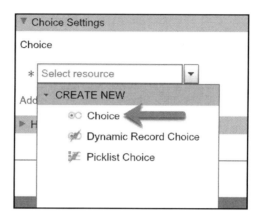

3. A new window will pop up where you have to enter Label, **Unique Name**, and **Value Data Type**. For **Stored Value**, use 1 and uncheck the **Show Input on Selection** checkbox, as shown in the following screenshot:

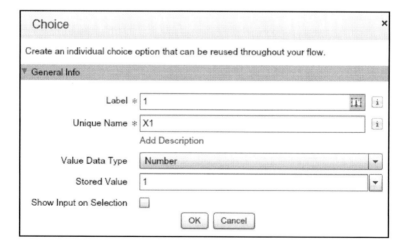

4. If you leave **Stored Value** blank, then, in runtime, if the user leaves a choice blank or unselected, its stored value is set to null. If you select the **Show Input on Selection** checkbox, then the user input field appears below the choice option. This option is not available if the choice's data type is Boolean. Repeat the same process and create choices 2, 3, 4, and 5, and use 2, 3, 4, and 5 as the stored values, respectively, as shown in the following screenshot:

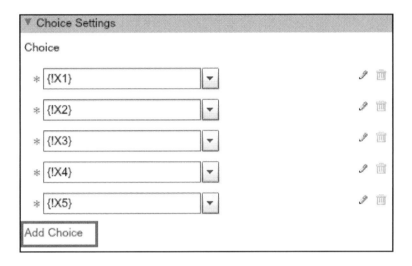

5. Use **Add Choice** to add multiple choices.
6. Once you are done, click on the **OK** button.

You can also create a choice from the **Resources** tab, double-click on **Choice**, which is available under the **CREATE NEW** section, and use it with radio buttons, drop-down lists, multi-select checkboxes, and multi-select picklists as **Choice**.

7. The final task is to connect all the elements using connectors. As we are using the **Decision** element, when you connect the **Decision** element **Check Age** to the **Screen** element **Feedback form**, you will get an option to select the outcome. In this case, select **Greater than 18**, as shown in the following screenshot:

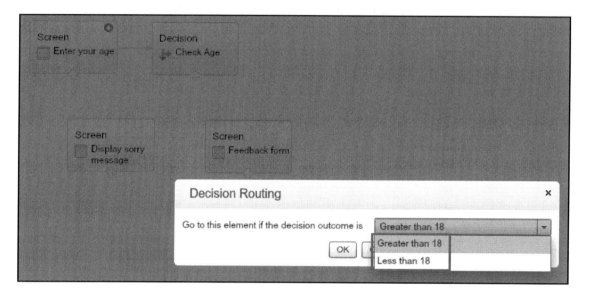

8. Navigate to the element that you want to use as the first screen in your Flow. Now, set the **Screen** element **Enter your age** as the Start element, as shown in the following screenshot:

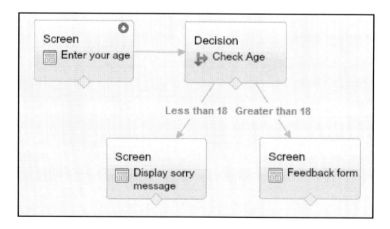

9. Save the Flow with the name **Displaying feedback form based on age** and click on the **Run** button to test your Flow. Now, enter any date on the screen:

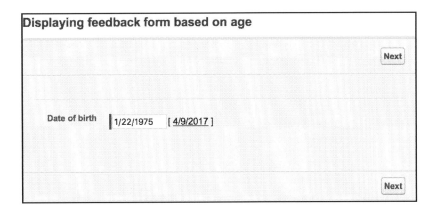

10. Once done, click on the **Next** button, as shown in the preceding screenshot. If the age difference is greater than 18, then it will display the feedback form, as shown in the following screenshot:

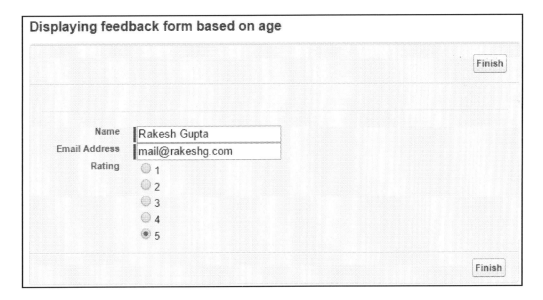

11. Finally, click on the **Finish** button and it will redirect you to the first screen. We will discuss the concepts related to exposing the Flow for unauthenticated access in Chapter 3, *Manipulating Records in Visual Workflow*.

# Hands on 4 - displaying related records based on search functionality

Let's start with an example: Helina Jolly is working as a system administrator for Universal Containers. She wants to develop a Flow using which a user can search for leads based on the lead's e-mail address and select multiple leads as well.

To develop this Flow, it's first required to ask for an e-mail address as the user input. Then, we will use dynamic record choice to display the leads with the same e-mail address. To develop the Flow, perform the following instructions:

1. Navigate to **Setup** | **Build** | **Create** | **Workflow & Approvals** | **Flows**.
2. Click on the **New Flow** button; it will open the Flow canvas for you.
3. Then navigate to the **Palette** tab, and drag and drop the **Screen** element onto the canvas; this will open a **Screen** element window.
4. Enter the **Name** field as `Enter the lead details`; you can also add a description. Under the **Navigation Options** section, select **Don't show Previous button** from the drop-down. Optionally, you can add **Help Text** as well.
5. The next task is to add a **Textbox** onto the screen to allow your users to enter an e-mail address. On the **Screen** element, navigate to the **Add a Field** tab and double-click on the **Textbox** field, which is available under **INPUTS**, to add it on to the screen. In the **Screen** overlays preview pane, click on the **Textbox** field to configure its settings by entering **Label**, **Unique Name**, and **Default Value**, and selecting the **Required** checkbox under the **General Info** section, as shown in the following screenshot:

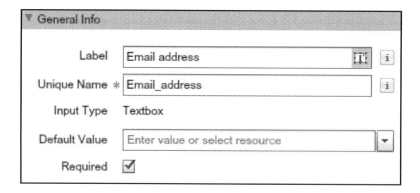

6. Create a variable (`VarLeadsID`) of the **Text** data type to store the lead's ID. We will use this variable in **Dynamic Choice** in the upcoming steps.

7. Now we will add one more screen to display the leads with the same e-mail address form. For this, drag and drop the **Screen** element onto the canvas; this will open a **Screen** element window. Enter the **Name**, and you can also add a description for it. Under the **Navigation Options** section, select **Don't show Previous button** from the dropdown. Optionally, you can add **Help Text** as well.

# Adding a Dynamic Record choice to a Flow

Dynamic Record choice is used to dynamically create a reusable set of choices based on a filtered list of Salesforce records. For dynamic display leads with the same e-mail address, we will use the **Multi-Select Picklist** field and follow these steps:

1. Double-click on the **Multi-Select Picklist** field, which is available under the **MULTI-SELECT CHOICES** section. In the **Screen** overlays preview pane, click on the **Multi-Select Picklist** field to configure its settings by entering **Label**, **Unique Name**, the **Required** checkbox, and **Default Value**, as shown in the following screenshot:

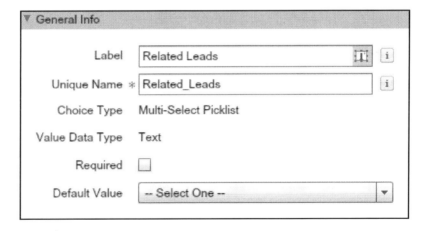

2. Under the **Choice Settings** section, create a new choice by expanding the **CREATE NEW** list and then clicking on **Dynamic Record Choice**, as shown in the following screenshot:

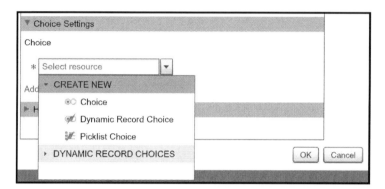

A new window will pop up where you have to fill in the following options:

- **Unique Name**: Enter a unique name. The name must begin with a letter and use only alphanumeric characters and underscores. Uniqueness applies only to elements within the current Flow. In this case, enter Leads as the unique name.
- **Description**: Enter the description for a dynamic record choice.
- **Value Data Type**: Select the data type for the choice's stored value.
- **Create a choice for each**: Select the object (in this case, select **Lead**), whose records contain the data for the created choices.
    - **Field**: To filter records we select the fields. In this case, select **Email**.
    - **Operator**: This depends on the data type selected for **Field** and **Value**. In this case, select equals as the **Operator.**
    - **Value**: This is used to compare with **Field**. The **Field** and **Value** for the same row must have the same data type. In this case, select {!Email_address} as the **Value.**
- **Choice Label**: This allows you to select the record's field, whose value appears as the choice's label at runtime. In this case, select Name as the **Choice Label.**
- **Choice Stored Value**: This allows you to select the field, whose value is saved when the user selects this choice at runtime.

- **Sort results by**: This also allows you to sort your results based on the object field and you can also limit the number of choices. In this case, use **Name** to sort the results.
- **Additional Options**: This section allows you to assign a field's value to variables at runtime when the user chooses **Field** and **Variable** from the generated sets. In this case, map **Id** with your variable (`{!VarLeadsID}`), which we created in step 5 of the *Hands on 4 - displaying related records based on search functionality* section.

This will look like the following screenshot:

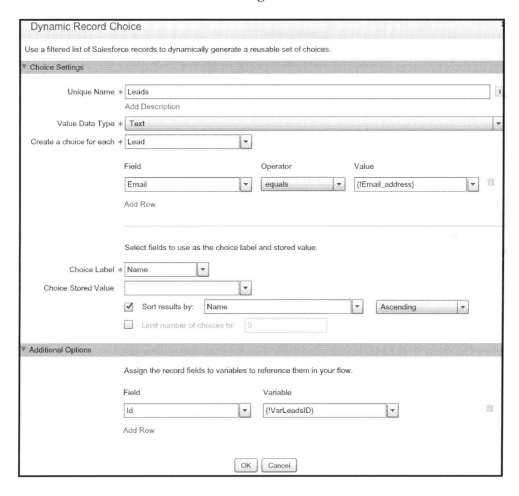

3. Once you are done, click on the **OK** button.

You can also create a **Dynamic Record Choice** from the **Resources** tab; double-click on **Dynamic Record Choice**, which is available under the **CREATE NEW** section, and use it with the radio button, drop-down list, multi-select checkboxes, and multi-select picklist as a dynamic choice.

4. The next task is to connect all the elements using connectors and set the **Screen** element **Enter the lead details** as the Start element, as shown in the following screenshot:

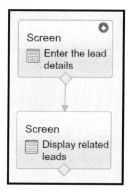

5. Click on the **Save** button, which is available in the top-left corner of the Flow canvas and enter **Name**, **Unique Name**, **Description**, and **Interview Label**, and select **Type** as the **Flow**. Save the Flow with the name of `Display leads`. To test this Flow, click on the **Run** button and enter the e-mail address:

6. Once you're done with the e-mail address, click on the **Next** button. Then the following screen will appear:

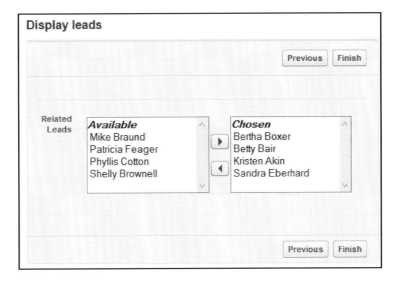

7. Finally, click on the **Finish** button and it will redirect you to the first screen.

# Hands on 5 - creating an opportunity form

Let's start with an example: Helina Jolly is working as a system administrator for Universal Containers. She wants to develop a Flow using which a user can create an opportunity. Later on, she wants to embed this Flow into a home page layout so that users can easily access it.

Before going ahead, the first task is doing the ground work; this means finding the fields that are required to create an opportunity in the system. In a new Salesforce organization, the following are the fields that are required to create an opportunity:

- Opportunity Name
- Close Date
- Stage

It means our forms must contain these fields to successfully create an opportunity in Salesforce. To develop this Flow, follow these instructions:

1. Navigate to **Setup** | **Build** | **Create** | **Workflow & Approvals** | **Flows**.
2. Click on the **New Flow** button, which will open the Flow canvas for you.
3. Then navigate to the **Palette** tab, and drag and drop the **Screen** element onto the canvas; this will open a **Screen** element window.
4. Enter the **Name** field as `Create Opportunities`; you can also add a description. Under the **Navigation Options** section, select **Don't show Previous button** from the dropdown. Optionally, you can add **Help Text** as well.
5. The next task is to add a **Textbox** onto the screen to allow your users to enter the `Opportunity_Name`. On the **Screen** element, navigate to the **Add a Field** tab and double-click on the **Textbox** field, which is available under **INPUTS**, to add it onto the screen. In the **Screen** overlays preview pane, click on the **Textbox** field to configure its settings by entering **Label**, **Unique Name**, and **Default Value**, and selecting the **Required** checkbox under the **General Info** section, as shown in the following screenshot:

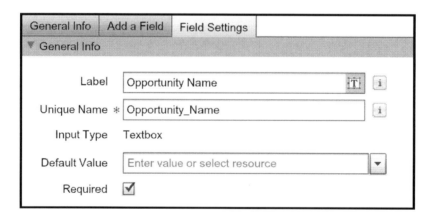

6. Likewise, add a **Date** field to allow users to enter Close Date, as shown in the following screenshot:

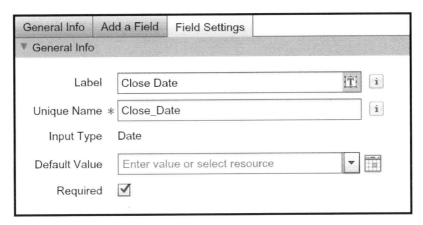

7. Now, we will add another that allow users to select opportunity Stage.

# Adding a Picklist choice to a Flow

Picklist choice is used to create a reusable set of choices using the values of a Salesforce picklist or multi-select picklist. It means that instead of creating a picklist in Flow, we can use Opportunity Stage standard picklist values here. The benefits of using out-of-the-box stage standard picklist values are that, anytime someone adds or removes values from the Stage picklist (by navigating to **Setup** | **Build** | **Customize** | **Opportunities** | **Fields**), they will available in Flow as well.

To display the stage values, we will use the **Dropdown List** field and follow these steps:

1. Double-click on the **Dropdown List** field, which is available under the **CHOICES** section. In the **Screen** overlays preview pane, click on the **Dropdown List** field to configure its settings, by entering **Label**, **Unique Name**, the **Required** checkbox, and **Default Value**, as shown in the following screenshot:

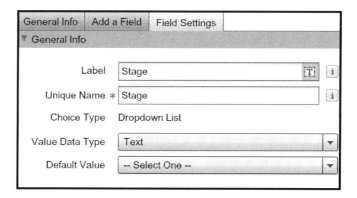

2. Under the **Choice Settings** section, create a new choice by expanding the **CREATE NEW** list and then clicking on **Picklist Choice**, as shown in the following screenshot:

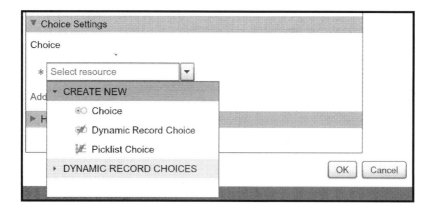

3. A new window will pop up where you have to fill in the following options:
    1. **Unique Name**: Enter a unique name. The name must begin with a letter, and use only alphanumeric characters and underscores. Uniqueness applies only to elements within the current Flow. In this case, enter Stages as the unique name.
    2. **Description**: Enter the description for a Picklist choice.
    3. **Value Data Type**: Select the data type of the choice's stored value. In this case, select Picklist as the **Value Data Type**.
    4. **Object**: Select the object (in this case, select **Opportunity**), whose picklist or multi-select picklist values you want to use in your Flow.
    5. **Field**: Select the picklist or multi-select picklist field to use to generate the list of choices. In this case, select StageName as the **Field.**
    6. **Sort Order**: This allows you to control the order that the choices appear in. The choices are sorted based on the translated picklist value for the running user's language. In this case, use **Ascending** to sort the choices.

This will look like the following screenshot:

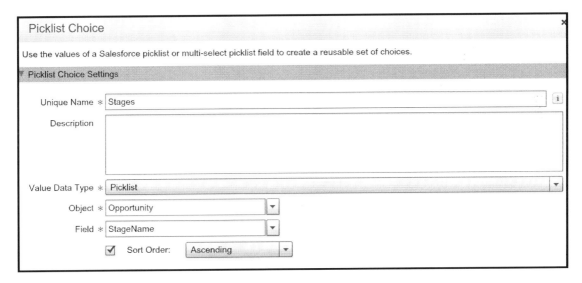

4. Once you are done, click on the **OK** button.

You can also create a **Picklist Choice** from the **Resources** tab; double-click on **Picklist Choice**, which is available under the **CREATE NEW** section, and use it with the radio button, drop-down list, multi-select checkboxes, and multi-select picklist for a picklist choice based on your business requirement.

5. The next task is setting the **Screen** element. In our case, select the **Screen** element **Create Opportunities** as the Start element, as shown in the following screenshot:

6. Click on the **Save** button, which is available on the top-left corner of the Flow canvas and enter **Name**, **Unique Name**, **Description**, and **Interview Label**, and select **Type** as the **Flow**. Save the Flow with the name Create Opportunities. To test this Flow, click on the **Run** button and enter the opportunity name, close date, and stage:

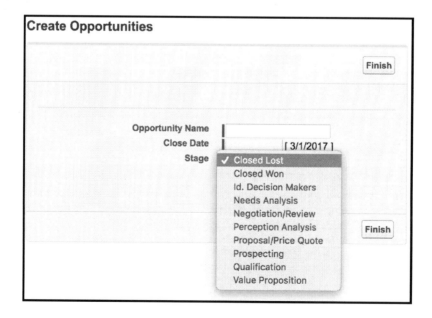

7. Finally, click on the **Finish** button and it will redirect you to the first screen.

# A few points to remember

The following are some noteworthy points about Flow design:

- As far as possible, use fewer elements in your Flow, so it will take less execution time.
- The limit on the number of executed elements at runtime is 2,000.
- One organization can have a maximum of 500 active Flows and processes.
- One organization can have a maximum of 1,000 Flows and processes.
- The date must be in MM/DD/YYYY format, and the date and time must be in MM/DD/YYYY HH:SS format.
- The Flow will return null at runtime if you leave any field or resource value blank.
- For a text value, if you want it to be treated as an empty string instead of null, then set it to `{!$GlobalConstant.EmptyString}`.
- At runtime, the date/time values reflect the time zone settings in Salesforce. For the running users and in the Flow designer, the date/time values reflect the time zone set on your computer.
- UTF-8 encoding for text in user input fields is not supported by Cloud Flow Designer.
- If you enter null as the default value for a text field in the Flow Designer, it will clear the default value after saving.
- If a Display Text screen field contains an invalid formula, then the Flow will display an empty string at runtime.
- If a Flow contains an invalid formula, then you can't activate the Flow.
- A Flow always displays every picklist value for that field, even if you are using record types to filter picklist choices in page layouts.
- A Flow always displays the label for each picklist value.

# Exercises

Starting from this chapter, at the end of each chapter, you will find a set of exercises for practice:

1. Create a Flow that allows users to enter two numbers, and on the next screen display its summation and multiplication.

2. Create a Flow that allows users to enter three texts (such as the first name, middle name, and last name), and on the next screen display their combination in one field.

3. Display the organization ID, name, division, city, street, FAX, and phone number that is defined under **Setup | Administer | Company Profile | Company Information** on the screen.

4. Create a Flow that allows users to enter their name, and on the next screen display a thanks message with the name (with the name in green and the thanks message in red).

5. Create a Flow and add a **Screen** element to it. On the screen, add one textbox that allows users to enter an e-mail address, and add a validation rule so that the user can only enter an e-mail address or else display, an error message.

6. Create a **Screen** element with 10 checkboxes and allow your user to select a maximum of five checkboxes out of 10. If the user selects more than five checkboxes, display an error message.

7. Create a Flow to allow users to search for accounts based on the billing city, and display all related account records in a drop-down list so that the user can select one of them.

8. Create a Flow that allows users to enter an account name, then display all related contacts from that account.

9. Create a Flow that allows users to create a case. Use a picklist choice to display the case status and case origin as a drop-down list.

10. Create a form that allows users to select the lead status. Then, on the next screen, display all leads with the selected status in a multi-select picklist. Use a picklist choice to display the lead status and a dynamic record choice to display the lead record with the selected status.

# Summary

In this chapter, we went through various concepts related to designing the screen, starting from the different types of variables in a Flow, and the naming conventions for them. We covered how you can use formulas, the Validation rule, the Decision element, and Choice in a Flow. We also went through how to add fields into a Flow and connect two screens using connectors. Then, we moved forward and discussed how you can add dynamic record choices and picklist choices to your Flow. Finally, we discussed the key points related to screen design. In the next chapter, we will discuss concepts related to manipulating records in Salesforce using a Flow.

# 3
# Manipulating Records in Visual Workflow

In the previous chapter, we discussed the various building blocks of the Flow design. We also discussed how to use the **Decision** element to display different screens to users based on the conditions. You also learned how to use choice, dynamic record choice, and picklist choice in a Flow. In this chapter, we will discuss how easily we can create, update, or delete records without using Apex, and we will also look at the various ways to invoke/trigger the Flow. This chapter will mainly focus on manipulating data in Salesforce. The following topics will be covered in this chapter:

- Creating the building blocks of a Flow
    - Creating a constant
    - Creating a text template
- Manipulating data: In this subtopic, we will cover the following:
    - Creating leads
    - Adding leads to a campaign
    - Quickly updating an account
    - Cleaning Chatter feeds
    - Adding an image to display text
    - Saving data in a feedback form
    - Creating a custom error message
    - Conditional execution of a Flow with JavaScript

# Creating the building blocks of a Flow

In Chapter 2, *Creating Flow through Point and Click*, we discussed a few Flow building blocks, such as **Variable**, **Decision**, and **Screen** elements. Before going ahead, you will learn about a few more resources that we can use in the Flow for various purposes. The two resources we are going to discuss here are:

- Creating a constant
- Creating a text template

# Creating a constant

A constant is used to store a fixed value. A constant value can't be changed throughout the execution once it has been assigned a value. You can use the constant all over your Flow, for example, while creating a record, performing an update, or with delete operations.

Let's look at a business scenario. Alice Atwood is working as a system administrator in Universal Containers. Currently, she is developing a Visual Workflow and wants to create a constant that can be used to store an organization's name.

To add a constant to your Flow, follow these instructions:

1. Navigate to **Setup** | **Build** | **Create** | **Workflow & Approvals** | **Flows**. This will open a window for you, where you have to enter the following details.
2. Click on the **New Flow** button; it will open the Flow canvas.
3. Then, navigate to the **Resources** tab and double-click on **Constant**, available under the **CREATE NEW** section:

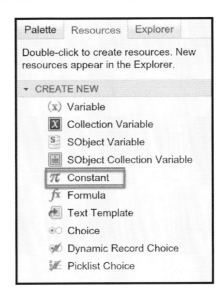

4. This will open a window for you where you have to enter the following details:

- **Unique Name**: Enter a unique name. The name must begin with a letter, and use only alphanumeric characters and underscores. Uniqueness applies only to elements within the current Flow. Use ConOrgName as the unique name.

- **Description**: Write some meaningful text so that another developer/administrator can easily understand why this constant variable has been created. When you select a variable in the **Explorer** tab, a description appears in the **Description** pane.

- **Data Type**: This determines which types of values a variable can store. Select the **Text** data type. Other available data types for a variable are as follows:

  - **Text**: This is used to store any combination of letters and numbers.
  - **Number**: This is used to store any number.
  - **Currency**: This is used to store the currency.
  - **Date**: This is used to store the date.
  - **Boolean**: This is used to store either true or false values.

- **Value**: This allows you to set a value for the constant. You can either manually enter the value or use the `{!$GlobalConstant.EmptyString}` drop-down list to assign the null value to Constant. In this case, enter the organization name, `Universal Container`.

This will look like what is shown in the following screenshot:

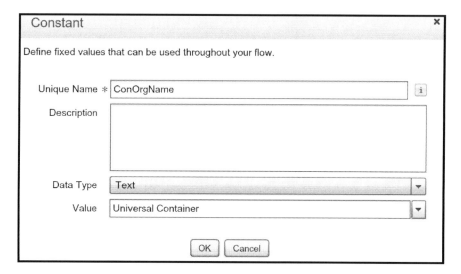

5. Once you are done, click on the **OK** button.

 For the best practice, in this book, we will use `Con` as the prefix for Constant. For the date value, you must use the MM/DD/YYYY format. For the date/time value, you must use the MM/DD/YYYY HH:SS format.

# Creating a Text Template

A Text Template is used to create text for use in your Flow. It also allows you to use HTML tags in it; this means that along with plain text, we can also create colorful text, tables, and so on. For example, using this, we can create an e-mail template and use it to send e-mails to people who submitted their feedback on the survey form, **Displaying feedback form based on age**, which we created in `Chapter 2`, *Creating Flow through Point and Click*.

Let's look at a business scenario. Joe Thompson is working as a system administrator in Universal Containers. His next assignment is to create a Flow and add the customer details in a table on the screen. Now he is looking for a way in which he can create a colorful table (2 x 2 to display the first name and the last name) and add it to the screen.

To add a Text Template to your Flow, follow these instructions:

1. Navigate to **Setup** | **Build** | **Create** | **Workflow & Approvals** | **Flows**.
2. Click on the **New Flow** button; it will open the Flow canvas.
3. Then, navigate to the **Resources** tab and double-click on **Text Template**, available under the **CREATE NEW** section.
4. This will open a window where you have to enter the following details:
    - **Unique Name**: Enter a unique name. The name must begin with a letter and use only alphanumeric characters and underscores. Uniqueness applies only to elements within the current Flow. Use `TTempDisplayTable` as the unique name.
    - **Description**: Write some meaningful text so that another developer/administrator can easily understand why this **Text Template** has been created. When you select **Text Template** in the Explorer tab, a description appears in the **Description** pane.
    - **Text Template**: Enter the text for the template. Use the dropdown to select the existing resources or create brand new resources.

This will look like what is shown in the following screenshot:

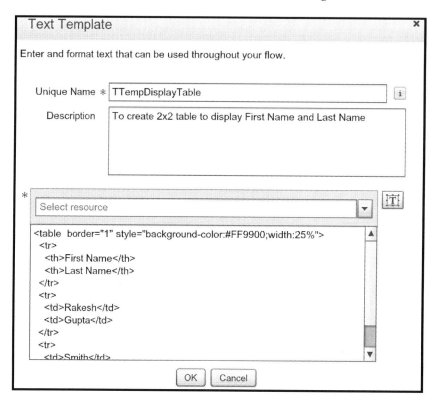

The following is the sample code:

```
<table border="1"  style="background-color:#FF9900;width:25%">
  <tr>
    <th>First Name</th>
    <th>Last Name</th>
  </tr>
  <tr>
    <td>Rakesh</td>
    <td>Gupta</td>
  </tr>
  <tr>
    <td>Smith</td>
    <td>Jackson</td>
  </tr>
</table>
```

5. Once you are done, click on the **OK** button.

6. To see the output of the **Text Template**, add a **Screen** element onto the canvas.

7. Now, add **Display Text** onto the screen and select the **TEXT TEMPLATES** resource that we created from the dropdown, as shown in the following screenshot:

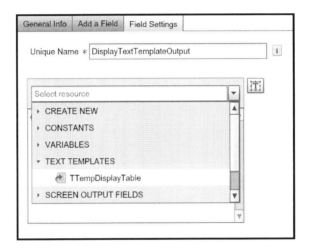

8. Click on the **OK** button and save your Flow.

9. To test it, click on the **Run** button available in the top-left corner. You can see the output in the following screenshot:

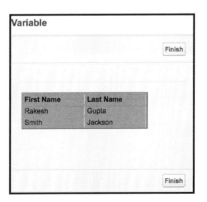

In the preceding example, we created a static table.

Refer to `automationchampion.com` to learn about how to create a dynamic table.

You can also use Text Variable, Assignment, Fast Lookup, and Screen elements to dynamically display data in a table, as shown in the following screenshot:

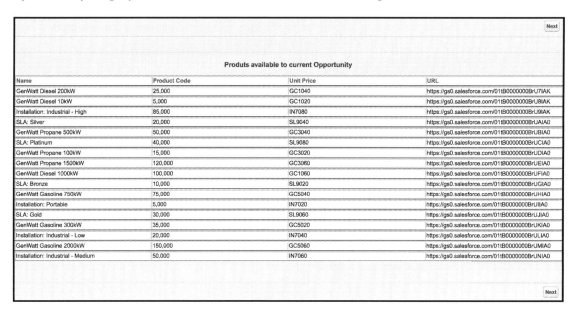

# Manipulating the data

Now we will discuss how you can use Flow elements, such as **Record Create**, **Record Update**, **Record Lookup**, **Record Delete**, and **Decision**, to modify the existing data or to create new data. We will pick up a few business scenarios and try to learn these concepts.

# Hands on 1 - creating leads

A lead is the prospect or people who are interested in your business. In Salesforce, we can capture the leads in various ways, for example, from Salesforce web-to-lead, data loader, data import wizard, manually, and so on.

Let's look at a business scenario. Helina Jolly is working as a system administrator in Universal Containers. She received a requirement to develop a Flow through which users can create leads. Basically, her manager wants to display a screen where users can enter their details (last name, company name, and e-mail address) that, after clicking on the **Finish** button, will create a lead into Salesforce.

Before going ahead, the first task is to do the ground work; this means finding the fields that are required to create a lead in the system. In a new Salesforce organization, the following are the fields that are required to create a lead:

- Last name
- Company
- Lead status (by default, this is set to **Open-Not Contacted**, so you can ignore it) or you can also use picklist choice to display Lead Status dropdown from the lead object

To develop this Flow, follow these instructions:

1. Navigate to **Setup** | **Build** | **Create** | **Workflow & Approvals** | **Flows**.
2. Click on the **New Flow** button; this will open the Flow canvas.
3. Then, navigate to the **Palette** tab, and drag and drop the **Screen** element onto the canvas; this will open a **Screen** element window.
4. Enter the **Name** field as `Create Leads`; you can also add **Description**. Under the **Navigation Options** section, select **Don't show Previous button** from the dropdown. Optionally, you can add **Help Text** as well.
5. The next task is to add a few field to the screen in order to capture lead details. Add three textbox fields on the **Screen** element by clicking on the **Add a Field** tab. Double-click on the **Textbox** field available under the **INPUTS** section, first for **Last Name**, second for **Email Address**, and third for **Company**, as shown in the following screenshot:

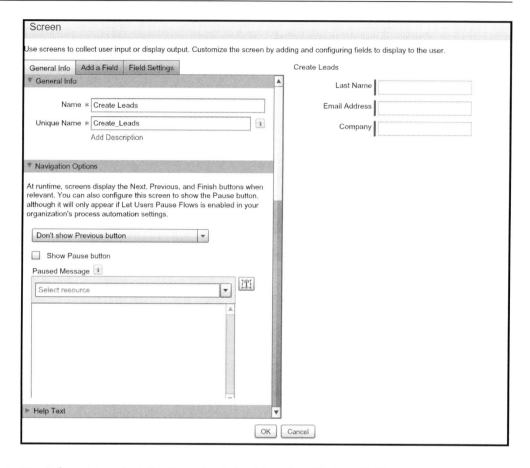

6. Don't forget to select the **Required** checkbox for all three fields.
7. Once you are done, click on the **OK** button.

# Adding the Record Create element to a Flow

The **Record Create** element allows you to create a record in Salesforce using the values from the Flow. This only creates a single record at a time. You can also use the SObject variable to create a single record with all field values. Now, we will add one **Record Create** element to this Flow:

1. Navigate to the **Palette** tab and drag and drop the **Record Create** element onto the canvas; this will open a new window, where you have to enter the following details:
   - **Name**: Enter the name for the **Record Create** element. In this case, enter `Create lead record` as the name.
   - **Unique Name**: This will be autopopulated based on the name.
   - **Description**: Write some meaningful text so that another developer/administrator can easily understand why this **Record Create** element was created. When you select the **Record Create** element in the **Explorer** tab, the description appears in the **Description** pane.
   - **Create**: Select the object for which you want to create the record, in this case, the **Lead** object.
   - The next task is to assign the value or resource to the object fields, so the data types must match. To assign values to multiple fields, click on the **Add Row** link. Map the **Company** field with the screen input field `{!Company}`, the **Email** field with the screen input field `{!Email_Address}`, and the **LastName** field with the screen input field `{!Last_Name}`, as shown in the upcoming screenshot.
   - **Variable**: Optionally, you can save the new record's ID in a variable, so you can use it later in the Flow. Let's create a **Text** variable with the name `VarTLeadID` by expanding the **CREATE NEW** section of the drop-down list and setting **Input/Output Type** as **Input and Output**.

This will look like what is shown in the following screenshot:

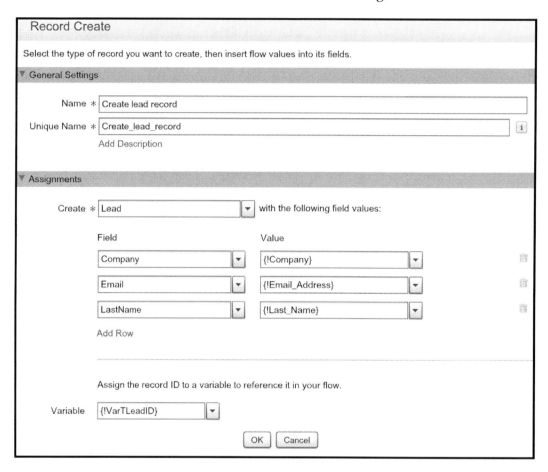

2. Once you are done, click on the **OK** button.
3. Use a connector to connect to the **Screen** and **Record Create** elements and set the **Screen** element **Create Leads** as the **Start** element, as shown in the following screenshot:

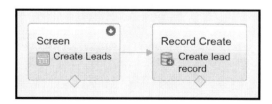

4. Save the Flow with the name **Create Leads** and click on the **Run** button to test the Flow. Enter the required data in all the fields;

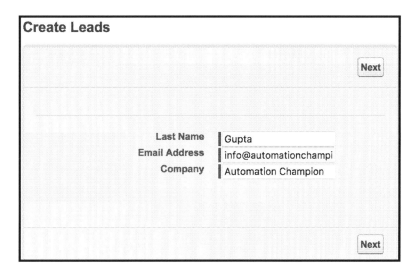

5. Once done, click on the **Next** button, as shown in the preceding screenshot, and Flow will create a lead record in Salesforce, as shown in the following screenshot:

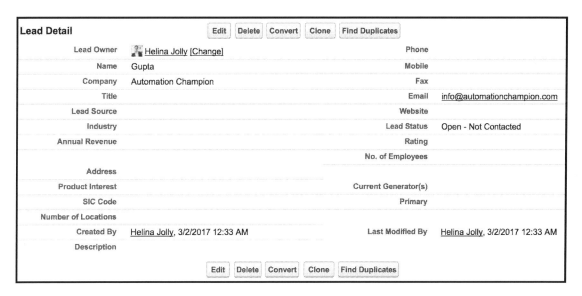

Here, you learned how to create a record using Flow and how to test it. In the next section, you will learn how to add a child record to a parent record (lookup, master-detail, or junction object), for example, how to add a new contact to an account.

# Hands on 2 - adding leads to a campaign

Most businesses associate leads with campaigns to help them calculate ROI and the success of their sales and marketing campaigns.

Let's look at a business scenario. Helina Jolly is very happy now, as she received appreciation from her manager. After a few hours, she receives another requirement, as follows:

- Put this Flow onto the campaign detail page as a detail button
- Auto-relate new leads to a campaign from which a user has created the lead

## Adding a record to a parent

First of all, create a **Text** variable in your Flow to pass the campaign ID to auto-relate leads with a campaign. Then, we will use a custom button to invoke the Flow and pass the campaign ID to the **Text** variable. To do this, follow these instructions:

1. Open the **Create Leads** Flow that we created in the previous case.
2. Create a **Text** variable `VarTCampaignID`, set **Input/Output Type** as **Input and Output**, and for **Default Value**, use `{!$GlobalConstant.EmptyString}`.
3. Drag and drop the **Record Create** element onto the canvas; this will open a new window. Now, enter `Add to Campaign` as **Name**, and **Unique Name** will be autopopulated based on the name. Select the **CampaignMember** object and the map object fields **LeadId** with the `{!VarTLeadID}` variable and **CampaignId** with the `{!VarTCampaignID}` variable, as shown in the following screenshot:

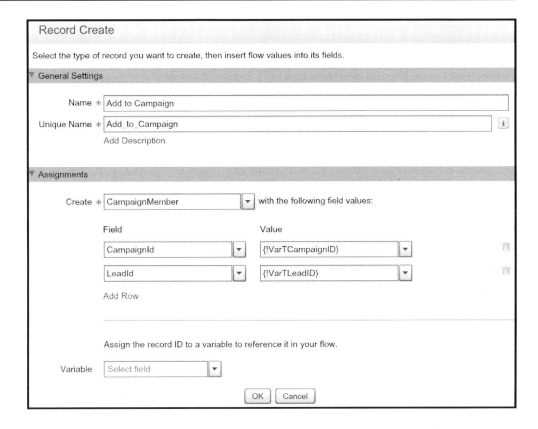

You can also save the newly created record ID in a variable and refer to it anywhere in the Flow.

The current user must have "Marketing User" on their user so they can access Campaign records. The **CampaignMember** object represents the relationship between a campaign and either a lead or a contact. For more details, visit,
`https://www.salesforce.com/developer/docs/api/Content/sforce_api_objects_campaignmember.htm`.

4. Once you are done, click on the **OK** button.

5. Use a connector to connect to the **Record Create** element, **Create lead record,** and the **Record Create** element **Add to Campaign,** as shown in the following screenshot:

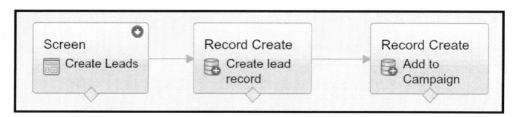

6. Save your Flow and close the Flow Designer using the **Close** button. This will redirect you to the **Flow Detail** page.

# Activating a version of a Flow

Once you have activated a Flow and you want to modify it, Salesforce doesn't allow you to do it. There are two possibilities (mentioned in step 1 and 2):

1. Create a new Flow by copying the activated Flow.

2. Modify the activated Flow and save it as **New Version** or save the activated Flow as **New Version** and modify it. Once you are done with the modifications, activate the new version of the Flow.

3. You can have multiple versions of a Flow, but you can only activate one version at a time. The **Flow Detail** page allows you to activate or deactivate one version of a Flow. Click on the **Activate** link, available next to version 1 of the Flow, as shown in the following screenshot:

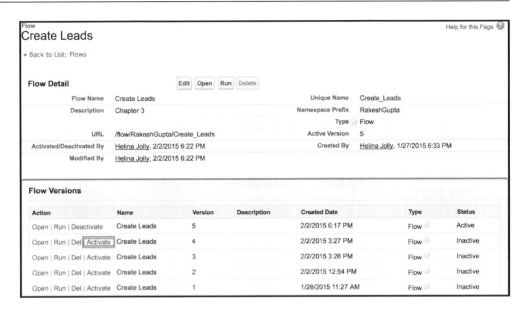

If the Flow doesn't have a start item, the **Activate** link will not be available.

4. From the **Flow Detail** page, copy the unique URL; it will look like `/flow/Create_Lead`.

# Passing values to Flow variables through a URL

There are many ways to call a Flow, as we discussed in `Chapter 1`, *Getting Started with Visual Workflow*. One of them is to call a Flow via a custom button or link. Using this, we can call a Flow and also pass the value to Flow variables. The next task is to create a custom button on a campaign object and add it to the campaign detail page:

1. To create a custom button, navigate to **Setup** | **Build** | **Customize** | **Campaigns** | **Buttons, Links, and Actions** and click on the **New Button or Link** button. Enter `Create Lead` in the **Name** field and for **Display Type**, and select **Detail Page Button**. For **Behavior**, select **Display in existing window without sidebar or header**; for **Content Source**, select **URL**, and then construct the URL as per the business needs.

To pass the value to a Flow variable, use `?VariableUniqueName=Value`. If you want to set values to multiple Flow variables, then append `?VariableUniqueName1=Value1&VariableUniqueName2=Value2` to the end of the URL. If you want to set values for a collection variable, then use `?VariableUniqueName=Value1&?VariableUniqueName=Value2`.

At the end, a custom button URL will look like `/flow/Create_Leads?VarTCampaignID={!Campaign.Id}`. Note that these parameters have to exactly match the Flow input variables and also have to have the same case (upper or lower). We have used `VarTCampaignID` because we named our input variable in the Flow.

2. Once you are done, click on the **Save** button.
3. The next task is to add a custom button on a page layout. Navigate to **Setup | Build | Customize | Campaigns | Page Layouts**, click on the **Edit** link, drag and drop a custom button **Create Lead** on to the page layout, and save the changes.
4. To test it, identify a campaign record and go to the campaign detail page and then click on the **Create Lead** button. This will open the Flow on the same window, where you can fill in all the details. Click on the **Next** button, and Flow will create a new lead and attach it to the campaign.

Let's look at a business scenario. Helina Jolly received an e-mail from the marketing manager saying that he and his team are very happy with the Flow created by her. Marketing teams want an enhancement in the current Flow so that as soon as users are done with the data entry, and after they click on the **Next** button, they will be redirected to the campaign detail page.

# Setting the finish location or redirecting the URL for a Flow

To set the finish location or to redirect a user to a specific page after completing the Flow execution for a custom button/link, navigate to the custom button, **Create Lead,** that we have created in the preceding example and append the `retURL` function to the button URL. For this scenario, append `&retURL={!Campaign.Id}` at the end of the URL.

Finally, the Flow URL will look like this:

```
/flow/Create_Leads?VarTCampaignID={!Campaign.Id}&retURL={!Campaign.Id}
```

At the end, the custom button will look like what is shown in the following screenshot:

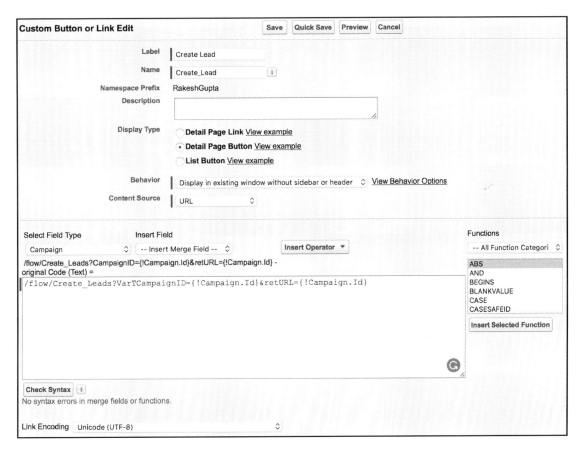

Once you are done, click on the **Save** button. To verify, go the campaign detail page and try to create a lead on clicking the **Create Lead** button. At the end, after entering the data and clicking on the **Next** button, Flow will redirect you to the campaign detail page, from where you initiated this process.

# Hands on 3 - quickly update an account record

An account represents the customer, partner, or competitor. We can update an account through the Web, data loader, Workflow rule, Process Builder, and Apex code.

Let's look at a business scenario. Alice Atwood is working as a system administrator in Universal Containers. She has received a requirement from her manager to develop a Flow that allows users to update an account rating to **Cold** in a single click.

To develop this Flow, follow these instructions:

1. Navigate to **Setup** | **Build** | **Create** | **Workflow & Approvals** | **Flows**.
2. Click on the **New Flow** button; it will open the Flow canvas.
3. Create **Text** variable `VarTAccountID`, set **Input/Output Type** as **Input and Output**, and for **Default Value**, use `{!$GlobalConstant.EmptyString}`; we will use this variable to pass the account ID through the Flow URL.

## Adding Record Update elements to a Flow

The **Record Update** element allows you to update a group of records in Salesforce using Input, Constant, Variable, or other values from the Flow. This allows you to update either a single record or multiple records at a time depending on how you fixed the filter criteria. Now, we will add a **Record Update** element onto the canvas:

1. Click on the **Palette** tab and drag and drop the **Record Update** element onto the canvas; this will open a new window, where you have to enter the following details:
    - **Name**: Enter the name for the **Record Update** element. In this case, enter `Update account rating` as the name.
    - **Unique Name**: This will be autopopulated based on the name.
    - **Description**: Write some meaningful text so that another developer/administrator can easily understand why this **Record Update** element was created. When you select the **Record Update** element in the **Explorer** tab, the description appears in the **Description** pane.

- **Update**: Select the object for which you want to update the record. In this case, select the **Account** object.
- The next task is to set filter the criteria to identify which record gets updated; in this case, select **Id** as `{!VarTAccountID}`. Then, select the fields from the object that you want to update and assign the value or resource (input, Constant, and so on) to the data type, which must match. In this case, select the **Rating** field, and for the value, from the **PICKLIST VALUES** dropdown, select **Cold**. To add multiple fields, click on the **Add Row** link.

This will look like what is shown in the following screenshot:

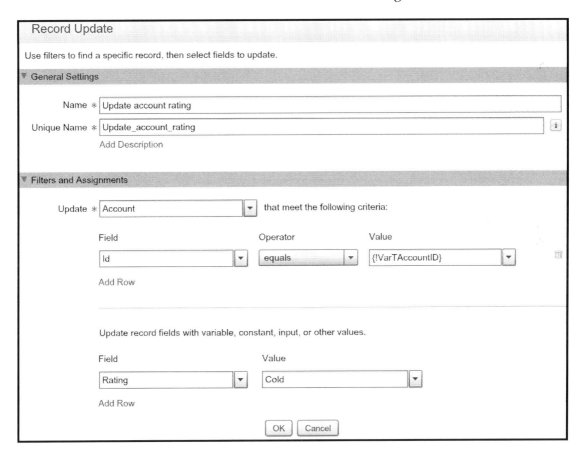

2. Once you are done, click on the **OK** button.

3. Set the **Record Update** element, **Update account rating,** as the **Start** element, as shown in the following screenshot:

4. Save the Flow with the name `update an account` and close the Flow Designer using the **Close** button; this will redirect you to the **Flow Detail** page. Don't forget to activate the Flow.

5. From the **Flow Detail** page, copy the unique URL; it will look like `/flow/Update_an_account`.

6. Now we will create a custom button on the account object to launch the Flow. To create a custom button, navigate to **Setup | Build | Customize | Accounts | Buttons, Links, and Actions** and click on the **New Button or Link** button. Enter the **Name** field as `Update Rating`; for **Display Type**, select **Detail Page Button**; for **Behavior**, select **Display in existing window without sidebar or header**; for **Content Source**, select **URL**, and construct the URL. At the end, a custom button URL will look like this: `/flow/Update_an_account?VarTAccountID={!Account.Id}&retURL={!Account.Id}`.

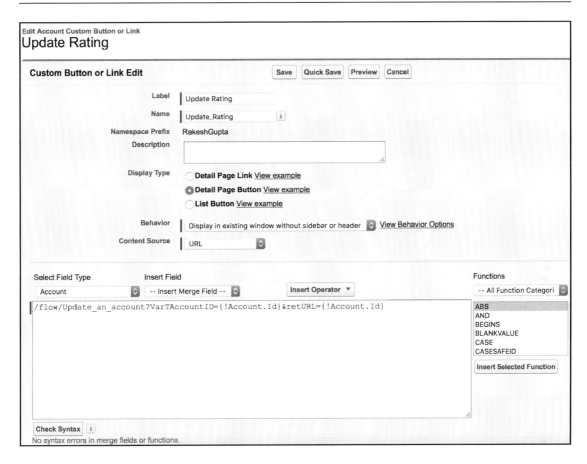

7. Once you are done, click on the **Save** button.

8. The next task is to add a custom button on a page layout. Navigate to **Setup** | **Build** | **Customize** | **Accounts** | **Page Layouts**, click on the **Edit** link, and drag and drop a custom button, **Update Rating,** onto the page layout, and click on the **Save** button to save the changes.

9. To test this, identify an account record and go to the account details page; click on the **Update Rating** button.

Flow will update the account status to **Cold**, as shown in the preceding screenshot. You can use this concept to create a wizard that allows your users to update the Opportunity stage by a single click. Also, make sure your Flow sets all fields to values that meet your active validation rules.

# Hands on 4 - cleaning Chatter group feed

A Chatter group is a place where all internal communication can happen. Here, users can post statuses, files, links and announcements, add records, and so on. We are going to discuss ways to use the **Record Delete** element and images to display messages.

Let's look at a business scenario. Helina Jolly is working as a system administrator in Universal Containers. She has received a requirement from one of the Chatter group managers. She is looking for a way to delete Chatter posts (only textposts), and she also wants to define a date (to delete all textposts created before this date).

To develop this Flow, follow these instructions:

1. Navigate to **Setup** | **Build** | **Create** | **Workflow & Approvals** | **Flows**.
2. Click on the **New Flow** button; it will open the Flow canvas for you.
3. Then, navigate to the **Palette** tab, and drag and drop the **Screen** element onto the Canvas; this will open a **Screen** element window.
4. Enter the **Name** field as `Delete Feeds`; you can also add **Description**. Under the **Navigation Options** section, select **Don't show Previous button** from the dropdown. Optionally, you can add **Help Text** as well.
5. The next task is to add a few fields onto the screen to capture the details. Add a **Textbox** field and a **Date** field on the screen by navigating to the **Add a Field** tab. Double-click on the **Textbox** field available under the **INPUTS** section; there is one for **Chatter Group ID** and one **Date** field for **Date**, as shown in the following screenshot:

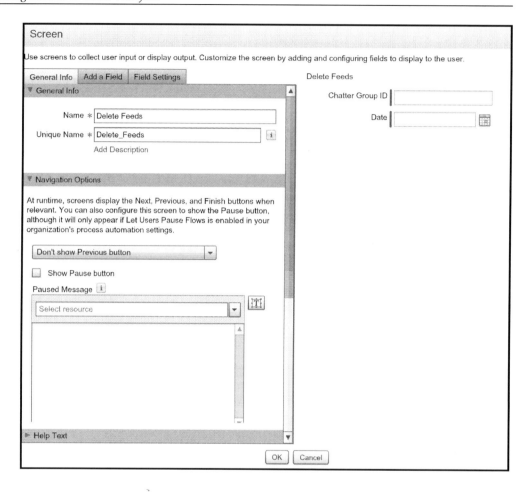

Don't forget to select the **Required** checkbox for all two fields. Click on **OK** once you are done.

# Adding the Record Delete element to a Flow

The **Record Delete** element allows you to delete a group of records in Salesforce using input, constant, variable, or other values from the Flow. It allows you to update either a single record or multiple records at a time, depending on how you fixed the filter criteria. Now, we will add a **Record Delete** element to this Flow:

1. Navigate to the **Palette** tab and drag and drop the **Record Delete** element onto the canvas; this will open a new window, where you have to enter the following details:
   - **Name**: Enter the name for the **Record Delete** element. In this case, enter `Delete Chatter Group Feed` as **Name**.
   - **Unique Name**: This will be autopopulated based on the name.
   - **Description**: Write some meaningful text so that another developer/administrator can easily understand why this **Record Delete** element was created. When you select the **Record Delete** element in the **Explorer** tab, the description appears in the **Description** pane.
   - **Delete**: Select the object you want to delete the record of. In this case, select the **CollaborationGroupFeed** object.

2. The next task is to set the filter criteria to identify which record gets deleted. In this case, select **ParentId**, which equals to the `{!Chatter_Group_ID}` screen input element, select **CreatedDate**, which is less than the `{!Date}` screen input element, and for the **Type** field, from the **PICKLIST VALUES** dropdown, select **TextPost**. To add multiple fields, click on the **Add Row** link.

The **CollaborationGroupFeed** object represents a single feed item on a Chatter group feed. For more details,
visit `https://www.salesforce.com/developer/docs/api/Content/sforce _api_objects_collaborationgroupfeed.htm`.

3. This will look like what is shown in the following screenshot:

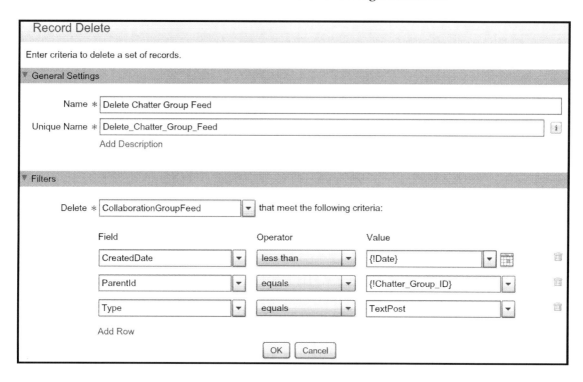

4. Once you are done, click on the **OK** button.

5. Use the connector to connect the **Screen** and **Record Delete** elements and set the **Screen** element **Delete Feeds** as the **Start** element, as shown in the following screenshot:

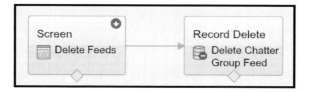

6. Save the Flow with the name **Delete Chatter Group Feed** and close the Flow Designer using the **Close** button; this will redirect you to the **Flow Detail** page. Don't forget to activate the Flow.

7. From the **Flow Detail** page, copy the URL; it will look like `/flow/Delete_Chatter_Group_feeds`.

# Hands on 5 - adding Flow to the home page layout

Now we will create a home custom link and add it to the home page layout; to call the Flow user, we have to click on this custom link:

1. To create a home custom link, navigate to **Setup** | **Build** | **Customize** | **Home** | **Custom Links** and click on the **New** button. Enter the **Name** field as `Clean Chatter Group Feeds`; for **Behavior**, select **Display in existing window without sidebar or header**; for **Content Source**, select **URL**, and construct the URL.

   At the end, the custom button URL will look like `/flow/Delete_Chatter_Group_feeds?retURL=/home/home.jsp`. The `retURL=/home/home.jsp` part will redirect the user to the home page after completion of the Flow execution. Your custom button should look like what is shown in the following screenshot:

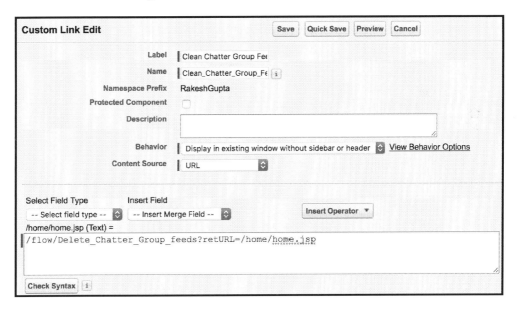

2. Now we will add a home custom link to a new home page component. To create this, navigate to **Setup** | **Build** | **Customize** | **Home** | **Home Page Components** and click on the **New** button. Enter the **Name** field as `Clean Chatter Group Feeds`; for **Type**, select **Link** and then move a custom **Clean_Chatter_Group_Feeds** link from the **Custom Links not to show** pane to the **Custom Links to show** pane, as shown in the following screenshot:

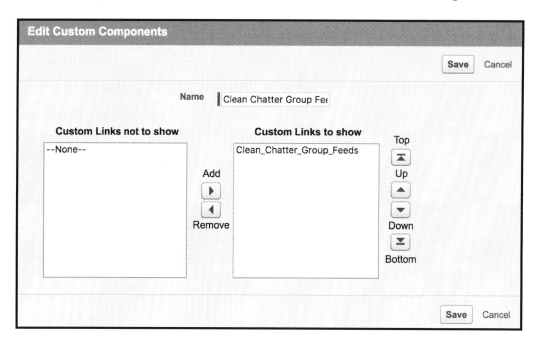

3. Once you are done, click on the **Save** button.
4. Finally, add this custom component to the home page layouts. To do this, navigate to **Setup** | **Build** | **Customize** | **Home** | **Home Page Layouts**, click on the **Edit** link available in front of all home page layouts, and then select the **Clean Chatter Group Feeds** component and save the changes.
5. To test this Flow, navigate to the **Home** tab and click on the **Clean Chatter Group Feeds** link available in the narrow (left) component:

6. This will redirect you to a new window, where you have to enter **Chatter Group ID** and **Date** and click on the **Next** button:

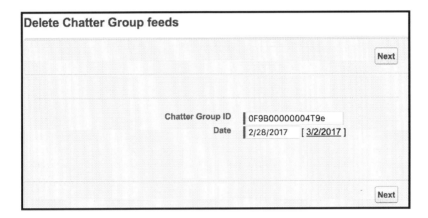

Flow will delete all the textposts where the **CreatedDate** is earlier than the date you have entered.

The problem with the preceding Flow, **Delete Chatter Group feeds**, is that if the **Record Delete** element doesn't find any textpost based on the filter criteria, then it will fail at runtime and the Flow owner will receive an e-mail with an error message, **Encountered unhandled fault**, as shown in the following screenshot:

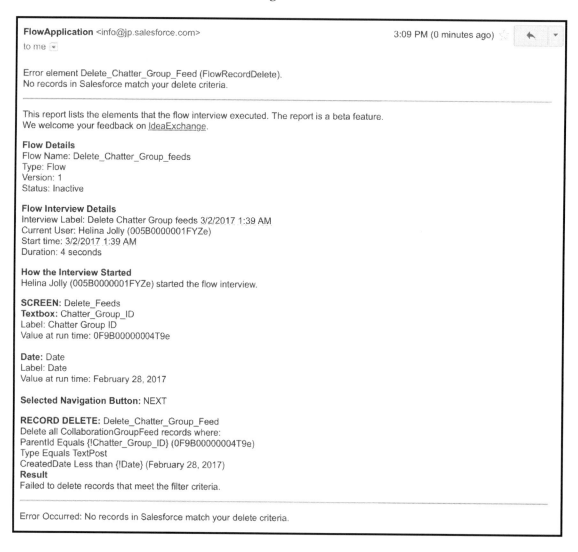

Error element Delete_Chatter_Group_Feed (FlowRecordDelete).
No records in Salesforce match your delete criteria.

This report lists the elements that the flow interview executed. The report is a beta feature.
We welcome your feedback on IdeaExchange.

**Flow Details**
Flow Name: Delete_Chatter_Group_feeds
Type: Flow
Version: 1
Status: Inactive

**Flow Interview Details**
Interview Label: Delete Chatter Group feeds 3/2/2017 1:39 AM
Current User: Helina Jolly (005B0000001FYZe)
Start time: 3/2/2017 1:39 AM
Duration: 4 seconds

**How the Interview Started**
Helina Jolly (005B0000001FYZe) started the flow interview.

**SCREEN:** Delete_Feeds
**Textbox:** Chatter_Group_ID
Label: Chatter Group ID
Value at run time: 0F9B00000004T9e

**Date:** Date
Label: Date
Value at run time: February 28, 2017

**Selected Navigation Button:** NEXT

**RECORD DELETE:** Delete_Chatter_Group_Feed
Delete all CollaborationGroupFeed records where:
ParentId Equals {!Chatter_Group_ID} (0F9B00000004T9e)
Type Equals TextPost
CreatedDate Less than {!Date} (February 28, 2017)
**Result**
Failed to delete records that meet the filter criteria.

Error Occurred: No records in Salesforce match your delete criteria.

This means if a Flow fails at runtime or if any unhandled exception occurs, then the user who created the Flow will receive a fault e-mail from Salesforce with a fault message. The e-mail includes the error message from the failure and details about every flow element that the interview executed. To resolve this error, we have to add a few elements (**Record Lookup** and **Decision**) to the Flow, **Delete Chatter Group feeds**.

# Saving a Flow as a different version

As we have already activated the Flow **Delete Chatter Group feeds**, you're not permitted to modify it. If you want to modify an existing Flow, then save it as either **New Flow** or **New Version**. Now, we will save the Flow **Delete Chatter Group feeds** as **New Version**. To do this, follow these instructions:

1. Navigate to **Setup** | **Build** | **Create** | **Workflow & Approvals** | **Flows**.
2. Open the Flow **Delete Chatter Group feeds**.
3. Click on the **Save As** button available in the top-left corner of the Flow canvas; this will pop up a window, where you have to enter the following details:
    - **Save As**: From the dropdown, you can select **New Version** or **New Flow**; in this case, select **New Version**.
    - **Name**: Enter the name for the Flow or Flow version. Let it be the old Flow name.
    - **Description**: Enter the description for the Flow or Flow version. In this case, enter `Version 2`.
    - **Type**: This is the type for the Flow or Flow version.
    - **Interview Label**: This displays the label for the Flow interview.

You can create a maximum of 50 versions of a Flow; however, you're not allowed to update its **Unique Name** when you save it as **New Version**. This will look like what is shown in the following screenshot:

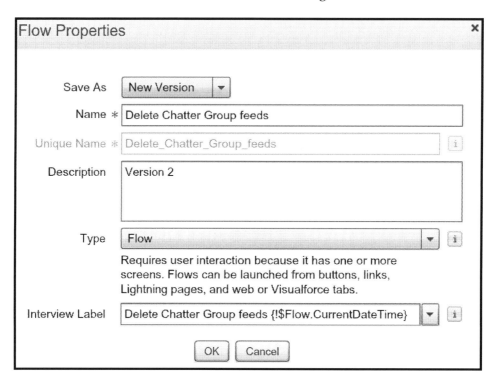

Note that Salesforce allows you to save the description for each version of a Flow, but in the **Flow Detail** page, you will see the description of the active version of a Flow. It also allows us to change the description of the Flow from the **Flow Detail** page, as shown in the following screenshot:

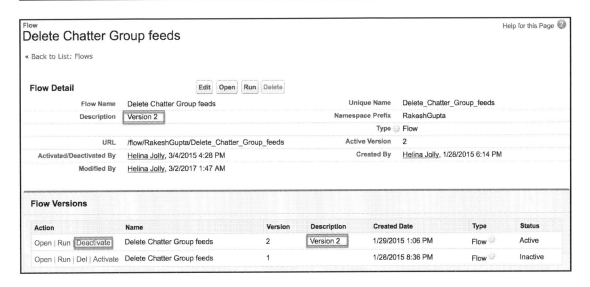

4. Once you are done with data entry, click on the **OK** button to save the changes.

5. Now we will modify **New Version** to make it bug-free. For this, first of all, we have to add a **Record Lookup** element on the Flow and then add a **Decision** element to decide whether a Chatter group contains any textposts that match the **Record Delete** entry criteria similar to the following screenshot:

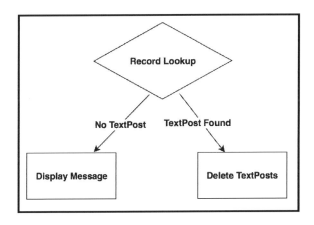

# Adding the Record Lookup element to a Flow

The **Record Lookup** element allows you to search a record in Salesforce and save the field's value in variables. Now we will add a **Record Lookup** element to this Flow with these instructions:

1. Navigate to the **Palette** tab and drag and drop the **Record Lookup** element onto the canvas; this will open a new window, where you have to enter following details:

   - **Name**: Enter the name for the **Record Lookup** element. In this case, enter `Search for TextPosts` as **Name**.
   - **Unique Name**: This will be autopopulated based on the name.
   - **Description**: Write some meaningful text so that another developer/administrator can easily understand why this **Record Lookup** element was created. When you select the **Record Lookup** element in the **Explorer** tab, the description appears in the **Description** pane.
   - **Look up**: Select the object you want to search the record of. In this case, select the **CollaborationGroupFeed** object. The next task is to define the search criteria. If you want to add multiple fields for the search criteria, then click on the **Add Row** link to add a new row. You can refer to the upcoming screenshot to define the search criteria.
   - **Assign the record's field value to variables**: Optionally, you can save the field's values into variables so that you can use them later in the Flow. Let's create a **Text** variable with the name `VarTGroupFeed` by expanding the **CREATE NEW** section of the drop-down list and set **Input/Output Type** as **Input and Output**; for **Default Value**, use `{!$GlobalConstant.EmptyString}`.

Don't forget to select the **Assign null values to the variable(s) if no records are found** checkbox, as shown in the following screenshot:

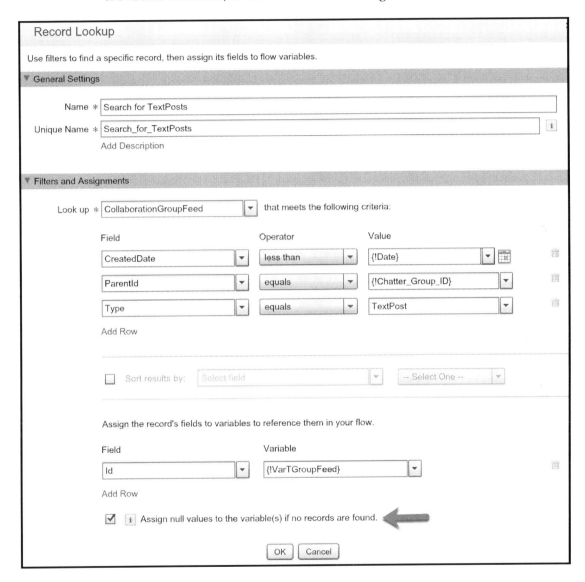

2. Once you are done, click on the **OK** button.

3. Now we will add the **Decision** element to evaluate the variable `VarTGroupFeed`. Drag and drop the **Decision** element onto the Flow canvas. Enter **Name** as `Decide the next step` and **Unique Name** will autopopulate based on **Name**. Optionally, you can also add **Description** for the **Decision** element. Then, create two outcomes for the **Decision** element, which are as follows:

   - **Not Found**: Select the `VarTGroupFeed` variable with the **is null** operator and the `{!$GlobalConstant.True}` value.
   - **Found**: Enter the name `Found` as **DEFAULT OUTCOME**.

This is shown in the following screenshot:

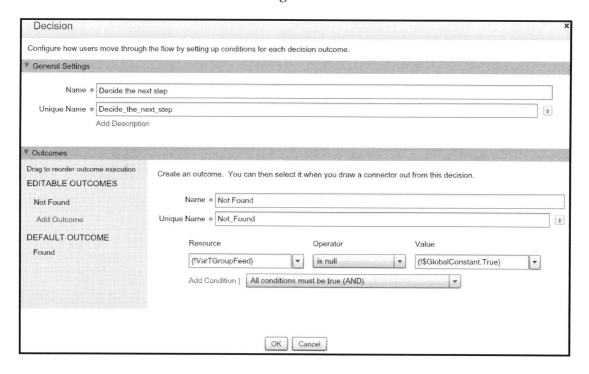

4. Once you are done, click on the **OK** button.
5. The next step is to add a **Screen** element with the name **Display Message** onto the canvas in order to display messages when no textpost is found. Add **Display Text** to the screen and configure the message, as shown in the following screenshot:

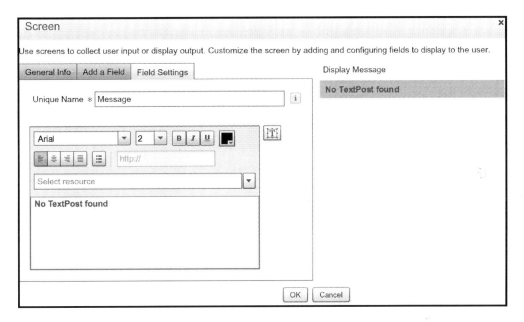

6. You can switch to the Rich Text editor to add color and HTML code; for more details, refer to the *Hands on 2 - real estate commission calculator* section of `Chapter 2`, *Creating Flow through Point and Click*.
7. Once you are done, click on the **OK** button.
8. Use the connector to connect the **Screen**, **Record Lookup**, **Decision**, and **Record Delete** elements; set the **Screen** element **Delete Feeds** as the starting point, as shown in the following screenshot:

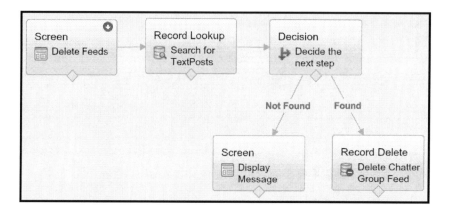

9. Save the Flow and close the Flow Designer using the **Close** button; this will redirect you to the **Flow Detail** page. Don't forget to activate the Flow version 2.

10. To test it, navigate to the **Home** page and click on the **Home** custom link that we added to **Clean Chatter Group Feeds**; refer to step 4 of the *Hands on 5 - adding Flow to the home page layout* section for more details. If the Flow is unable to find any textpost, it will display the following message:

You can also use an image with **Display Text**; to do this, switch to the normal editor and use the HTML code.

# Hands on 6 - adding an image to Display Text

We will add an image to the **Display Message** screen (refer to step 5 of the *Adding the Record Lookup element to a Flow* section of *Hands on 5 - adding Flow to the home page layout*) under the **Display Text** field's message. To add an image, follow these instructions:

1. First of all, copy the URL of the image.
2. Open the Flow **Delete Chatter Group Feeds** version 2. Then, double-click on the **Screen** element **Display Message** to open it and navigate to the **Display Text** message. Switch to the normal editor and append the following HTML image tag:

```
<img src="https://rakeshistom.files.wordpress.com
/2017/03/untitled.png" height="80" width="80" align="middle">
```

After this, it will look like what is shown in the following screenshot:

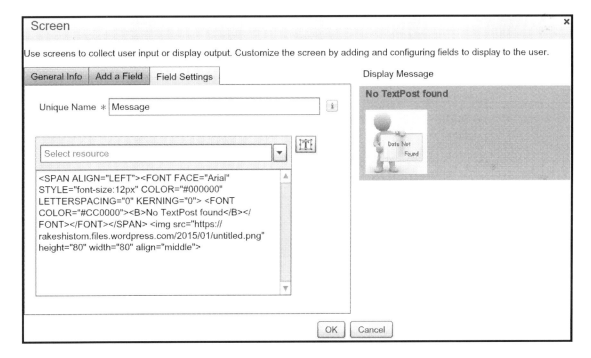

3. Once you are done, click on the **OK** button.
4. Click on **Save As** to save the Flow as **New Version**, that is, Version 3.

# Hands on 7 - saving data from a feedback form

In Chapter 2, *Creating Flow through Point and Click*, in the *Hands on 3 - displaying a feedback form based on conditions* section, we created a Flow for survey purposes, which is **Displaying feedback form based on age**. Now, a business user wants to save the survey detail in a custom object so that in future, they can run the report and get consolidated feedback. To do this, follow these instructions:

1. First of all, create a custom object Survey to save the survey data and set the record name as **Text** data type. Create two fields, as shown in the following screenshot, and grant permission to the respective profiles:

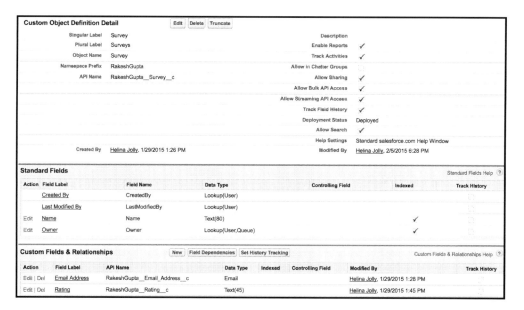

2. Navigate to **Setup** | **Build** | **Create** | **Workflow & Approvals** | **Flows**.

3. Open the Flow **Displaying feedback form based on age**.

4. Remember that we haven't activated this Flow yet. Now we will add a **Record Create** element to this Flow. Navigate to the **Palette** tab and drag and drop the **Record Create** element onto the canvas; this will open a new window, where you have to enter following details:

   - **Name**: Enter the name for the **Record Create** element. In this case, enter `Create Survey Record` as **Name**.

   - **Unique Name**: This will be autopopulated based on the name.

   - **Description**: Write some meaningful text so that another developer/administrator can easily understand why this **Record Create** element was created. When you select the **Record Create** element in the **Explorer** tab, the description appears in the **Description** pane.

   - **Create**: Select the object for which you want to create the record. In this case, select the `Survey__c` object.

   - The next task is to assign the value or resource to the object fields (data types must match). Map the **Name** field with the screen input field `{!Name}`, the **Email_Address__C** field with the screen input field `{!Email_Address}`, and the **Rating__c** field with the screen input field `{!Rating}`, as shown in the upcoming screenshot. To assign value to multiple fields, click on **Add Row** link.

   - **Variable**: Optionally, you can save the new record's ID into a variable so that you can use it later in the Flow.

This will look like what is shown in the following screenshot:

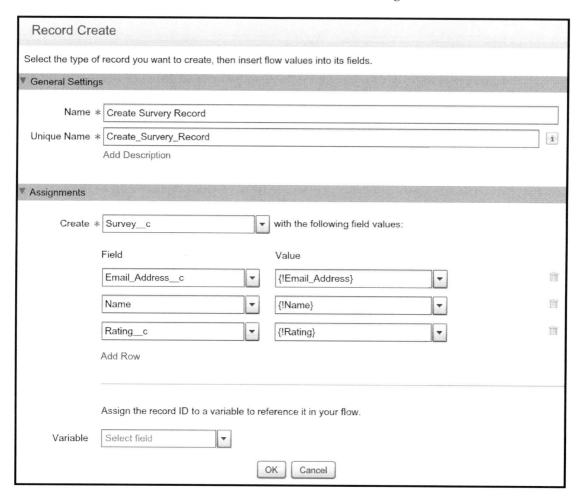

5. Once you are done, click on the **OK** button.

6. Use the connector to connect the **Screen** and **Record Create** elements with the rest of the Flow, as shown in the following screenshot:

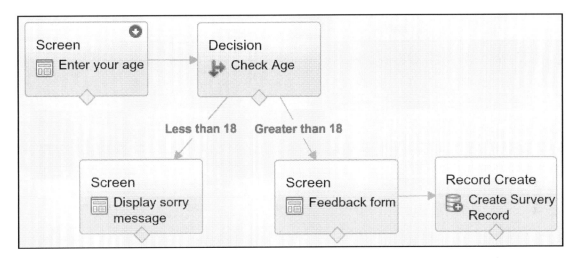

7. If you are done with the Flow designs, click on the **Save** button to save the changes and don't forget to close the Flow Designer.

# Hands on 8 - sending an e-mail

Let's look at a business scenario. Sara Bareilles, who is working on the Flow **Displaying feedback form based on age**, received a new requirement to send a thank you e-mail to participants on their successful completion of a survey. To implement this, follow these instructions:

1. Click on the **Resource** tab and add **Text Template** to create an e-mail template. Enter **Unique Name** as EmailTemplate and create an e-mail template, as shown in the following screenshot. You can also use an HTML tag here:

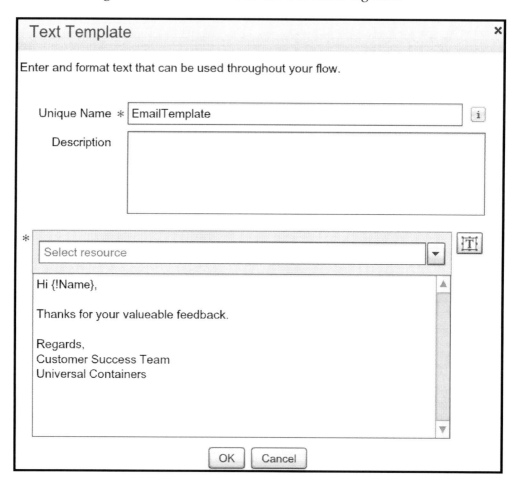

2. Once you are done, click on the **OK** button.

3. Now we will use the **Send Email** static action to send out an e-mail to participants. Click on the **Palette** tab and drag and drop the **Send Email** static action onto the canvas; this will open a new window, where you have to enter the following details:

   - **Name**: Enter the **Name** field for the **Send Email** element. In this case, enter `Thank you email` as **Name**.

   - **Unique Name**: This will be autopopulated based on the name.

   - **Inputs**: Enter text in **Body** for the e-mail. In this case, use **Text Template** that we created in previous steps. For **Subject**, enter `Thank you for completing our survey!`. For **Email Addresses (comma-separated)**, select `{!Email_Address}` screen input fields. If you want to use an organization-wide e-mail address instead of a current user's e-mail address to send an e-mail, add **Sender Type** as `OrgWideEmailAddress` and **Sender Address** as the organization-wide e-mail address that is used to send the e-mails. If you are using organization-wide email addresses to send out an e-mail, you have to enter the organization-wide e-mail address in **Sender Address**.

This is shown in the following screenshot:

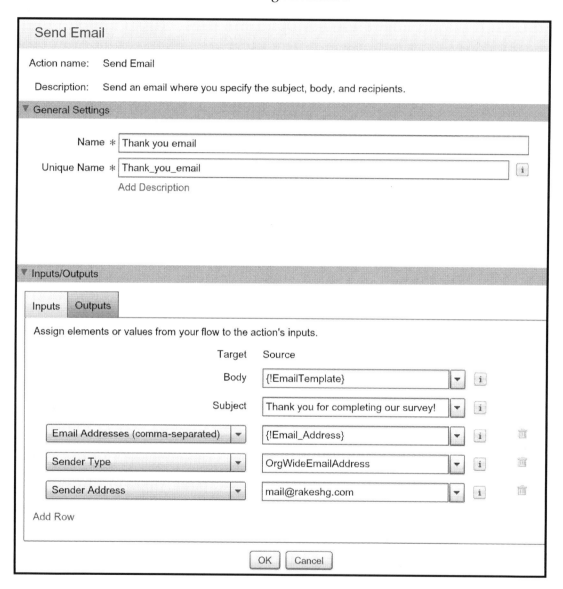

4. Once you are done, click on the **OK** button.

To find the organization-wide e-mail address for the current organization, navigate to **Setup** | **Administer** | **Email Administration** | **Organization-Wide Addresses**.

5. Use the connector to connect the **Record Create** element and the **Send Email** static action with the rest of the Flow, as shown in the following screenshot:

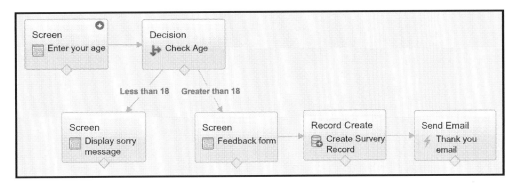

6. Save your Flow and close the Flow Designer using the **Close** button; this will redirect you to the **Flow Detail** page. Don't activate the Flow now; as a system administrator, you can test it without activating it.

7. To test this Flow, click on the **Run** button and enter the date 1/29/1984. Then, click on the **Next** button, fill in all the details and check your e-mail inbox (remember, you have to enter your e-mail address on the survey page). You should receive an e-mail that looks similar to what is shown in the following screenshot:

8. Navigate to the **Survey** tab and check the record created by the Flow:

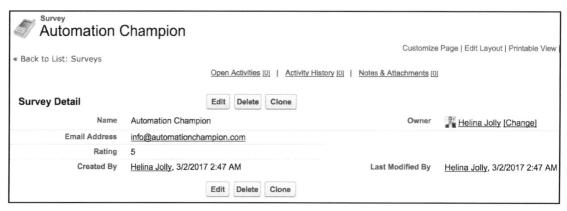

In Chapter 4, *Debugging and New Ways to Call a Flow*, you will learn the ways to expose this Flow for unauthenticated access using the Force.com site and the Visualforce page.

# Hands on 9 - creating a custom error message

If a runtime error occurs in any Flow while interacting with a database, it will display a common message to users. To display a custom message to users, we have to use the **Screen** and **FAULT** connectors.

Let's look at another business scenario. Joe Thompson is working as a system administrator in Universal Containers. He wants to add a custom error message to the Flow **Displaying feedback form based on age**.

First of all, create a **Screen** element and add **Display Text** to it. To do this, follow these instructions:

1. Navigate to **Setup** | **Build** | **Create** | **Workflow & Approvals** | **Flows**.
2. Open the Flow **Displaying feedback form based on age**.
3. Drag and drop the **Screen** element onto the Canvas. Enter the **Name** field as **Fault Screen**; you can also add **Description**. Under the **Navigation Options** section, select **Don't show Previous button** from the dropdown. Optionally, you can add **Help Text** as well.
4. The next task is to add **Display Text** onto the **Screen** element to display an error message. Navigate to the **Add a Field** tab. Double-click on the **Display Text** field available under the **OUTPUTS** section, as shown in the following screenshot:

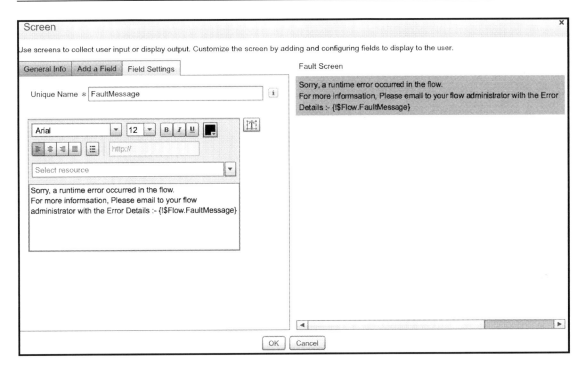

5. Once you are done, click on the **OK** button.
6. Now we will use the **FAULT** connector to connect it to the **Record Create** element. To connect the new **Screen** to the **Record Create**, element use the **FAULT** connector. Drag the node from the bottom of the **Record Create** element to the **Screen** element, as shown in the following screenshot:

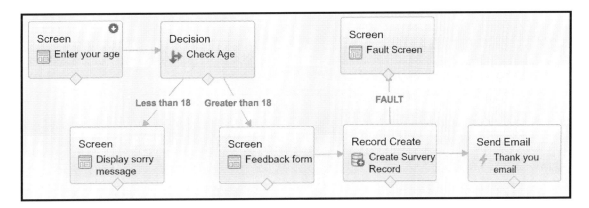

7. Once you are done, save your Flow and close the Flow Designer using the **Close** button.

 You can use the **FAULT** connector only with the **Record Create**, **Record Update**, **Record Delete**, **Record Lookup**, **Fast Create**, **Fast Update**, **Fast Delete**, **Fast Lookup**, and **Apex Plug-in** elements.

# Hands on 10 - conditional execution of a Flow with JavaScript

Until now, you learned how to execute Flow from a custom button or link and how to pass values to variables. Now, you will learn how to use JavaScript to pop up the Flow with the **Screen** element without human interaction.

Let's look at a business scenario. Helina Jolly is working as a system administrator in Universal Containers. She has created a Flow **Create Leads** that allows users to quickly create a lead and attach it to the campaign from the campaign detail page. For more details, refer to the **Create Leads** Flow under the *Hands on 1 - creating leads* section. She has received a requirement from her manager stating that users are not allowed to create leads if a campaign is not active.

We have already created a custom **Create Leads** button to invoke it in the *Hands on 1 - creating leads* section. We will modify the existing code of the custom button and add JavaScript to fulfill the previously mentioned requirement. To do this, follow these instructions:

1. Navigate to **Setup** | **Build** | **Customize** | **Campaigns** | **Buttons, Links, and Actions** and click on the **Create Lead** button. Then, click on **Edit** to modify the button code. Change the **Behavior** field to Execute JavaScript; for **Content Source**, select **OnClick JavaScript** and then replace the old script with the new script mentioned in the following code:

```
//Mandatory by Salesforce to run OnClick JavaScript

{!RequireScript("/soap/ajax/10.0/connection.js")}

if ({!Campaign.IsActive } == true)
{
window.open('/flow/Create_Leads?CampaignID=
{!Campaign.Id}&retURL={!Campaign.Id}');
}
```

```
else
{
alert('You are not authorized to create Leads for Inactive
Campaign');
}
```

2. Once you are done, click on the **Save** button:

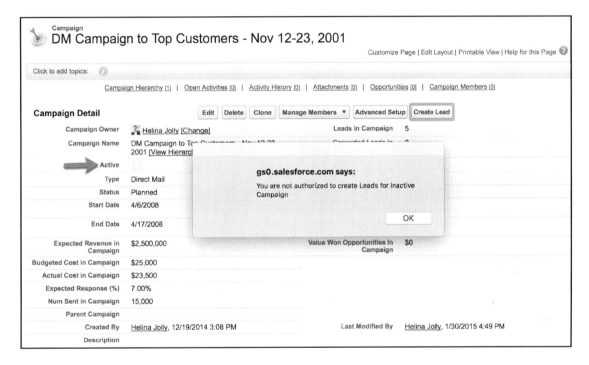

Now if the user tries to click on the **Create Lead** button, and the campaign is not active, it will prompt an alert or send a message to the users, as shown in the preceding screenshot.

   As of Spring'17 release, Onclick Javascript Buttons are not supported on Lightning Experience.

# A few points to remember

The following are some noteworthy points regarding data manipulation in Flow:

1. If the Flow doesn't have a starting point, then you will not get an Activate link on the **Flow Detail** page.
2. You have a maximum of 50 versions in a Flow.
3. Use the ID of the record type in a Flow to set the record type for a record.
4. It's not possible to redirect Flow users to a URL that is outside your Salesforce organization.
5. Make sure that the variable is set as **Input and Output** in order to pass values from the URL.
6. In the send e-mail static action, it's allowed to use **Email Addresses (comma-separated)** or **Email Addresses (collection)**, but the limit is a combined number of addresses of five or less.
7. You can use string values in **Email Addresses (comma-separated)**.
8. Use Text Template for formatted e-mail alerts. The Text Template allows HTML tags.
9. If you have used the **Record Delete** element to delete records, it can delete records that are between an approval process.
10. In the **Decision** element, you can use the contains operator with collections to identify whether it contains a particular value.
11. If you haven't activated the "Enable governor limits on all executed flows" critical update, Flow can only update or delete a maximum of 200 records.
12. Once you have enabled the "Enable governor limits on all executed flows", Flows can process a maximum of 10,000 records as a part of DML operations.
13. Sometimes, you may face unexpected problems while using Cloud Flow Designer, for example, when you lose Internet access. Salesforce doesn't save your changes automatically, so it is best practice to save as often as possible so that you don't accidentally lose a few hours' worth of work.
14. File type custom fields aren't supported in Visual Workflow.

# Exercises

1. Create a Flow that allows users to create an account and contact by entering data on a Single Screen. Add this Flow to the **Home** page's component on the left-hand side.

2. Create a Flow that allows users to delete accounts whenever an account's parent account is empty, and its related contacts, by clicking on a button. Put this button on the account details page.

3. In the last requirement, make sure that it won't work when the account is **Active** and it doesn't have parent account.

> To achieve this, modify your button code and use JavaScript.

4. Whenever an account's rating gets updated to **Cold**, update all related Opportunity stages to Closed-Lost by clicking on a button available on the account details page.

5. Create a Flow that allows users to update the Opportunity stage to Closed-Won by a single click (this means that by clicking on a single button, they can update the Opportunity stage to Closed-Won).

6. Create a Flow that clones Opportunity with the required fields only and clears out all other fields. Close date should be Opportunity cloned date plus 45 days, and stage should be **Prospecting**. New Opportunity name should include the word "Copy" after the name (**Burlington Textiles Corp of America - Copy**, where **Burlington Textiles Corp of America** is **existing opportunity name**). Place this button on the Opportunity detail page. Don't allow system administrators to use this Flow.

7. Create a Flow that allows users to create three leads at a time and also places it on the campaign detail page. After completion, redirect users to the lead's views, that is, today's leads.

8. Create a Flow that allows you to unfollow all users and records with a single click.

9. Create a Flow that allows users to add followers in an account record. Add this Flow to the account details page, and after the completion of the Flow execution, redirect users to the account tab.

10. Create a Flow that allows opportunity owners to create assets from Opportunity product by clicking on a button. Place this button on the Opportunity product detail page.
11. Create a Flow that allows users to create Closed Opportunity from an order. Set the Opportunity details, as mentioned here:

- **Opportunity name**: Order number
- **Account name (Opportunity)**: Account name (order)
- **Stage**: Closed-Lost
- **Close date (Opportunity)**: PO date (order)

Place this Flow as a button on the order detail page.

# Summary

In this chapter, we looked at various concepts related to manipulating data through Flow. We looked at ways to create Constant and Text Template. We also covered how to use the **Record Create**, **Record Update**, **Record Delete**, and **Record Lookup** elements in Flow. We went through ways to activate a Flow and pass values to Flow variables using URL and custom buttons. Then, we moved forward and discussed how to redirect a user to the desired screen after the completion of the Flow. We also discussed a way to send e-mails from Flow, that is, the **Send Email** static action. In the next chapter, we will discuss concepts related to the automation of your business processes and expose Flow for unauthenticated access.

# 4
# Debugging and New Ways to Call a Flow

In the previous chapter, we discussed how we can create, update, and delete records using Flow. We also discussed how to pass variable values through a custom button or link and redirect users to a page after completion of the Flow. We also learned a way to display a custom error message in a Flow and how to use JavaScript with a Flow. In this chapter, we will discuss how to use the style sheet with Flow, OpenFlow access for unauthenticated access, and use a controller to pass the value into Flow variables. We will also discuss a few more ways to call Flow and learn how to access cross-object fields in Flow. The following topics will be covered in this chapter:

- Debugging your Flow
- Who can run the Flow and how
- Automating your business process:
  - Copying the followers from an Opportunity
  - Opening a Flow for unauthenticated access
  - Setting finish behavior in the Visualforce page
  - Accessing a Flow through Salesforce1
  - Setting Flow variable values from a Visualforce page
  - Invoking a Flow using a controller
  - Invoking a Flow using an Inline Visualforce page
  - Using Flow to save the data from a Visualforce page
  - Using cross-object fields in Flow

# Debugging your Flow

In Chapter 3, *Manipulating Records in Visual Workflow*, we discussed a way to display a meaningful error message to users when an unhandled exception occurred at runtime. But apart from displaying the custom error message to users, it's also important to understand the various ways through which you can debug the Flow.

# On screen debugging

There are various ways through which you can debug the Flow on screen, which are discussed in the upcoming sections.

## Inbuilt debugging tools

While working, sometimes, you may get an error generated by Visual Workflow, which may be too general, for example, **We're sorry but a serious error occurred. Please don't close the Cloud Flow Designer window. Contact Salesforce Customer Support as soon as possible**. Visual Workflow has a prebuilt debugger tool that allows you to debug your Flow from the Flow canvas itself. To open the debug window, press *Ctrl + Shift + M* (Windows) or *command + Shift + M* (Mac) while you open the Flow canvas. This will look like what is shown in the following screenshot:

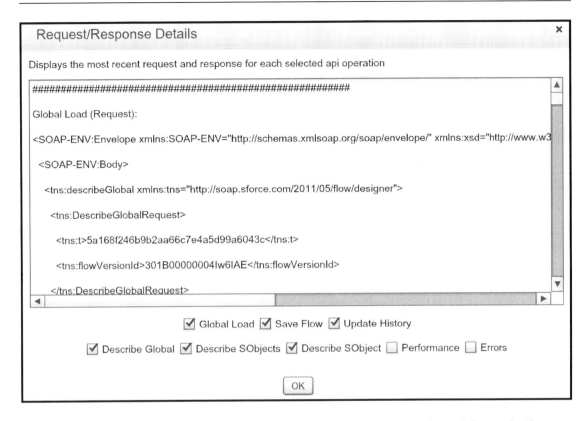

To view more details about this kind of error, you can use the Visual Workflow inbuilt debugging tool. To get more information about an error, make sure that you select the **Errors** checkbox.

# Using debug screens

Another way to debug the Flow is to keep a debug screen after each of the Flow elements (for example, after **Record Lookup**, **Record Create**, **Record Delete**, **Record Update**, **Assignment**, or **Decision**) while developing it. This will help you check each variable or field value in every step, and you can also check whether the Flow is working as designed (Flow follows the correct path) or not. You can add any field onto the debug screen for which you want to check values at runtime. Once you are done, disconnect screens for the normal running of Flow and in future, you can use it if required.

Let's look at a business scenario. In Chapter 3, *Manipulating Records in Visual Workflow*, we developed a Flow, that is, **Create Leads**. Say, Helina Jolly is working as a system administrator in Universal Containers and she worked on this Flow. She received a few messages from business users saying that Flow stops the creation of leads into the system.

She is planning to add a debug screen after the **Create Lead Record** element to make sure that the **Record Create** element is working fine. The steps to debug the Flow are as follows:

1. Open the existing Flow **Create Leads** that we created in the previous chapter.
2. From the **Palette** tab, drag and drop the **Screen** element onto the canvas; it will open a **Screen** element window for you. Enter **Name** as Verify Lead Creations; you can also add **Description**. Under the **Navigation Options** dropdown, select the **Don't show Previous button** option.
3. The next task is to add a field onto the screen in order to display the new lead's ID. Add **Display Text** to the **Screen** element by clicking on the **Add a Field** tab. Double-click on the **Display Text** field available under the **OUTPUTS** section, enter the **Unique name** field as Verify Lead Creation, and select the **{!VarTLeadID}** resource from **Variables**, as shown in the following screenshot:

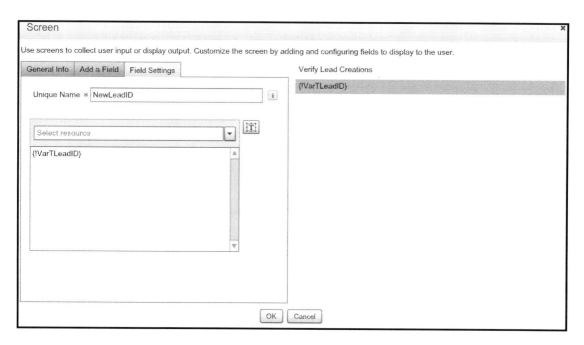

4. Once you are done, click on the **OK** button.

5. Use the connector to connect the **Verify Lead Creation** debug screen with the **Record Create** element and **Create lead record**, as shown in the following screenshot:

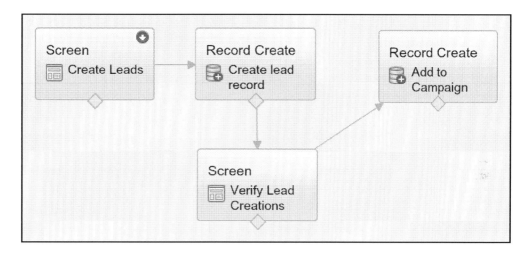

6. Save this Flow as the new version. From now, when Helina tries to create a new lead, the debug screen will display the newly created lead's ID.

# Debug log

If a Flow or process (created in Process Builder) fails at runtime or if any unhandled exception occurs, the system administrator who created the Flow or process will receive a fault e-mail from Salesforce with a fault message. The e-mail includes the error message from the failure and details about every Flow element that the interview executed.

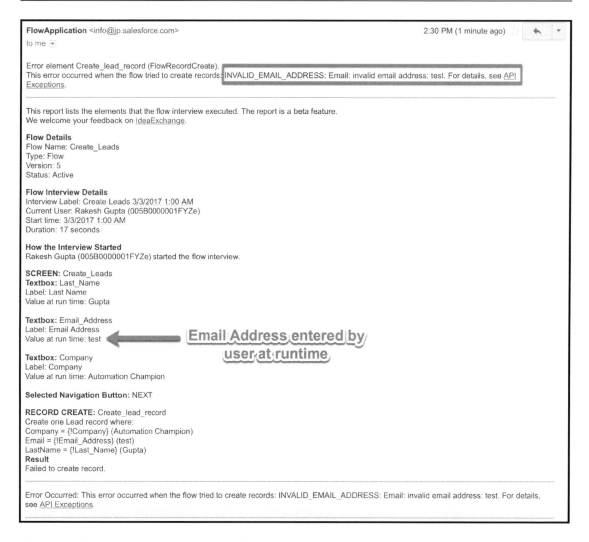

FlowApplication <info@jp.salesforce.com>                    2:30 PM (1 minute ago)

to me

Error element Create_lead_record (FlowRecordCreate).
This error occurred when the flow tried to create records: INVALID_EMAIL_ADDRESS: Email: invalid email address: test. For details, see API
Exceptions.

This report lists the elements that the flow interview executed. The report is a beta feature.
We welcome your feedback on IdeaExchange.

**Flow Details**
Flow Name: Create_Leads
Type: Flow
Version: 5
Status: Active

**Flow Interview Details**
Interview Label: Create Leads 3/3/2017 1:00 AM
Current User: Rakesh Gupta (005B0000001FYZe)
Start time: 3/3/2017 1:00 AM
Duration: 17 seconds

**How the Interview Started**
Rakesh Gupta (005B0000001FYZe) started the flow interview.

**SCREEN:** Create_Leads
**Textbox:** Last_Name
Label: Last Name
Value at run time: Gupta

**Textbox:** Email_Address
Label: Email Address
Value at run time: test  ⬅ **Email Address entered by user at runtime**

**Textbox:** Company
Label: Company
Value at run time: Automation Champion

**Selected Navigation Button:** NEXT

**RECORD CREATE:** Create_lead_record
Create one Lead record where:
Company = {!Company} (Automation Champion)
Email = {!Email_Address} (test)
LastName = {!Last_Name} (Gupta)
**Result**
Failed to create record.

Error Occurred: This error occurred when the flow tried to create records: INVALID_EMAIL_ADDRESS: Email: invalid email address: test. For details,
see API Exceptions.

The preceding screenshot displays a Flow error generated at runtime because the user has entered an invalid format of an e-mail address. If the system administrator who created the Flow or process leaves the organization (that is, if the the user gets deactivated in Salesforce), and if a Flow fails at runtime or if any unhandled exception occurs, they will receive a fault e-mail from Salesforce with a fault message.

The best way to troubleshoot runtime issues is to use **Debug Logs**. In the debug log, you will see the Flow action events in the workflow category of **Debug Logs**, which shows the Flow version and the values passed into Flow variables.

# Setting the debug log filter

Before going ahead with the debug log, the one thing you have to do is set the correct log filters, the steps for which are as follows:

1. Navigate to **Setup** | **Monitor** | **Logs** | **Debug Logs**.
2. Click on **New** available under the **Monitored Users** related list. Using a magnifying glass, add the users whose debug logs you would like to monitor and retain. In the current case, select your name.
3. Click on **Save**.
4. Navigate to the **Monitored Users** related list and click on the **Filters** link to change the debug logs filter. There are mainly three kinds of setting available:
   - **Log category**: The type of information logged.
   - **Log level**: For the Workflow and Visualforce page, set it as **FINER**. If you set the log level for the running user to be **FINER**, it will show your assignment actions and values.
   - **Events**: This is the combination of **Log category** and **Log level**.
5. Click on **Save**.

For example, if you try to run the **Create Leads** Flow that we created in `Chapter 3`, *Manipulating Records in Visual Workflow*, from canvas Flow by clicking on the **Run** button, then you will receive a runtime error or fault error. If you go to the debug log and open it, you can easily identify the reason behind it: the campaign ID is null (inside Flow, the **Record Create** element, **Add_to_campaign**). This is because we are passing the campaign ID through the custom button and not through the Flow, as shown in the following screenshot:

```
39.0 APEX_CODE,FINEST;APEX_PROFILING,INFO;CALLOUT,INFO;DB,FINEST;SYSTEM,FINE;VALIDATION,INFO;VISUALFORCE,INFO;WAVE,INFO;WORKFLOW,FINER
01:35:44.11 (11690516)|USER_INFO|[EXTERNAL]|005B0000001FYZe|rakeshistom-ulvj@force.com|India Standard Time|GMT+05:30
01:35:44.79 (79464305)|USER_INFO|[EXTERNAL]|005B0000001FYZe|rakeshistom-ulvj@force.com|India Standard Time|GMT+05:30
01:35:44.79 (80322960)|FLOW_ELEMENT_BEGIN|386461cf4df9776d3c2d7fef818c15a90925922-442b|FlowRecordCreate|Add_to_Campaign
01:35:44.79 (216835169)|FLOW_BULK_ELEMENT_DETAIL|FlowRecordCreate|Add_to_Campaign|1
01:35:44.79 (313404110)|FLOW_VALUE_ASSIGNMENT|386461cf4df9776d3c2d7fef818c15a90925922-442b|Add_to_Campaign|false
01:35:44.79 (313525137)|FLOW_ELEMENT_ERROR|This error occurred when the flow tried to create records: REQUIRED_FIELD_MISSING:
Attempted to add a campaign member where either the member id '00QB0000003AbMQ' or the campaign id 'null' is null.. For details,
see <a href='https://developer.salesforce.com/docs/atlas.en-us.api.meta/api/sforce_api_calls_concepts_core_data_objects.htm#'>API
Exceptions</a>.|FlowRecordCreate|Add_to_Campaign
01:35:44.79 (313695562)|FLOW_ELEMENT_END|386461cf4df9776d3c2d7fef818c15a90925922-442b|FlowRecordCreate|Add_to_Campaign
01:35:44.79 (456715779)|FLOW_ELEMENT_ERROR|This error occurred when the flow tried to create records: REQUIRED_FIELD_MISSING:
Attempted to add a campaign member where either the member id '00QB0000003AbMQ' or the campaign id 'null' is null.. For details,
see <a href='https://developer.salesforce.com/docs/atlas.en-us.api.meta/api/sforce_api_calls_concepts_core_data_objects.htm#'>API
Exceptions</a>.|FlowScreen|New_Lead_ID
```

Through the debug log, you can easily track a bug or error in your Flow.

 If a Flow or process fails at runtime, Flow or process creators receive an e-mail from Salesforce with a fault message. If the interview failed at multiple elements, Flow or process creators receive multiple e-mails, and the final e-mail includes an error message for each failure. If a flow uses fault connectors, its interviews can fail at multiple elements.

If Flow creators want to receive an e-mail for each fault/error, whether it's the same or not, enable critical updates, **Flow Creators Receive Email for Each Unhandled Fault**.

# Who can run the Flow and how

There are various concepts related to who can run the Flow and how, what kind of permission is required to run a Flow, and what happens when an organization wants to open a Flow for external users or unauthenticated access. To see the Flow detail page, users must have the **View Setup and Configuration** system permission; users who have the **Manage Force.com Flow** system permission can open, create, delete, activate, deactivate, or delete Flows.

# Debugging insufficient privileges on the custom button/link

Let's look at a business scenario. Helina Jolly is working as a system administrator in Universal Containers. She has developed a Flow, that is, **Create Leads** in Chapter 3, *Manipulating Records in Visual Workflow,* and embedded it into the custom button. She has received several e-mails from users saying that they are getting **Insufficient Privileges Errors** when they click on the **Create Lead** button, as shown in the following screenshot:

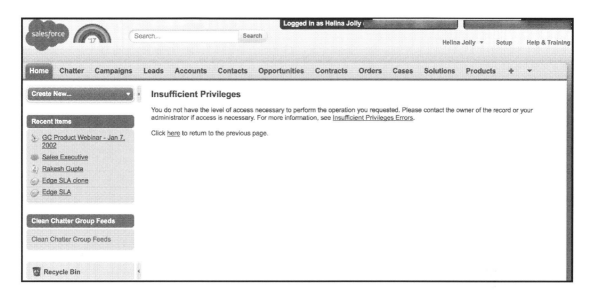

If a system administrator embeds a Flow into the custom button or link, then to run a Flow, the user must have either run Flow system permission under profile or the **Force.com Flow User** feature license selected in the user record.

# Embedding a Flow into a Visualforce page

Let's look at a business scenario. Alice Atwood, who is working as a system administrator at Universal Container, received a requirement from her manager to grant the **Create Leads** Flow access to partner community users.

The partner community profile doesn't have the **Run Flow** system permission, and you can't assign the **Force.com Flow User** feature license to them. So, the workaround is to use the Visualforce page in this case. The steps to grant permission to partner community users of a Flow are as follows:

1. Create a Visualforce page by navigating to **Setup | Build | Develop | Pages** and click on the **New** button. Use the **standard controller** for campaign in this case, as shown in the following code:

   ```
   <apex:page standardController="Campaign">
   <flow:interview name="Create_Leads"> // Flow interview
   component is used to embed flow in a Visualforce page.
   Create_Leads is flow Unique Name.
   <apex:param name="VarTCampaignID" value="{!Campaign.ID}"/>
   // apex:param is used to pass variable CampaignID value
   ```

```
to a flow
</flow:interview>
</apex:page>
```

You can download the example code files from your account at
`http://www.packtpub.com` for all the Packt Publishing books you have
purchased. If you purchased this book elsewhere, you can visit
`http://www.packtpub.com/support` and register to have the files e-
mailed directly to you.

2. Save this Visualforce page with the name `Flow_Partner_Community`.

3. The next task is to grant the Visualforce page access to the partner community
users. To do that, navigate to **Setup** | **Administer** | **Manage users** | **Profiles** and
select the partner community profile that you want to grant access to. Then,
navigate to **Apps** under the **Profile Overview** page, and select **Visualforce pages
access**. Next, click on **Edit** and move the desired Visualforce Page from **Available
Visualforce Pages** to the **Enabled Visualforce Pages** pane.

4. Once you are done, click on the **Save** button.

5. The next step is to create a custom button to call a Visualforce page on the campaign object. To create a custom button, navigate to **Setup** | **Build** | **Customize** | **Campaigns** | **Buttons, Links, and Actions** and click on the **New Button or Link** button. Enter the **Name** field as `Create Lead VF`; for **Display Type**, select **Detail Page Button**; for **Behavior**, select **Display in existing window without sidebar or header**; for **Content Source**, select **Visualforce Page**; and from the **Content** dropdown, select the Visualforce Page of **Flow_Partner_Community** and click on **OK**. It will look like what is shown in the following screenshot:

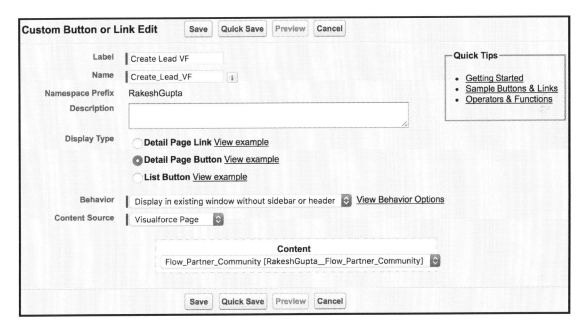

6. The next task is to add a new custom button on the campaign page layout. Navigate to **Setup** | **Build** | **Customize** | **Campaigns** | **Page Layouts**, click on the **Edit** link, and drag and drop the custom button **Create lead VF** on to the page layout and save the changes.

7. Now log in through partner community users and try to create leads by clicking on the **Create lead VF** custom button.

To create a lead, a user must create the permission on the lead object.

If you have embedded the Flow into a Visualforce page, then there are few ways in which users can use it to run a Flow. They are as follows:

- Custom buttons or links
- Visualforce tabs
- Force.com sites
- Salesforce1 action
- Salesforce1 navigation menu
- Inline Visualforce page

We will see these one by one later on in this chapter.

# Invoking a Flow using Process Builder

Until now, we have seen many Flows, but invoking or calling a Flow requires user intervention. There are many requirements for which we want a way so it will automatically call without a manual intervention.

To improve user adoption in the organization, management at Universal Container wants to implement a business process: if a user has not logged in in the last 15 days, then auto-freeze their user account and send out an e-mail to the user as well as the system administrator.

To solve this requirement, we have to use Flow, and to autofire Flow, we can use Process Builder. We will see similar types of examples in detail in `Chapter 7`, *Building Applications without Code*.

# Automating your business process

There are multiple scenarios that a business wants to automate. For example:

- Allow external users to fill the survey form, and after submitting, capture the data into Salesforce.
- To improve the collaboration, an organization wants to send a Chatter group link in the e-mail, and as soon as the users click on it, they are automatically added to the Chatter group.
- Whenever the Opportunity contact role is updated as a primary, update the Opportunity lead source, which is the same as the contact lead source.

We are going to discuss how we can use Flow elements with **Fast** elements (**Fast Create**, **Fast Update**, **Fast Delete**, and **Fast Lookup**) and the **Loop** element to implement the preceding business scenarios.

# Hands on 1 - copying the record followers

A user can follow records and users in Salesforce. As an owner or manager of a Chatter group or as a system administrator, you can add or remove members from Chatter groups. But you can't add or remove followers from or to the records.

Let's look at a business scenario. Alice Atwood is working as a system administrator at Universal Container. On a daily basis, she receives plenty of requests for Opportunity owners to add the same followers from old Opportunity X to new Opportunity Y. Currently, she is handling this through data loader, but before that, she used to spend time on data massaging.

We will create a Flow that will allow the system administrator to copy followers from Opportunity record X (old) to Opportunity record Y (new). We can assume that as the Opportunity owner wants to copy followers to a new record, it means that currently, records don't have any followers.

The steps to develop this Flow are as follows:

1. Navigate to **Setup** | **Build** | **Create** | **Workflow & Approvals** | **Flows**.
2. Click on the **New Flow** button, and it will open the Flow canvas for you.
3. Create a **Text** variable `VarT_NewOppID` to pass the new Opportunity ID (where the user wants to add followers) from the custom URL.
4. Then, navigate to the **Palette** tab, and drag and drop the **Screen** element onto the canvas; it will open a **Screen** element window for you. Enter **Name** as `Enter Old Opportunity ID`; you can also add **Description**. Under the **Navigation Options** section, select **Don't show Previous button** from the dropdown. Optionally, you can add **Help Text** as well.

5. The next task is to add a field onto the screen in order to capture the old Opportunity ID (from where the Opportunity owner wants to copy the followers). Add a **Textbox** field on **Screen** by clicking on the **Add a Field** tab. Double-click on the **Textbox** field available under the **INPUTS** section, as shown in the following screenshot:

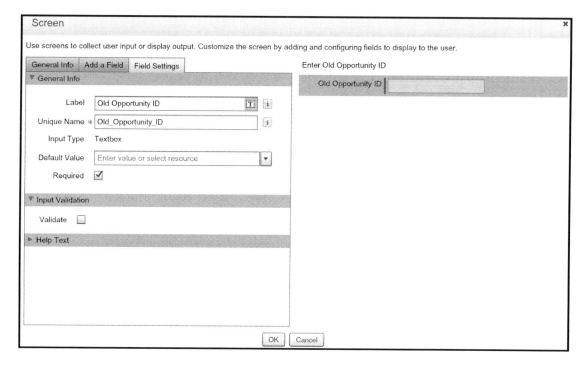

6. Once you are done, click on the **OK** button.
7. Now our next task is to get the list of followers from the old Opportunity. For this, we have to use the **Fast Lookup** element. The reason behind using **Fast Lookup** is that it allows you to save the outcomes into SObject Collection variable. Create an SObject Collection variable SocvOld_Opportuntiy_Followers for the object type **EntitySubscription** and set **Input/Output Type** as **Input and Output**, as shown in the following screenshot:

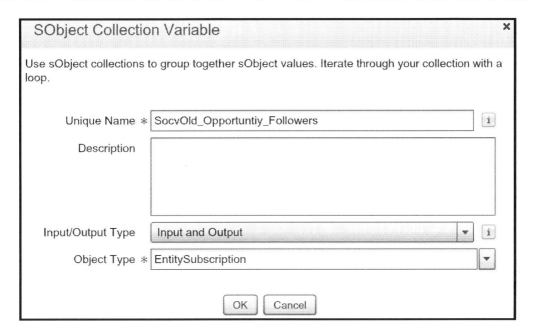

8. Once you are done, click on **OK**. We will use it in **Fast Lookup** to store the record details. Similarly, create another SObject Collection variable `SocvNew_Opportuntiy_Followers` and one SObject variable `SovIndividual_Follower_Details` for the object **EntitySubscription**.

# Adding the Fast Lookup element to a Flow

The **Fast Lookup** element allows you to search records in Salesforce and save results into SObject variable or SObject Collection variable. The difference between **Record Lookup** and **Fast Lookup** is as follows:

| Record Lookup | Fast Lookup |
| --- | --- |
| This allows you to save only one record field value. | This allows you to save all the records that **Fast Lookup** found after applying the filter criteria. |
| You can use variables or SObject variables to save the record details. | You can use SObject variable or SObject Collection variable to save the record details. |
| You have to map the record fields one by one with either variables or SObject variable. | You don't have to map the record fields. Here, you have to just select the fields whose data you want to save. |

Now we will add a **Fast Lookup** element to this Flow:

1. Click on the **Palette** tab and drag and drop the **Fast Lookup** element onto the canvas; it will open a new window for you, where you have to enter the following details:
   - **Name**: Enter the name for the **Fast Lookup** element. In this case, enter the name as `Followers from old Opportunity`.
   - **Unique Name**: This will be autopopulated based on the name.
   - **Description**: Write some meaningful text so that another developer/administrator can easily understand why this **Fast Lookup** element was created. When you select the **Fast Lookup** element in the **Explorer** tab, a description appears in the **Description** pane.
   - **Lookup**: Select the object for which you want to search the records. In this case, select the **EntitySubscription** object.
   - The next task is to define the search criteria. For this, map **ParentId** with the **Screen** element `{!Old_Opportunity_ID}`. If you want to add multiple fields for the search criteria, then click on the **Add Row** link to add a new row. You can take help from the following screenshot to define the search criteria. You can use the **Sort** option to sort the result.
   - **Variable**: Select SObject variable or SObject Collection variable to store the field's values for all records returned by **Fast Lookup**. In our case, select the SObject Collection variable `SocvOld_Opportuntiy_Followers`. Don't forget to select the **Assign null to the variable if no records are found.** checkbox. Finally, select fields whose values you want to store in SObject variable or SObject Collection variable. In this case, select **ParentId** and **SubscriberId**.

Refer to the following screenshot for more details:

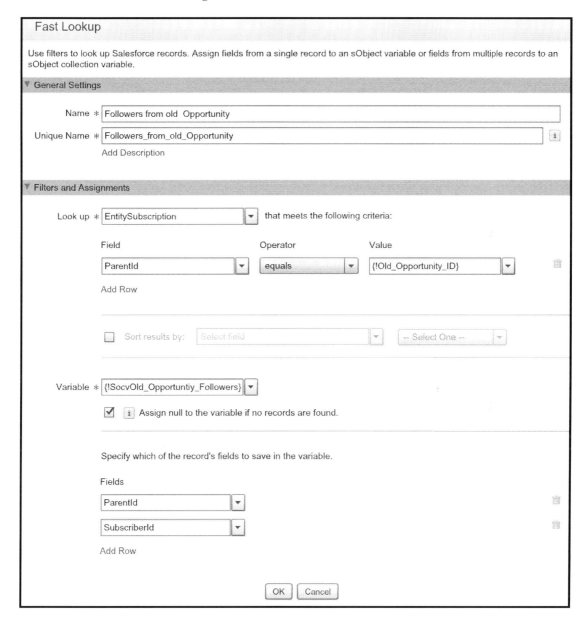

2. Once you are done, click on the **OK** button.

3. The next step is to check whether SObject Collection variable `SocvOld_Opportuntiy_Followers` contains any values or not. For this, we will use the **Decision** element. Drag and drop the **Decision** element onto the Flow canvas. Enter the **Name** field as `Check SObject Collection Variable` and **Unique Name** will be autopopulated based on the name. Optionally, you can also add **Description** for the **Decision** element. Then, create two outcomes for the **Decision** element, which are as follows:

    1. **Is null False**: Select the collection variable `SocvOld_Opportuntiy_Followers`; it is null `{!$GlobalConstant.False}`.

    2. **True**: Enter the name `True` for **DEFAULT OUTCOME**.

It will look like what is shown in the following screenshot:

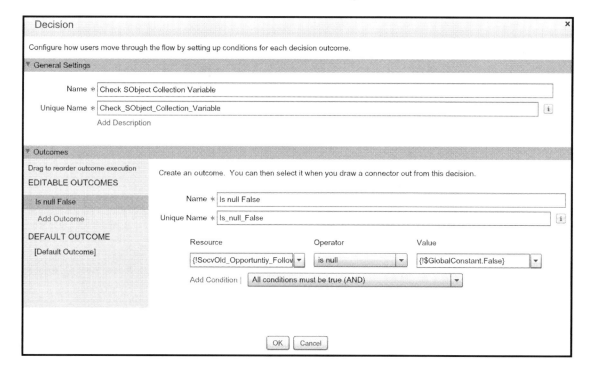

It is a best practice to use the decision element to check the SObject Collection variable or SObject variable data before performing a DML operation to avoid the runtime error.

# Adding the Loop element to a Flow

The **Loop** element is used to check each item in a collection variable and execute an action on it. For example, you can use the **Loop** element to store SObject Collection variable values into a **Loop** variable, that is, SObject variable, and both must have the same object as the collection. You can also use the **Loop** element to examine the collection variable (data type text) and copy its value into a **Text** variable.

If the SObject Collection variable is not null, it means that the old Opportunity record has some followers. We will use the **Loop** element to extract records from the SObject Collection variable (`SocvOld_Opportuntiy_Followers`) and store it to the SObject variable (`SovIndividual_Follower_Details`):

1. Click on the **Palette** tab and drag and drop the **Loop** element onto the Flow canvas. It will open a new window for you, where you have to enter the following details:
    - **Name**: Enter the name for the **Loop** element. In this case, enter **Name** as `Extract each followers`.
    - **Unique Name**: This will be autopopulated based on the name.
    - **Description**: Write some meaningful text so that another developer/administrator can easily understand why this **Loop** was created. When you select **Loop** in the **Explorer** tab, the description appears in the **Description** pane.
    - **Loop through**: In the **Assignments** section, select the collection or SObject Collection variable you want to loop through. In this case, select the SObject Collection variable **{!SocvOld_Opportuntiy_Followers}**. Select the order as **Ascending** in order to loop through the collection.
    - **Loop Variable**: Select SObject variable or variable as a **Loop** variable. In this case, select SObject variable. **{!SovIndividual_Follower_Details}** as the **Loop Variable**.

For more details, refer to the following screenshot:

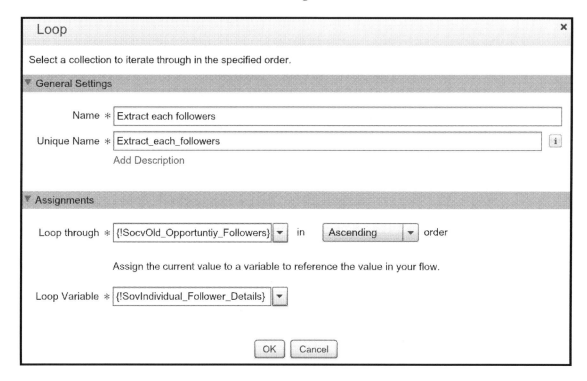

2. Once you are done, click on the **OK** button.
3. To add followers to a record, two things are required: one is **Subscriber Id** (user ID) and the other is **Parent ID** (record ID). The SObject Variable SovIndividual_Follower_Details already has a user ID, so we will assign a new Opportunity ID to the **Parent ID** field using the **Assignment** element.

# Adding an Assignment element to a Flow

The **Assignment** element is used to assign values to the Flow resources:

1. Navigate to the **Palette** tab and drag and drop the **Assignment** element onto the Flow canvas. This will open a new window for you, where you have to enter the following details:
    - **Name**: Enter the name for the **Assignment** element. In this case, enter Assign New OppID as the name.
    - **Unique Name**: This will be autopopulated based on the name.

- **Description**: Write some meaningful text so that another developer/administrator can easily understand why this **Assignment** element was created. When you select the **Assignment** element in the **Explorer** tab, the description appears in the **Description** pane.
- **Assignment**: In the **Assignment** section, select the **Variable** field whose value you want to modify; in this case, select **{!SovIndividual_Follower_Details.ParentId}**. Then, select the operator; it will depend on the data type of the selected variable. In this case, select **equals**. For **Value**, select an existing resource from the Flow, such as **Variable**, **Formula**, or **Constant**, whose value you want to assign. In this case, select **{!VarT_NewOppID}** as **Value**. To assign a value to multiple variables, use **Add Assignment** to enter new rows.

It will look like what is shown in the following screenshot:

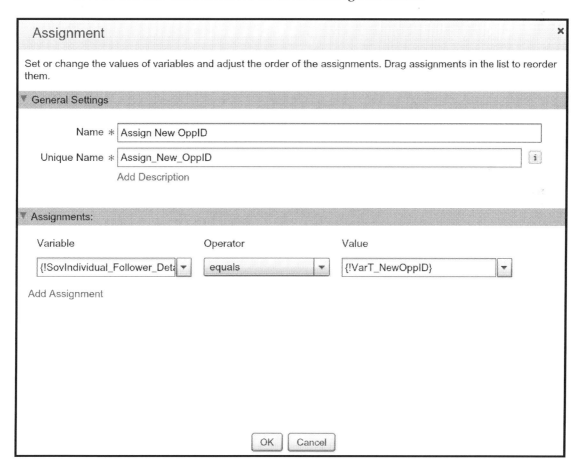

2. Once you are done, click on the **OK** button.
3. The next steps are to add all SObject variables into an SObject Collection variable. So at the end, we will create records in **EntitySubscription** at once. If you add a record using SObject variable for each record separately, you will easily hit the governor limit.
4. Drag and drop the **Assignment** element onto the Flow canvas, and it will open a new window for you. Enter `Add Sobject Variable into SObject Collection` as **Name** and add the SObject variable `SovIndividual_Follower_Details` to the SObject Collection variable `SocvNew_Opportuntiy_Followers`.

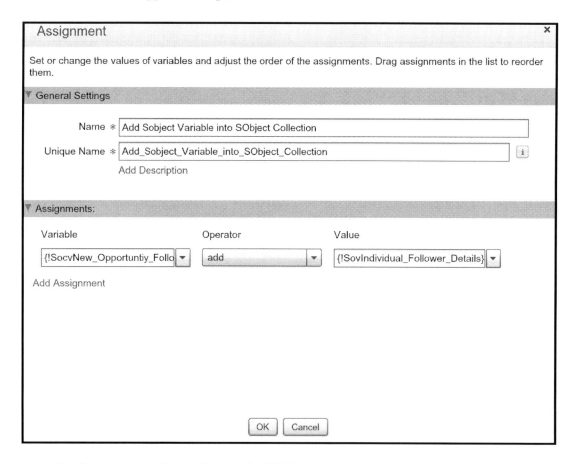

5. Once you are done, click on the **OK** button.
6. The final task is to create records in the **EntitySubscription** object. For this, we will use the **Fast Create** element.

# Adding the Fast Create element to a Flow

The **Fast Create** element allows you to create records using values stored in the SObject Collection variable or SObject variable. The difference between **Record Create** and **Fast Create** is as follows:

| Record Create | Fast Create |
| --- | --- |
| It allows you to create one record at a time. | It allows you to create single or multiple records at a time. |
| You can use variables or SObject variables to create a record. | You can use SObject variables or SObject Collection variables to create the record. |
| One by one, you have to map the record fields with either variables or SObject variable. | You don't have to map the record fields. Here, you have to just select the SObject variable or SObject Collection variable to create the records. |
| If you use multiple **Record Create** elements in a Flow, or the **Record Create** element inside the **Loop** element, then it will easily hit the governor limit. | To avoid the governor limits, add the multiple record details to a SObject Collection variable and refer to a **Fast Create** element. |

Now, we will add a **Fast Create** element with the following steps:

1. Click on the **Palette** tab and drag and drop the **Fast Create** element onto the Flow canvas. It will open a new window for you, where you have to enter the following details:
    - **Name**: Enter the name for the **Fast Create** element. In this case, enter `Add_Followers_to_new_Opportunity` as the name.
    - **Unique Name**: This will be autopopulated based on the name.
    - **Description**: Write some meaningful text so that another developer/administrator can easily understand why this **Fast Create** element was created. When you select the **Fast Create** element in the **Explorer** tab, the description appears in the **Description** pane.
    - **Variable**: To create a record or multiple records, you can either use SObject variable or SObject Collection variable. The object types must match, and each ID field must not have a value. In this case, select the SObject Collection variable `SocvNew_Opportuntiy_Followers`.

It will look like what is shown in the following screenshot:

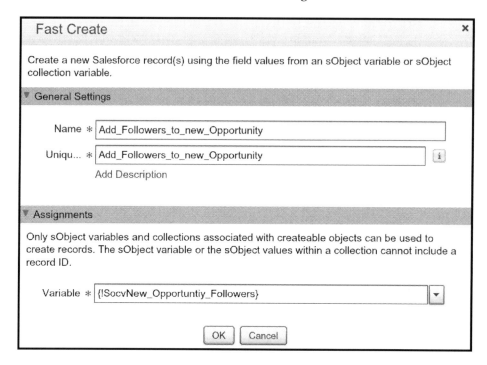

2. Once you are done, click on the **OK** button.
3. Use the connector to connect **Screen**, **Fast Lookup**, **Decision**, **Assignment**, and **Fast Create** elements, and set the **Screen** field **Enter Old Opportunity ID** as the start point, as shown in the following screenshot:

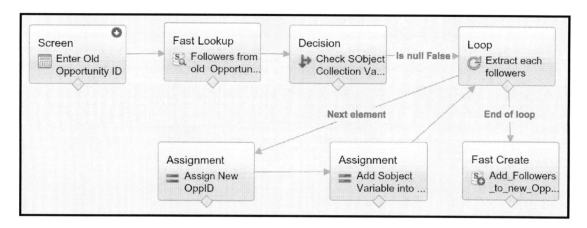

4. Save your Flow with the **Name** field `Copying the record followers` and close the Flow Designer using the **Close** button; it will redirect you to Flow detail page. Form here, copy the Flow URL.

5. To execute the Flow, we will create a custom button on the Opportunity object. To create a custom button, navigate to **Setup** | **Build** | **Customize** | **Opportunities** | **Buttons, Links, and Actions** and click on the **New Button or Link** button. Enter the name `Copy Followers`, for **Display Type** select **Detail Page Button**, for **Behavior** select **Display in existing window without sidebar or header**, for **Content Source** select **URL**, and then construct the URL as per the business needs. In this case,
`/flow/Copying_the_record_followers?VarT_NewOppID={!Opportunity.Id}&&retURL={!Opportunity.Id}`.

6. Once you're done, click on **Save**. The next task is adding a custom button on Opportunity page layouts. Navigate to **Setup** | **Build** | **Customize** | **Opportunities** | **Page Layouts**, click on the **Edit** link and drag and drop custom button **Copy Followers** onto the page layout, and save the changes.

7. To test it, create a new Opportunity record. Now identify an existing Opportunity record in which there are few followers, and copy the record ID from URL. Then navigate to newly create Opportunity, click on the **Copy followers** button and paste existing Opportunity ID (that you copied) and click on the **Next** button.

Flow will copy followers from the existing Opportunity record to a newly created Opportunity record.

# Hands on 2 - open a Flow for unauthenticated access

Until now, we have learned the different ways to call a Flow, and a Visualforce page is one of them. Once you have embedded Flow into a Visualforce page, business users can use it without having the **Run Flow** system permission or the **Force.com Flow User** feature license. In the beginning of this chapter, we had already discussed ways to embed a Flow into a Visualforce page.

In `Chapter 2`, *Creating Flow through Point and Click*, we created a Flow for survey purposes, **Displaying feedback form based on age**. Now we will open it for unauthenticated access using Force.com sites. This means that anyone can use this Flow to share their feedback without logging in to Salesforce.

# Customizing the Flow user interface

To customize the Flow user interface, first of all, you have to embed the Flow into a Visualforce page. Create a Visualforce page and embed your Flow (**Displaying feedback form based on age**) into it, as shown in the following code:

```
<apex:page>
<br/>
<Center>
<Font size ="6" color ="gold">Customer Service Feedback Form </font>
</Center>
<br/>
<flow:interview name="Displaying_feedback_form_based_on_age"/>
// Flow interview component is used to embed Flow in a Visualforce  Page.
Displaying_feedback_form_based_on_age is Flow Unique Name.
</apex:page>
```

It will display the embeded survey form into the Visualforce page and look like what is shown in the following screenshot:

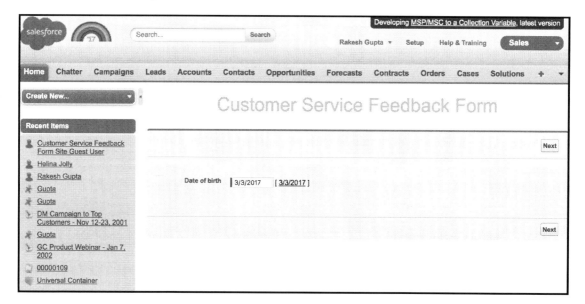

Flow allows you to modify the user interface by applying a custom style using CSS. It allows you to customize specific parts of a Flow, such as the button style, button location, background, and look and feel of the screen and labels using a combination of Flow attributes and CSS classes.

Let's look at a business scenario. Sara Bareilles, who is working on the Flow **Displaying feedback form based on age**, received a new requirement to change the **Date of birth** field label color to blue and display the **Next** button in green at the top.

To modify the Flow user interface, we have to use Flow style classes with CSS styles. First of all, we will add a CSS style into Visualforce page to change the color of the **Date of birth** field label:

```
<style type="text/css">
.FlowDate {
  color: Blue;
}
</style>
```

If you want to use the custom font (for example, **Courier New**) for the date label, then use the font-family attribute inside the **FlowDate** class:

```
<style type="text/css">
.FlowDate {
  color: Blue;
  font-family: Courier New;
}
</style>
```

The next task is to modify the **Next** button's location and color. For that, we will add the `flow:interview` **attributes**, `buttonLocation` and `buttonStyle`, as shown in the following code:

```
<flow:interview name="Displaying_feedback_form_based_on_age"
                buttonLocation="top"
                buttonStyle=" color:Green; border:1px solid;"/>
```

So finally, the Visualforce page code will look like what is shown in the following code snippet:

```
<apex:page >
  <br/>
    <Center>
      <Font size ="6" color ="gold">Customer Service Feedback Form </font>
    </Center>
  <br/>
  <style type="text/css">
```

```
     .FlowDate {
        color: Blue;
        font-family: Courier New;
     }
     </style>
     <flow:interview name="Displaying_feedback_form_based_on_age"
                     buttonLocation="top"
                     buttonStyle=" color:Green; border:1px solid;"/>
  </apex:page>
```

The Visualforce page will look like what is shown in the following screenshot:

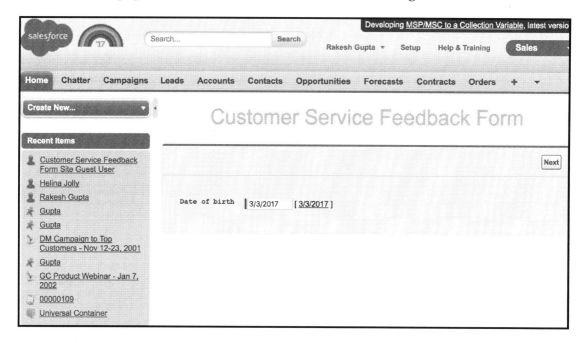

You can change the CSS style sheet as per your requirement.

To learn more about which fields can be customized in Flow, go to
https://www.salesforce.com/us/developer/docs/pages/Content/pages
_flows_customize_runtime_ui.htm.

Once you are done with the design, save the Visualforce page with the name `Flow for Force.com Sites`. The next step is to open Flow for unauthenticated access using Force.com sites.

Using Force.com site, open a Flow for unauthenticated access. Once you have embedded the Flow into a Visualforce page, then with the help of Force.com sites, you can open it for unauthenticated access. This means that users can access Flow without logging in to Salesforce. To open the access of Flow **Displaying feedback form based on age**, we have to add the Visualforce page **Flow for Force.com Site** to Force.com sites. For more details, perform the following steps:

1. Navigate to **Setup** | **Build** | **Develop** | **Sites**.
2. If you haven't registered the Force.com domain for your organization, then do that first. The sites page allows you to register the Force.com domain for your organization. Once you have successfully registered it, you can see a sites-related list on the **Sites** page. It will look like what is shown in the following screenshot:

3. To create a new site, click on the **New** button, as shown in the preceding screenshot. It will redirect you to the **Site Edit** page, where you have to enter the following details:

   - **Site Label**: Enter the site label. it will appear in the user interface. Enter `Customer Service Feedback Form` as **Site Label**.
   - **Site Name**: This will be autopopulated based on the site name.
   - **Site Description**: Write some meaningful text so that another developer/administrator can easily understand why this site was created.
   - **Site Contact**: Select the user who is responsible for receiving communication from site visitors and Salesforce.com.
   - **Default Web Address**: Create a unique URL for Force.com site by entering the Visualforce page unique name. Enter `SurveyForm` in the default web address textbox.
   - **Active**: Select this checkbox to activate the site after saving.

- **Active Site Home Page**: From the lookup dialog, select the Visualforce page you have created to embed Flow. In this case, select **Flow for Force.com Sites** as the active site home page.

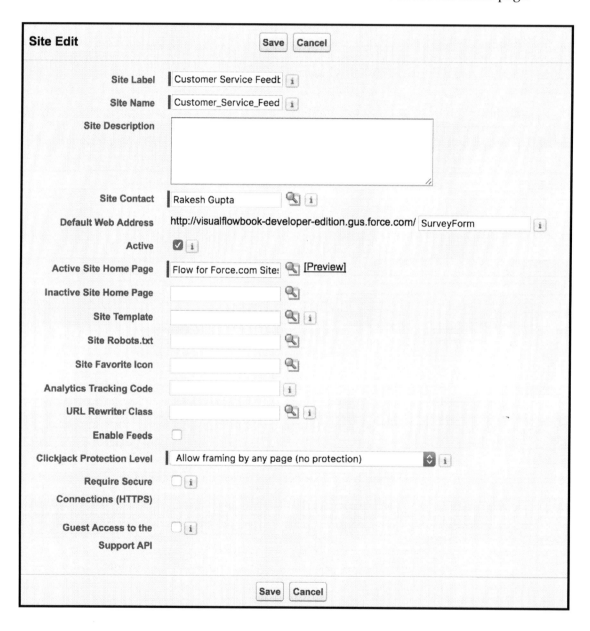

4. You can enter other details as well. Once you are done, click on the **Save** button. It will redirect you to the site detail page, which will allow you to configure your site.

5. Now we have to grant the Visualforce page access to the site user. To do this, navigate to site Visualforce pages-related list on the site detail page, click on the **Edit** button, and make sure that you have granted Visualforce pages to those you have used in **Active Site Home Page** and on your site.

6. The next step is to grant the custom object **Survey__c** permission to site guest users. For this, click on **Public Access Setting**, available on the site detail page, by clicking on the **Survey** object to grant, create, read, and edit permissions and also grant custom fields permission.

7. Once you are done, navigate to the site by following the path **Setup | Build | Develop | Sites** and click on the **Site URL**, which will appear as follows:

```
http://visualflowbook-developer-edition.gus.force.com/SurveyForm
```

The site will look like what is shown in the following screenshot:

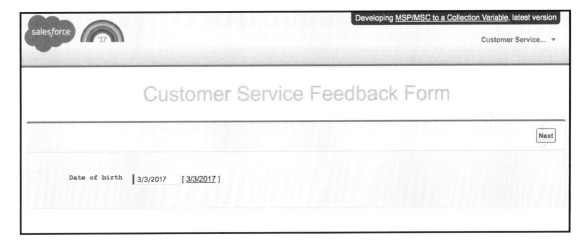

 Make sure that you have activated the Flow, or else you will get an authorization required error while trying to access the site you have developed.

You can check site usages history by clicking on the **24-Hour Usage History** related list available on the site detail page.

# Hands on 3 - setting finish behavior on the Visualforce page

The custom button/link allows you to redirect your user to some page within your Salesforce organization using the retURL attribute once they click on the **Finish** button. If you used the standard controller in a Visualforce page to display a record on the same page as the Flow, then users who click on the **Finish** button will be redirected to a new Flow interview, and they will see the first screen of the Flow without moving to the record detail page. This is because the ID query string parameter is not conserved in the page URL. If you want to redirect the user to another page, then use finishLocation. If you have embedded your Flow in a Visualforce page and want to achieve the same thing once the user clicks on the **Finish** button, you can achieve it by adding the finishLocation attribute to the <flow:interview> component. But you can't redirect your users to a URL that is external to your Salesforce organization. If you have created a Flow for a lead and embedded it into a Visualforce page that uses a standard controller, and after completion you want to redirect users to the same page from where they have started, you can use the following method:

```
<flow:interview name="FlowUniqueName" finishLocation="/{!Lead.Id}">
```

There are a few other ways in which you can configure the finishLocation attribute in the <flow:interview> component, and those are as follows:

## Using the URLFOR function

If you want to redirect a user to a specific page, such as home tab, detail page, or specific record, then use the URLFOR function. Let's take an example: if you want to redirect your Flow user to a lead tab after completion of the Flow, then use the following method:

```
<flow:interview name="FlowUniqueName"  finishlocation="{!URLFOR('/00Q/o')}"
/>
```

## Using the $Page variable

If you want to redirect your Flow user to another Visualforce page without using the URLFOR function, then you can use the $Page variable. Use the name of the Visualforce page with the $Page variable, as shown in the following example:

```
<flow:interview name="FlowUniqueName"
finishlocation="{!$Page.Flow_Partner_Community}"/>
```

## Using a controller

Using a custom controller, you can set the finish location for a Flow. Imitate a new page reference by passing the URL (as string) to define the location, as shown in the following controller example:

```
public class FlowRedirect {
    public PageReference getPageA() {
        return new PageReference('/001');
    }
}
```

The following is the code for the Visualforce page that uses a custom controller and sets the Flow's finish behavior:

```
<apex:page controller="myFlowController">
  <flow:interview name="flowname" finishLocation="{!pageA}"/>
</apex>
```

Using the preceding options, you can redirect Flow users to another page/URL but not a URL that is external to your Salesforce organization.

# Hands on 4 - accessing a Flow through Salesforce1

Until now, we have learned the way to embed a Flow into a Visualforce page, and then users can access Flow through sites or Salesforce web application without having the **Run Flow** system permission or **Force.com Flow User** feature license. There are a few ways through which Flow user can access Flow on Salesforce1 mobile application.

# Through the Salesforce1 navigation menu

If you have created a Flow and allow your users to access it from the Salesforce1 mobile application, then you have to embed the Flow into a Visualforce page.

Let's look at a business scenario. Helina Jolly, who is working as a system administrator at Universal Container, developed the **Clean Chatter Group Feeds** Flow in Chapter 3, *Manipulating Records in Visual Workflow*. She's received another requirement from her manager to make this Flow available for Salesforce1 users.

To make a Flow available for Salesforce1 users through the navigation menu, perform the following steps:

1. Create a Visualforce page by navigating to **Setup** | **Build** | **Develop** | **Pages** to embed the flow. The following is the sample code, where Delete_Chatter_Group_feeds is the Flow's unique name:

   ```
   <apex:page>
     <flow:interview name="Delete_Chatter_Group_feeds"/>
   </apex:page>
   ```

2. Save this Flow with the name Clean Chatter Group Feed, and don't forget to select the **Available for Salesforce mobile apps** checkbox to make this Visualforce page available for Salesforce1.

3. The next step is to create a Visualforce tab for it; to do this, navigate to **Setup** | **Build** | **Create** | **Tabs**, and then navigate to the **Visualforce Tabs** related list and click on the **New** button. It will redirect you to another page, where you will be required to enter the following details:

   - **Visualforce Page**: Select a Visualforce page to display in the Visualforce tab.
   - **Tab Label**: Enter the tab label. It will appear in the user interface. Enter Clean Chatter Group as the tab label.

- **Tab Name**: This will be autopopulated based on the tab label.
- **Tab Style**: Select the tab style.

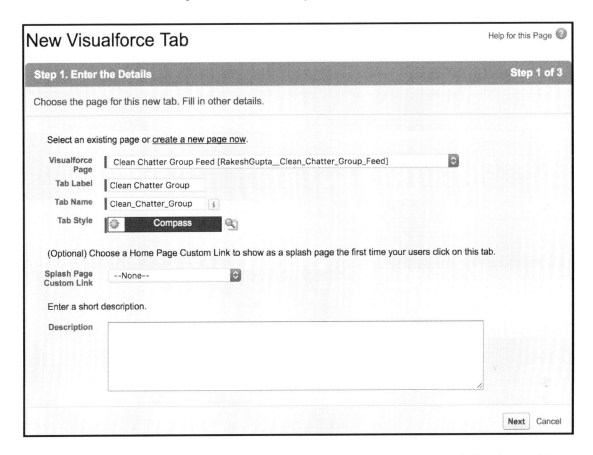

4. Once you are done, click on the **Next** button, and select tab visibility for profiles, followed by adding the tab to apps.
5. The final task is to add this Visualforce tab to the Salesforce1 navigation menu. To do that, navigate to **Setup** | **Administer** | **Mobile Administration** | **Mobile Navigation**, and move the **Clean Chatter Group** Visualforce tab from **Available** to the **Selected** pane, as shown in the following screenshot:

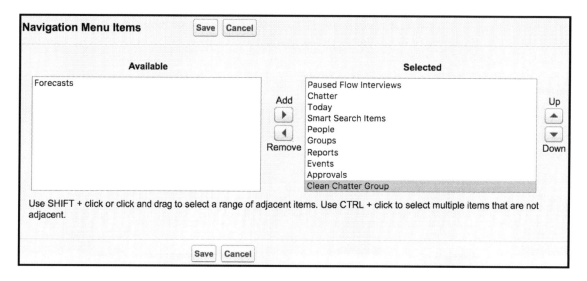

6. Once you are done, click on the **Save** button.
7. Now log in to Salesforce through the Salesforce1 mobile application; you can find it under the navigation menu.

# Through publisher actions

To use Flow as the publisher action, you have to embed it into a Visualforce page with a standard controller.

Let's look at a business scenario. Alice Atwood is working as a system administrator at Universal Containers and has developed a Flow to copy Opportunity followers in this chapter. She's received another requirement to make it available for a Salesforce1 publisher action on an Opportunity object.

To make a Flow available for the publisher action, perform the following steps:

1. Create a Visualforce page with the standard controller by navigating to **Setup** | **Build** | **Develop** | **Pages** to embed the Flow. The following is the sample code where `Copying_the_record_followers` is Flow's **Unique Name**:

```
<apex:page Standardcontroller="Opportunity">
  <flow:interview name="Copying_the_record_followers" >
    <apex:param name="VarT_NewOppID" value="
      {!Opportunity.Id}"/>
  </flow:interview>
</apex:page>
```

2. To create an action, navigate to **Setup** | **Build** | **Customize** | **Opportunities** | **Buttons, Links, and Actions** and click on the **New Action** button and then enter the following details:

3. Save this Flow with the name `Copy record followers`, and don't forget to select **Available for Salesforce1**:

    - **Action Type**: Select an action type. In this case, select the **Custom Visualforce** page.
    - **Visualforce Page**: Select a Visualforce page, **Copy record followers**.
    - **Height**: Set the height of the custom action composer. Enter `300px`.
    - **Standard Label Type**: Select a standard label, **Add Member**.
    - **Name**: Enter the action name, **Copy_Follower**.
    - **Description**: Write some meaningful text so that another developer/administrator can easily understand why this action was created.

At the end, publisher action should looks like what is shown in the following screenshot:

4. Once done, click on **Save**.
5. The next task is to add custom action on the Opportunity page layout. Navigate to **Setup** | **Build** | **Customize** | **Opportunities** | **Page Layouts**, click on the **Edit** link, and drag and drop the custom action **Copy Follower** onto the page layout and save the changes.
6. Now you will be able to use Flow from Publisher actions.

# Hands on 5 - setting Flow variables value from a Visualforce page

Once you embed a Flow into the Visualforce page, it allows you to set the initial values of variables, collection variables, SObject Variables, and SObject Collection Variables through the `<apex:param>` component. The `<apex:param>` tags evaluated at the time of Flow launched mean that you can set Flow variables values only once. This allows you to set values for those variables that allow input access, which means variables that **Input/Output Type** selected as **Input and Output** or **Input only**. There are some ways in which you can set Flow variables from a Visualforce page, which are discussed in the upcoming sections.

## Without a controller

You can set variables value without using the controller; this means that you have to hardcode the variables' values. Here's an example that sets the initial value of `VarT_NewOppID` to `006B0000002REv1` when the interview starts, as shown in the following sample code:

```
<apex:page Standardcontroller="Opportunity">
  <flow:interview name="Copying_the_record_followers" >
    <apex:param name="VarT_NewOppID" value="006B0000002REv1"/>
  </flow:interview>
</apex:page>
```

Without a controller, you can only set the value of variables.

## With the standard controller

Using the standard controllers, you can set variables or SObject variables by passing in data from a record. Let's look at an example that sets the initial value of `VarT_NewOppID` to the Visualforce expression `{!Opportunity.Id}` when the interview starts, as shown in the following sample code:

```
<apex:page Standardcontroller="Opportunity">
  <flow:interview name="Copying_the_record_followers" >
    <apex:param name="VarT_NewOppID" value="{!Opportunity.Id}"/>
  </flow:interview>
</apex:page>
```

With the standard controller, you can set the value of variables and SObject variables.

## With the custom controller

You can set Flow variable values using the custom controller as well. You can write a custom controller that sets the variables values, and then you can reference that controller in your Visualforce page. The following example sets the variable OppId value to specific Opportunity IDs when the interview starts using the custom controller, as shown in the following sample code for the controller. The controller is used to get the value in the variable OppId and pass it to the Visualforce page.

```
public class FlowCustomController {
    public Opportunity OppId {get; set;}
    public FlowCustomController () {
        OppId = [
            SELECT Id, Name FROM Opportunity
            WHERE Name = 'Edge Installation' LIMIT 1];
    }
}
```

The following is the code for the Visualforce page that embeds Flow and the passing value to the OppId variable with help of the custom controller:

```
<apex:page controller="FlowCustomController">
  <flow:interview name="Copying_the_record_followers" >
    <apex:param name="VarT_NewOppID" value="{!OppId}"/>
  </flow:interview>
</apex:page>
```

Using the custom controller, you can set the value of variables, collection variables, SObject variables, and SObject Collection variables.

If you try to attempt to set the variable that doesn't allow input, access is ignored and compilation may fail for the Visualforce page.

Don't forget to grant the Visualforce page and custom controller access to users; it's only then that they can access the Flow.

# Calling a Flow using the custom controller

The Visualforce page allows you to call a Flow using the custom controller. To launch an autolaunched Flow from Apex, you have to use the `start()` method in the `Flow.Interview` class.

Let's look at a business scenario. Joe Thompson is working as a system administrator at Universal Container and has developed a Flow to update the account rating in Chapter 3, *Manipulating Records in Visual Workflow*. He embedded the Flow into a Visualforce page and also added a **Start** button on the Visualforce page. Now he wants to call the Flow as soon as users click on the **Start** button without showing the Flow in the user interface.

Create a Visualforce page using a custom controller and add a command button to it:

```
<apex:page controller="FlowController">
    <apex:outputLabel id="text">
        <b>Click on Start button to call the flow</b>
    </apex:outputLabel>
    <apex:form >
        <apex:commandButton action="{!start}" Value="Start"/>
    </apex:form>
</apex:page>
```

The following is the sample code for the custom controller, and it launches the Flow using the `start()` method:

```
public with sharing class FlowController {
    public Flow.Interview.Update_an_account myFlow {get; set;}  //Instance
of the Flow
        public void start() {
        Map<String, Object> Var= new Map<String, Object>();
        myFlow = new Flow.Interview.Update_an_account(Var);
        myFlow.start();
    }
}
```

You can use `getVariableVale(String)` in the custom code to get the value of the specified Flow variable.

# Hands on 6 - invoking a Flow using an Inline Visualforce page

It is also possible to call a Flow through an Inline Visualforce page. Let's start with a business scenario.

Sara Bareilles, who is working as a system administrator with Universal Containers, receives a requirement as soon as a contact is added to an Opportunity (that is, using an Opportunity contact role) as a primary contact to the copy contact's lead source to the Opportunity lead source.

There are no out-of-the-box solutions for this. You can't achieve a preceding business requirement using Workflow Rule. You can achieve it through the Apex code. We will use Flow and an Inline Visualforce page to achieve it, the steps to create which are as follows:

1. Navigate to **Setup** | **Build** | **Create** | **Workflow & Approvals** | **Flows**, and then click on the **New Flow** button; it will open the Flow canvas for you.

2. Create three **Text** variables, `VarTOppId` (to pass the Opportunity ID from the Visualforce page), `VarTConId` (to save the primary contact ID), and `VarTLeadSource` (to store the primary contact lead source).

3. The first task is to get the primary contact from the Opportunity; for this, we will use the **Record Lookup** element. Click on the **Palette** tab and drag and drop the **Record Lookup** element onto the canvas; it will open a new window for you, where you have to enter the following details:
   - **Name**: Enter the name for the **Record Lookup** element. Enter `Get Primary Contact` as the name.
   - **Unique Name**: This will be autopopulated based on the name.
   - **Description**: Write some meaningful text so that another developer/administrator can easily understand why this **Record Lookup** element is added to Flow.
   - **Look up**: Select the object for which you want to search the record. In this case, select the `OpportunityContactRole` object. The next task is to define the search criteria. If you want to add multiple fields for search criteria, then click on the **Add Row** link to add the new row. For the field, select `IsPrimary` equal to `{!$GlobalCOnstant.True}` and `OpportunityId` equal to `{!VArTOppId}`. You can get help from the following screenshot to define the search criteria.

- **Assign the record's fields to variables to reference them in your flow**: Optionally, you can save the field's value into variables so that you can use it later in the Flow. Save `ContactId` into the `varTConId` variable.

Don't forget to select the **Assign null values to the variable(s) if no records are found** checkbox, as shown in the following screenshot:

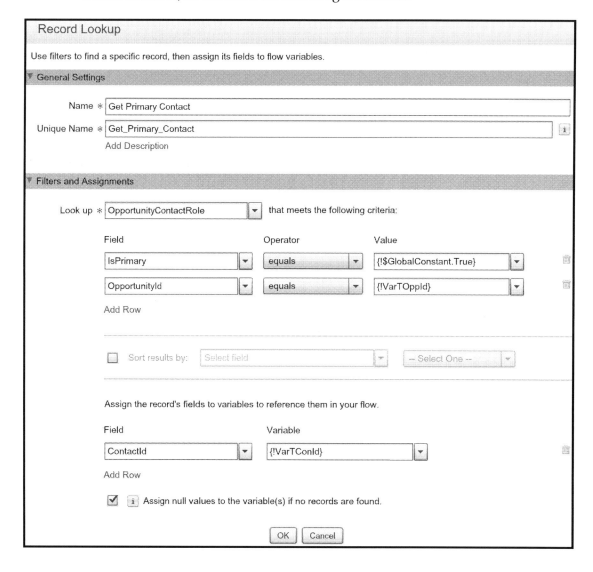

4. Once you are done, click on the **OK** button.

5. The next task is to check whether Opportunity has any contact role or not. To check this, we will use the **Decision** element and check whether the `ContactId` variable contains any value or not. To do that, drag and drop the **Decision** element onto the Flow canvas. Enter the **Name** field as `Verify Primary Contact Role` and **Unique Name** will get autopopulated based on the name. Optionally, you can also add **Description** for the **Decision** element. Next, create two outcomes for the **Decision** element, which are as follows:

   - **Exist**: Select variable `VarTConId` does not equal to `{!$GlobalConstant.EmptyString}`.
   - **Not Exist**: Enter the name `Not Found` as **DEFAULT OUTCOME**.

It will look like what is shown in the following screenshot:

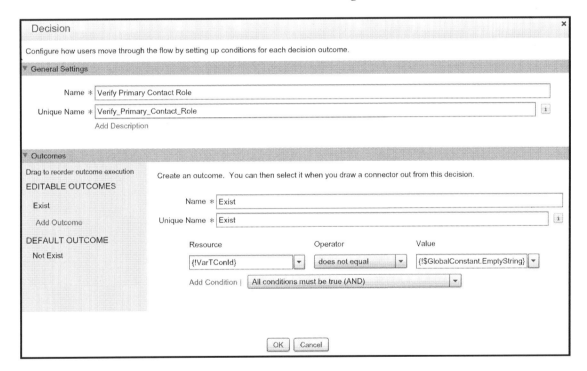

6. Once you are done, click on the **OK** button.
7. The next step is to find the lead source for the Opportunity primary contact role. For this, we will use the **Record Lookup** element. Drag and drop the **Record Lookup** element onto the canvas; it will open a new window for you, where you have to enter the following details:

   - **Name**: Enter the name for the **Record Lookup** element. Enter Get Contact Lead Source as the name.
   - **Unique Name**: This will be autopopulated based on the name.
   - **Description**: Write some meaningful text so that another developer/administrator can easily understand why this **Record Lookup** element is added to Flow.
   - **Look up**: Select the object for which you want to search the record. In this case, select the Contact object. The next task is to define the search criteria. Add **Id** of Contact equals the VarTConId variable.
   - **Assign the record's fields to variables to reference them in your flow**: Optionally, you can save the field's value into variables, so you can use it later in the Flow. Save **LeadSource** into the varTLeadSource variable.

Don't forget to select the **Assign null values to the variable(s) if no records are found** checkbox; it will look like what is shown in the following screenshot:

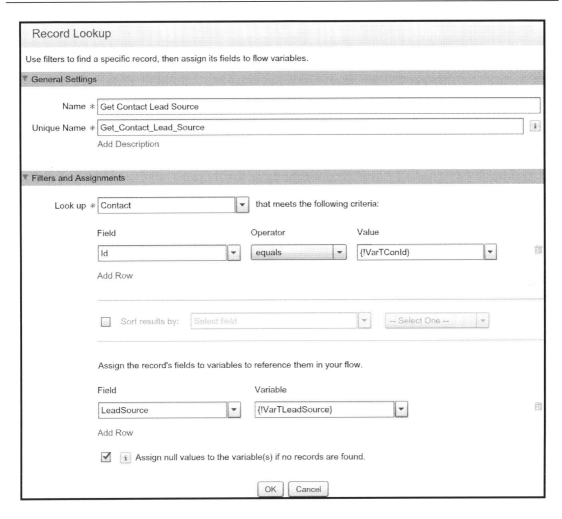

8. Once you are done, click on the **OK** button.
9. The final task is to add the **Record Update** element to update the Opportunity lead source. Drag and drop the **Record Update** element onto the canvas, and it will open a new window for you, where you have to enter the following details:
    - **Name**: Enter the name for the **Record Update** element. Enter `Update Opportunity Lead Source` as the name.
    - **Unique Name**: This will be autopopulated based on the name.
    - **Description**: Write some meaningful text so that another developer/administrator can easily understand why this **Record Update** element was added to a Flow.

- **Update**: Select the object for which you want to update the record. In this case, select the `Opportunity` object. The next task is to set the filter criteria to identify which record gets updated; in this case, select **Id** of Opportunity equals `VarTOppId`. Then, select the fields from the object that you want to update and assign the value or resource (input, constant, and so on ) to it; (data types must match) in this case, select the **LeadSource** field and for the value from drop-down variables, select `VarTLeadSource`. To add multiple fields, click on the **Add Row** link.

The **Record Update** element should look like what is shown in the following screenshot:

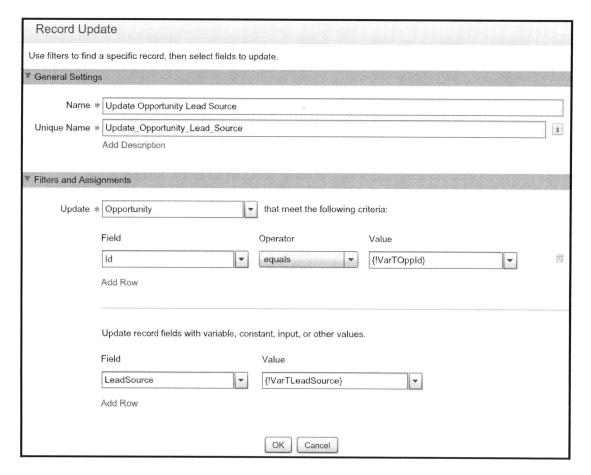

10. Once you are done, click on the **OK** button.

11. Save your Flow with the name `Update Opportunity Lead Source` and close the canvas using the **Close** button; it will redirect you to the Flow detail page. Don't forget to activate the Flow.

12. The next task is to add the Flow to a Visualforce page. Navigate to **Setup** | **Build** | **Develop** | **Pages** and click on **New** to add a new Visualforce page, embed the Flow into the Visualforce page, and pass the value the `VarTOppId` variable using the standard controller. In the following code, `apex:param` is used to pass the value in the `VarTOppId` variable:

```
<apex:page standardController="Opportunity">
  <flow:interview name="Update_Opportunity_Lead_Source">
    <apex:param name="VarTOppId" value="{!Opportunity.id}"/>
  </flow:interview>
</apex:page>
```

13. Save the Visualforce page with the name `Update Opportunity Lead Source`.

14. Now we have to add the Visualforce page to the Opportunity page layout. Navigate to **Setup** | **Build** | **Customize** | **Opportunities** | **Page Layouts**, click on the **Edit** link and drag and drop the Visualforce page **Update Opportunity Lead Source** on to the page layout, and set the Visualforce page width to 0 px and height to 0. Once you are done, click on the **Save** button to save the changes.

It will look like what is shown in the following screenshot:

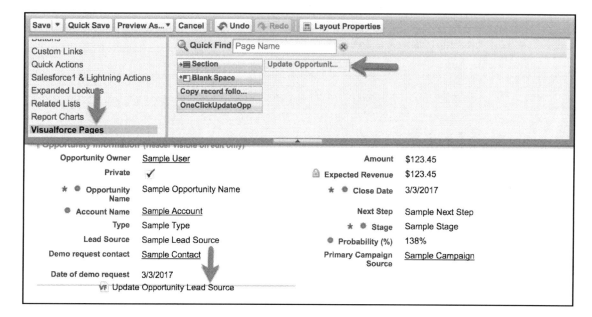

Now onward, if the user adds or updates the opportunity contact role as primary, then Flow will fire and automatically update the Opportunity lead source to be the same as the primary contact role lead source.

# Hands on 7 - using Flow to save the data from Visualforce page

In *Hands on 2 - open a Flow for unauthenticated access* section, we discussed a way to open a Flow access for unauthenticated access by embedding it to a Visualforce page. There is another possibility of using the Flow as the backend class to save the data from the Visualforce page. Let's start with a business scenario.

Robby Williams, who is working as a system administrator with Universal Containers, receives a requirement to create an event registration form to save the data in a custom object. For the frontend, they want to use Visualforce page and for the backend, they want to use Flow to save the data.

There are many possible solutions for the preceding business scenario. We will use the Visualforce page as the user interface screen (frontend) to allow users to enter the data and Flow to save the data in a custom object. To achieve this, perform the following steps:

1. First of all, create a custom object **Event Registration**, set record name as `Auto Number data Type`. Also, create few fields **Title**, **First Name**, **Last Name**, **Email Address**, and **Company**. Make a schedule for the required field and grant permissions to respective profiles. For more details, refer to the following screenshot:

Later on, we will use this object to save the event data from the Visualforce page.

2. The next step is to create a Flow. Navigate to **Setup** | **Build** | **Create** | **Workflow & Approvals** | **Flows** and click on the **New Flow** button, and it will open the Flow canvas for you. Create some variables in the Flow, as shown in the following table:

| Name | Data Type | Input/Output Type |
|---|---|---|
| VarT_Company | Text | Input and output |
| VarT_EmailAddress | Text | Input and output |
| VarT_FirstName | Text | Input and output |
| VarT_LastName | Text | Input and output |
| VarT_Title | Text | Input and output |

We will use these variables in the Flow.

3. Now we will add a **Record Create** element to the Flow to create the data in the custom object **Event Registration**. Click on the **Palette** tab and drag and drop the **Record Create** element onto the canvas. It will open a new window for you, where you have to enter the following details:

   - **Name**: Enter the name for the **Record Create** element. In this case, enter Create event registration as **Name**.
   - **Unique Name**: This will be autopopulated based on the name.
   - **Description**: Write some meaningful text so that another developer/administrator can easily understand why this **Record Create** element was created. When you select the **Record Create** element in the **Explorer** tab, the description appears in the **Description** pane.
   - **Create**: Select the object for which you want to create the record. In this case, select the Event_Registration__c object. The next task is to assign the value or resource to the object fields, and data types must match. To assign values to multiple fields, click on the **Add Row** link.
   - **Variable**: Optionally, you can save the new record's ID in a variable so that you can use it later in the flow.

It will look like what is shown in the following screenshot:

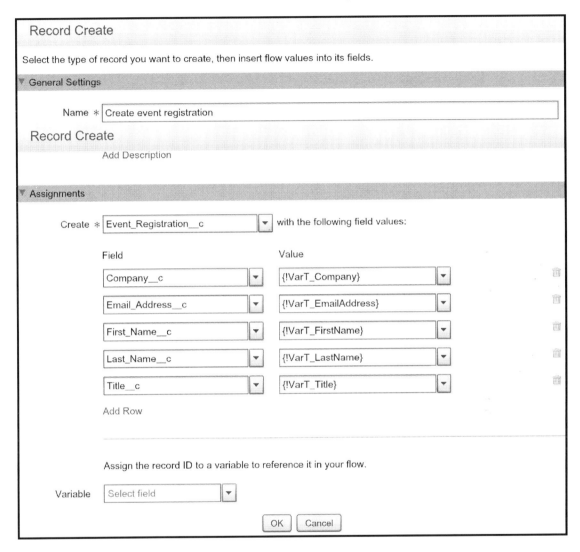

4. Once you are done, click on the **OK** button.

5. Set the **Record Create** element **Create event registration** as the Start element.

6. Save the Flow with the name `Event Registration Form` and close the Flow designer using the **Close** button. It will redirect you to the Flow detail page. Don't forget to activate the Flow.

7. From the Flow detail page, copy **Unique Name**; it will look like this: **Event_Registration_Form**.

8. The next task is to create a Visualforce page to allow users to enter the data. Navigate to **Setup** | **Build** | **Develop** | **Pages** and click on **New** to add a new Visualforce page. Create a Visualforce page with the name `EventRegistrationForm`. To add the input field to the Visualforce page, use the following code:

```
<apex:inputText id="Title" Value="{!Title}" required="true"/>
```

Likewise, use the same code to get user input for other fields.

9. Add a button to the Visualforce page that allows users to submit the event registration form. Use the following code to add the command button onto the Visualforce page:

```
<apex:commandButton action="{!Save}" value="Save"
reRender="myFlow"/>
```

10. To embed the Flow into a Visualforce page and then pass the value from the custom controller to the Flow variables, use the following code:

```
<flow:interview name="Event_Registartion_Form" id="myFlow"
rendered="{!renderOrNot}">
  <apex:param name="VarT_Title" value="{!inputTitle}"/>
  <apex:param name="VarT_FirstName" value="{!inputFirstName}"/>
  <apex:param name="VarT_LastName" value="{!inputLastName}"/>
  <apex:param name="VarT_EmailAddress" value="
{!inputEmailAddress}"/>
  <apex:param name="VarT_Company" value="{!inputCompany}"/>
</flow:interview>
```

Finally, the Visualforce page will look like what is shown in the following screenshot:

**Event Registration Form**

| | |
|---|---|
| Title : | |
| First Name : | |
| Last Name : | |
| Email Address : | |
| Comapny : | |

Submit

11. The next step is to add a custom controller to the Visualforce page in order to pass the input data to the Flow variables. Navigate to **Setup** | **Build** | **Develop** | **Apex Classes** and click on **New** to add a new Apex class. Create an Apex class with the name `EventRegistrationFormController`. Use the following code to pass the user input from the Visualforce page to Flow variables using the custom controller:

```
Public void Submit()
{
  renderOrNot = true;
  inputTitle = Title;
  inputFirstName = FirstName;
  inputLastName = LastName;
  inputEmailAddress = EmailAddress;
  inputCompany = Company;
}
```

You can download the example code files from your account at `http://www.packtpub.com` for all the Packt Publishing books you have purchased. If you purchased this book elsewhere, you can visit `http://www.packtpub.com/support` and register to have the files e-mailed directly to you.

12. Once you are done with the Visualforce page and custom controller, you can also expose this page for unauthenticated access using Force.com site, as mentioned in the *Hands on 2 - open a Flow for unauthenticated access* section.

# Hands on 8 - using cross-object fields in Flow

When working with related (parent-child relationship) records in Flow, sometimes, you may want to refer to parent record fields. For example, when working with a contact record in Flow, you may want to refer to the **Account Phone** field or **Contact Phone** field. To get the accounts phone, you may need to use Record Lookup, which means you have to perform a DML operation. Now you can refer to parent record fields without performing any query (Record Lookup), that is, using a cross-object field reference similar to the cross-object formula in Salesforce.

Let's look at a business scenario. Helina Jolly is working as a system administrator at Universal Containers. She received a requirement to develop a Flow through which sales directors can update the Asset's owner from the Asset's account's owner. Basically, her manager wants to place a button on the Asset detail page through which the sales director can invoke the Flow.

To develop this Flow, follow these instructions:

1. Navigate to **Setup** | **Build** | **Create** | **Workflow & Approvals** | **Flows**.
2. Click on the **New Flow** button; this will open the Flow canvas.
3. Create a **Text** variable to pass the Asset ID from the custom URL. To do that, navigate to the **Resources** tab and double-click on **Variable**, available under the **CREATE NEW** section. Create a Text variable `VarTAssetID` and set **Input/Output Type** as **Input and Output**.
4. Now our next task is to get the complete details of the Asset's record. For this, we have to use the **Fast Lookup** element. The reason behind using **Fast Lookup** is that it allows you to save the outcomes in the SObject variable. Create an SObject variable `SovAsset` for the object type **Asset**, and set **Input/Output Type** as **Input and Output**, as shown in the following screenshot:

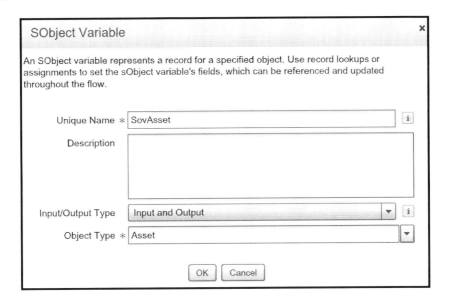

5. Once you are done, click on the **OK** button.
6. Now we will use the **Fast Lookup** element to store the asset's fields, including AccountId in an SObject variable called `SovAsset`. Navigate to the **Palette** tab and drag and drop the **Fast Lookup** element onto the canvas; it will open a new window for you, where you have to enter the following details:

   - **Name**: Enter the name for the **Fast Lookup** element. In this case, enter the name as `Get asset details`.
   - **Unique Name**: This will be autopopulated based on the name.
   - **Description**: Write some meaningful text so that another developer/administrator can easily understand why this **Fast Lookup** element was created. When you select the **Fast Lookup** element in the **Explorer** tab, a description appears in the **Description** pane.
   - **Lookup**: Select the object for which you want to search the records. In this case, select the **Asset** object.
   - The next task is to define the search criteria. For this, map **Id** with the text variable `VarTAssetID`.
   - **Variable**: Select the SObject variable `SovAsset` to store the asset details. Don't forget to select the **Assign null to the variable if no records are found.** checkbox. Finally, select fields whose values you want to store, in this case, select **Id, OwnerId,** and **AccountId**.

Refer to the following screenshot for more details:

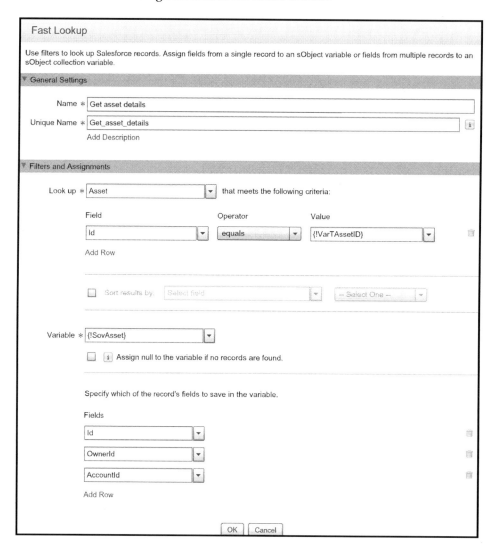

7. Once you are done, click on the **OK** button.
8. Now we will add the **Decision** element to evaluate the SObject variable `{!SovContract.AccountId}`. If **AccoundId** is not null, then we can use cross-object field reference to update the asset's owner without using another record lookup element to get the account owner's ID. This will save you from performing one more DML operation to get the account owner's ID. Drag and drop the **Decision** element onto the Flow canvas. Enter the name as `Was account set for asset` and the **Unique Name** field will get autopopulated based on the name. Optionally, you can also add Description to the **Decision** element. Then, create two outcomes for the **Decision** element, which are as follows:
   - **Found**: Select the SObject variable `SovAsset.AccountId` for **operator** and select **is null** and the **value** `{!$GlobalConstant.False}`.
   - **Not Found**: Enter the name as `True` for **DEFAULT OUTCOME**.

It will look like what is shown in the following screenshot:

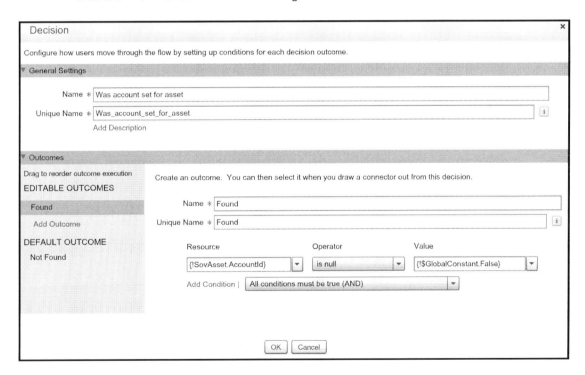

9. Once you are done, click on the OK button.

# Referencing a cross-object field in Flow

You can now reference fields for records that are related to the values that are stored in an sObject variable. This means that cross-object field values are valid wherever you can reference a Flow resource or manually enter a value. In other words, when you create an sObject variable to reference fields on related records, store the ID for the first related record in the variable. For example, to reference a quote's Opportunity, store Opportunity ID in the SObject variable or add a value for Opportunity ID using an Assignment element.

## Cross-object field references in simple relationships

In common relationships (where one child record can reference to only one parent record from a single object), you can reference parent record fields in a straightforward manner. For example, `Asset.AccountId` links directly to the Asset's parent account. If you know that a field relationship links your object to exactly one other object, use the following syntax to reference a field on a related record:

```
{!Sov.objectName1.objectName2.fieldName}
```

For example, to reference Asset's parent account owner, use the following syntax:

```
{!SovAsset.Account.OwnerId}
```

The explanation of the preceding syntax is as follows:

- `Sov`: This is the unique name for the SObject variable; in the preceding example, it is `SovAsset`.
- `objectName1`: This is the API name for an object that's related to SObject variable's object type. In the preceding example, it is `Account`.
- `fieldName`: This is the name for the field that you want to reference on the last object in the expression. In the preceding example, it is `OwnerId`.

## Cross-object field references in polymorphic relationships

A polymorphic relationship is a relationship between objects where one child record can reference to multiple parent objects of several different types. For example, the user field of a lead record could be a user or a queue. The `WhatId` field of an event could be an `Account`, a `Campaign`, or an `Opportunity`. If you're traversing from a lead to its owner ID, you have to add a special syntax to identify which object you want to refer when you say owner. Use the following syntax to reference a field on a related record:

```
{!Sov.polymorphicObjectName1:specificObjectName2.fieldName}
```

For example, to reference Lead's owner ID (user) who owns the lead record, use the following syntax:

```
{!SovLead.Owner:User.Id}
```

The explanation of preceding syntax is as follows:

- `Sov`: This is the unique name for the sObject variable; in the preceding example, it is `SovAsset`.
- `polymorphicObject`: This is the API name for a polymorphic relationship for sObjectVariable's object type. In the preceding example, it is `Owner`.
- `specificObjectName2`: This is the API name for the object that you want to select from the polymorphic relationship. In the preceding example, it is `User`.
- `fieldName`: This is the name for the field that you want to reference on the last object in the expression. In the preceding example, it is `Id`.

Now we will use the Assignment element to specify `{!SovAsset.Account.OwnerId}` as the value for `{!SovAsset.OwnerId}`.

1. To do this, navigate to the **Palette** tab and drag and drop the **Assignment** element onto the Flow canvas. It will open a new window for you, where you have to enter the following details:
    - **Name**: Enter the name for the **Assignment** element. In this case, enter `Assign OwnerID` as the name.
    - **Unique Name**: This will be autopopulated based on the name.
    - **Description**: Write some meaningful text so that another developer/administrator can easily understand why this **Assignment** element was created. When you select the **Assignment** element in the **Explorer** tab, the description appears in the **Description** pane.
    - **Assignment**: Select `SovAsset.OwnerId` as **Variable**; for **Operator**, select `equals` and for Value, manually enter `{!SovAsset.Account.ownerId}`.

It will look like what is shown in the following screenshot:

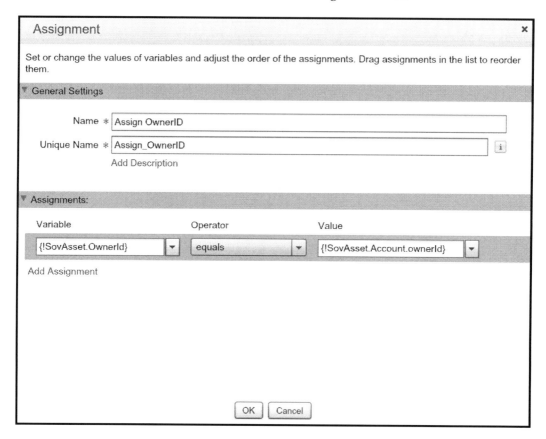

2. Once you are done, click on the **OK** button.
3. At the end, we will use the **Fast Update** element to update the Asset record. To do that, navigate to the **Palette** tab and drag and drop the **Fast Update** element onto the Flow canvas. It will open a new window for you, where you have to enter the following details:
    - **Name**: Enter the name for the **Fast Update** element. In this case, enter `Update asset owner` as the name.
    - **Unique Name**: This will be autopopulated based on the name.
    - **Description**: Write some meaningful text so that another developer/administrator can easily understand why this **Fast Update** element was created. When you select the **Fast Update** element in the **Explorer** tab, the description appears in the **Description** pane.

- **Variable**: To create a record or multiple records, you can either use SObject variable or SObject Collection variable. In this case, select the SObject Collection variable `SovAsset`.

4. Once you are done, click on the **OK** button.

5. Use the connector to connect **Fast Lookup, Decision, Assignment**, and **Fast Update** elements, and set the **Fast Lookup** element as the start point, as shown in the following screenshot:

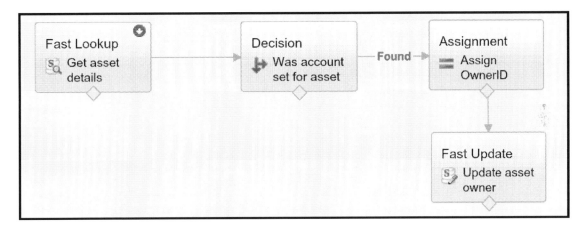

6. Save your Flow with the **Name** field `Update Assets owner` and close the Flow Designer using the **Close** button; it will redirect you to Flow detail page. Form here, copy the Flow URL.

7. To execute the Flow, we will create a custom button on the Asset object. To create a custom button, navigate to **Setup** | **Build** | **Customize** | **Assets** | **Buttons, Links, and Actions** and click on the **New Button or Link** button. Enter the name `Update owner`; for **Display Type**, select **Detail Page Button**; for **Behavior**, select **Display in existing window without sidebar or header**; for **Content Source**, select **URL**, and then construct the URL as per the business needs. In this case,
`/flow/Update_Assets_owner?VarTAssetID={!Asset.Id}&retURL={!Asset.Id}`.

8. Once you're done, click on **Save**. The next task is to add a custom button on the Asset page layouts. Navigate to **Setup** | **Build** | **Customize** | **Assets** | **Page Layouts**, click on the **Edit** link, drag and drop the custom button **Update Owner** onto the page layout, and save the changes.

9. To test this, identify an existing account where the account owner is another user. Then, create a new Asset for that account. Now you are the owner of that Asset record. Then, navigate to the newly created Asset, click on the **Update Owner** button, and it will update the Asset's owner from Asset's account owner. This means that Assets owner is now the same as the Account's owner.

# A few points to remember

The following are some noteworthy points regarding data manipulation in a Flow:

- Make sure that the field is set as Input and Output to pass values from the controller.
- Use the `<apex:param>` component in the Visualforce page to set the variables' value.
- Use the `start()` method in the `Flow.Interview` class to call a Flow from a controller.
- Using the standard list controller, you can set the SObject Collection Variable value from the standard controller.
- If you have embedded a Flow into a Visualforce page and Flow is not activated, then at runtime, Flow users will receive an error.
- Once you have deactivated a Flow, you can immediately delete it.
- If you are using the same choice in multiple screens on a Flow and you want to find the recent one, then use **was selected** in your query.
- To set the record type for a record, use the record type ID.
- If the Flow Designer doesn't show the custom object or fields you recently created, then close the Flow Designer and reopen it.
- If the Flow Designer doesn't show custom object or fields, make sure that you have permission to access it via a profile.
- Remember that Visual Workflow runs in the user mode.
- You can distribute a Flow through a package and deploy it through change sets.
- You can't redirect a Flow user to a URL that is external to your Salesforce organization.
- You can save 50 versions of a Flow, only one of which can be active.

- Don't forget to grant Visualforce page access to your Flow users, or else they may receive an error at runtime.
- The Flow or Process are using the AllOrNone header, which means if the runtime error occurs, Salesforce will roll back records because not all records were valid.
- The following relationships are not supported in cross-object field references:
    - `Lead.ConvertedAccount`
    - `Lead.ConvertedContact`
    - `Lead.ConvertedOpportunity`
- Cross-object field references in Flows do not count against your organization's limits for the following:
    - Cross-object relationships per object
    - DML operations per transaction
- If a Flow interview encounters a null value at any point in the cross object reference, the element containing the reference fails at runtime. The reference runs successfully if the last field value in the expression is null. For example, store an opportunity in `{!SovOpportunity}` and try to reference `{!SovOpportunity}.Account.Name`. The Flow will fail at runtime if Account ID on the stored opportunity is null (because there isn't an account to look at), but it succeeds if the name on the related account is null.
- If you are planning to set a value for a read-only field, then make sure that you are aware of its limitations. Refer to this help article for a detailed explanation: `https://help.salesforce.com/articleView?id=vpm_admin_inaccessiblefields_behavior.htm&language=en_US&type=0`

# Exercises

1. Create a Flow that allows a system administrator to mass activate archive Chatter groups. On the very first screen, display all archieved Chatter groups from your organization and allow them to select multiple Chatter groups. Next, click on the **Finish** or **Next** button and activate all selected Chatter groups. Make sure that the users are also able to access it from the Salesforce1 mobile app.

2. Create a Flow that allows Chatter group owners/managers to mass remove group members (add/remove multiple members). Make this available for Salesforce1 mobile app users as well. On the Visualforce page, display a button on the bottom.

3. Create a Flow that allows system administrators to add a user to multiple queues from a single screen. Currently, they have to go to each queue and assign the user manually, and it's a time-consuming process. Your Flow should look like what is shown in the following screenshot. It allows the system administrator to select multiple queues. Once they click on the **Next** button, the user automatically gets added to selected queues.

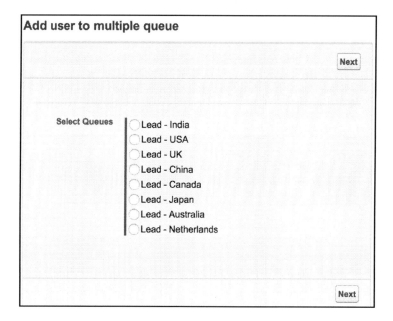

4. Create a Flow, and it will auto post Opportunity Closed Won information on Opportunity owner's profile page.

**Hint**: Use Inline Visualforce page to call the Flow. The preceding screenshot displays the sample output.

5. With the help of the Flow and Visualforce page, create a Contact Us page and expose it for non-Salesforce users so that they can reach your organization for any help. After submissions, send them a thank you e-mail with detailed information about your company and also include the company logo in the e-mail.

6. Create a Flow that allows the system administrator to select multiple user records and click on the **Finish** or **Next** button. Freeze selected users accounts.

7. Create a Flow that allows the system administrator to update the company information (contact details) from the Salesforce1 mobile application.

   **Hint**: Company information is available by navigating to **Setup** | **Administer** | **Company Profile** | **Company Information**. For this, you have to use the **Organization** Object.

8. Create a Visualforce page for **Contact us**, which includes the following fields, and save the data in a custom object. Also open it for unauthenticated access:
   - First name
   - Last name
   - Company
   - E-mail address
   - Mobile phone
   - Reason to contact
   - Preferred time to call

9. Create a Flow that allows the system administrator to mass delete topics. In the very first screen, display all topics and allow them to select multiple topics, and as soon as they click on the **Next** button, delete all the selected topics.

10. Create a Flow that allows Opportunity owners to add a topic to multiple Opportunity records from a single screen. Currently, they have to go to each record detail page and add a topic to it. On the very first page, allow them to enter the topic name (if the topic exists at runtime, create it via Flow) and criteria to search the Opportunity record. On the next screen, display all the related Opportunity records and allow them to select multiple Opportunity records. Next, click on the **Finish** or **Next** button and add the topic to all the selected Opportunity records.

11. Create a Flow that will automatically update the newly created contract's owner to the contract's account's owner.

**Hint**: Use the Inline Visualforce page to call the Flow. Use cross-object field reference to update the contract's owner.

# Summary

In this chapter, we went through various concepts related to debugging the Flow. In the beginning, we looked at who can run the Flow and the permissions required for it. We also covered the various ways to call a Flow. We discussed ways to set Flow variables values from the controller and ways to open Flow access for non-Salesforce users. Then, we moved forward and discussed ways to access Flow from Salesforce1 and use Flow though Inline Visualforce page. Finally, we discussed cross-object field reference in Flows and the key points related to manipulating the data. In the next chapter, we will discuss Process Builder and how this will help you automate your complex business process, for example, auto submit records into an approval process, and so on.

# 5
# Developing Applications with Process Builder

In the previous chapter, we discussed how to and who can access Flows. We also discussed various ways to call a Flow and open it for unauthenticated access. We also discussed a way to pass values in variables through Apex and the technique to access the Flow from the Salesforce1 mobile application. We also learned how you can reference cross-object fields in Visual Workflow. In this chapter, we will discuss Lightning Process Builder and how to use it to automate business processes. We will also discuss a way to access a Flow through it. The following topics will be covered in this chapter:

- An overview of Process Builder
- The differences between Process Builder and other tools
- Creating applications with Process Builder
- Various use cases of Process Builder
- Limitations of Process Builder

Just to remind you, we will now use Lightning Experience for all upcoming chapters.

# An overview of Process Builder

Lightning Process Builder and Process Builder are the same tool. Process Builder is a way of automating business processes. In other words, it is the upgraded version of the Workflow Rule. Whenever you create a process, the system automatically creates a **Flow** and a **Flow Trigger** to call this Flow. This happens behind the scenes, and the user doesn't need to interact with these shadow Flows. The Workflow Rule has several limitations. It doesn't allow you to update child records. Also, it doesn't allow you to Post to Chatter, create a child record on a specific action, or automatically submit a record for approval. To overcome these limitations, Salesforce introduced Process Builder in the **Spring '15** release. There are a few advantages of Process Builder, which are as follows:

- It allows you to create a complete process in a single screen, unlike Workflow Rules, where you have to move from screen to screen to create a complete rule
- Its visual layouts allow you to create a complete process using point-and-click
- It helps you minimize Apex code usage
- It allows you to call Apex from Process Builder, where Apex is still required
- It also allows you to create multiple scheduled actions for the criteria from Process Builder
- You can easily reorder the process criteria in your process with drag and drop
- It is also possible to execute multiple criteria of a process

As of the **Summer'17** release, Process Builder runs in the **system mode** so the object and field level permissions will both be ignored for the user who triggers the process. Visual Workflow runs in the **user mode**, which means that at runtime, the user who triggers the Flow, their access on the object, and field the level will be counted. However, if a process launching a Flow, the whole automation will run in the **system mode**. Let's take an example if you are trying to update the Opportunity **Next Step** field:

1. **If you use Process Builder to achieve it**: If the running user doesn't have access to the **Next Step** field, Process Builder will be able to update it.

2. **If you use Flow (custom button to call a Flow)**: If the running user doesn't have access to the **Next Step** field, they will get an error.

3. **If you use Flow to achieve the same thing and you are using the Process Builder to auto launch the Flow**: If the running user doesn't have access to the **Next Step** field, then too Flow will be able to update it.

If any of the actions fail at runtime, the entire transaction will fail and an error message will be displayed. There are some exceptions or settings around it, which we will discuss later in `Chapter 8`, *Enabling Flows to Work with Lightning Experience*.

# Business problems

As a Salesforce administrator or developer, you may get multiple requirements from the business to streamline sales or support processes. If something can't be achieved using Workflow Rule, then we may have to Apex code to automate it. Let's start with a business scenario.

The use case goes like this: Sara Bareilles is working as a Salesforce administrator in Universal Containers. She has a requirement to auto-update the related contacts **Other Phone** field with the account **Phone** once the account is activated.

There are several ways of solving the preceding business requirement. These are mentioned as follows:

1. To achieve this business requirement, we can create a Flow and embed it in a Visualforce page. Then, we can use it as an inline Visualforce page in an account page layout.

2. Since we can't achieve the business requirement using a Workflow Rule, the next possibility is to use an Apex trigger. A developer writes an Apex trigger on an **Account** object to update all **contacts** when the account gets activated.

3. You can also use Process Builder. We will discuss this in detail later in this chapter.

# Browser requirements for using Process Builder

Process Builder is available for the Lightning Professional (with a limited number of processes), Lightning Enterprise, Lightning Unlimited, and Developer editions. You can access Process Builder on any platform. The requirements are as follows:

- The most recent version of Google Chrome
- The most recent version of Mozilla Firefox
- The most recent version of Safari
- The most recent version of Internet Explorer

Process Builder is 508-compliant (which means that all users regardless of disability status can access Process Builder) with one exception:

```
they can close modal dialogs using the ESC key on their keyboard, but they
can't close side panels by using the ESC key.
```

# An overview of the Process Builder user interface

Process Builder is a tool that allows you to implement business requirements by creating a process (without any code). It has almost all the features that are offered by Workflow Rule, plus it also contains some new features, such as **Post to Chatter**, **Launch a Flow**, **Create a Record**, **Update Records**, and **Submit for Approval**. From now on, we will use Lightning Experience to create or manage processes using Process Builder and create or manage Visual Workflows. The Process Builder user interface has different functional parts, which are shown in the following screenshot:

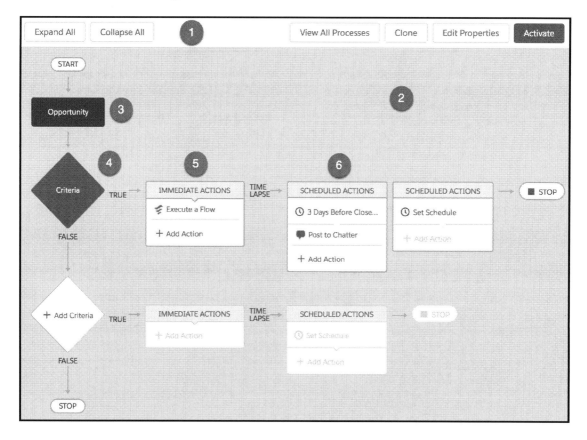

The different functional parts of the user interface of Process Builder are as follows:

1. **Button bar**: The following are the buttons available in the button bar:

   - **Activate**: Use this button to activate your process. You can't make any changes once a process is activated.
   - **Deactivate**: This button is available on the button bar only if the process is activated. Use this button to deactivate a process.

   - **Edit Properties**: This will show you the **Process Name**, **API Name**, and **Description** fields of your process. It allows you to change the process name and description as long as the process is not activated. You can't change the **API Name** field after you've saved it the first time. The **Properties** window will look like what is shown in the following screenshot:

   - **Clone**: The **Clone** button lets you make a copy of the current process. You can perform this activity with these two Clone As options using this button: **Version of current process** and **A new process**.

   - **View All Processes**: Once you click on this button, it will redirect you to the Processes management page. From there, you can see all the processes created in the current Salesforce organization.

- **Collapse All**: Collapse actions on the canvas.

- **Expand All**: Expand actions on the canvas.

2. **Process canvas**: This is the main area where you can use point-and-click to develop a process. To edit any element in the process canvas, double-click on it.

3. **Add object**: Select the object on which you want to create a process and choose the evaluation criteria (changes that will cause the process to run).

4. **Add criteria**: Use this to define the criteria and set the filter conditions.

5. **IMMEDIATE ACTIONS**: Use this to define immediate actions for the process.

6. **SCHEDULED ACTIONS**: Use this to define scheduled actions for the process.

# Actions available in Process Builder

Process Builder can perform almost all actions that are available for Workflow Rules, and it also contains some new actions, but it doesn't support outbound messages, among other things. With Process Builder, you can perform the following actions:

- **Apex**: This allows you to call an Apex class that contains an invocable method
- **Create a Record**: Using this, you can create a record
- **Email Alerts**: Use this to send e-mail alerts
- **Flows**: Use this action to call a Flow from the Process
- **Post to Chatter**: Use this to post a textpost on a Chatter group, record, or user's wall
- **Processes**: Use this action to call an existing process from another process
- **Quick Actions**: Use this action to call a Chatter global action or object specific action, for example, log a call, create a record, and so on
- **Submit for Approval**: Use this action to submit a record to an Approval Process
- **Update Records**: This allows you to update any related records

In this and the upcoming chapters, we will see each action in detail.

# Differences between Process Builder and other tools

Salesforce offers various tools to automate business processes, for example, Visual Workflow, Workflow Rule, and Process Builder. So, it is necessary to understand the difference between these tools and when to use which. The following table describes the difference between these tools:

| | Workflow | Flow | Process Builder |
| --- | --- | --- | --- |
| **Visual designer** | Not available | Available | Available |
| **Starts when** | A record is created or edited | • The user clicks on a custom button/link<br>• A process starts<br>• Apex is called<br>• Inline Visualforce page<br>• The user accesses a custom tab | A record is created or edited |
| **Supports time-based actions?** | Yes | Yes | Yes |
| **Call Apex code?** | No | Yes | Yes |
| **Create records** | Only task | Yes | Yes |
| **Invoke processes** | No | No | Yes |
| **Update records?** | Yes, but only fields from the same record or parent (in case of Master-detail relationship) | Yes, any record | Yes, any related record |
| **Delete records?** | No | Yes | No |
| **Launch a Flow?** | No | Yes | Yes |
| **Post to Chatter?** | No | Yes | Yes, but only textpost |
| **Send an e-mail?** | Yes | Yes | Yes |

| | Workflow | Flow | Process Builder |
|---|---|---|---|
| **Submit for approval?** | No | Yes | Yes |
| **Send Outbound Messages?** | Yes | No | No |
| **Supports user interaction?** | No | Yes | No |
| **Version control?** | No | Yes | Yes |
| **Supports user input at runtime?** | No | Yes (through screen elements) | No |
| **Supports unauthenticated access?** | No | Yes (through Force.com Sites) | No |
| **Can pause on runtime?** | No | Yes | No |
| **Allows modification** | After deactivation, you can modify the Workflow rule | Once Flow is activated, you can't modify it and the same applies after deactivation | Once process is activated, you can't modify it and the same applies after deactivation |
| **Delete** | Once Workflow is deactivated, you can immediately delete it | Once Flow is deactivated, you can immediately delete it | Once process is deactivated, you can immediately delete it |
| **Version Control** | No | Yes (number of versions you can create for a Flow is 50) | Yes (number of versions you can create for a Process is 50) |

# Creating applications with Process Builder

Before Process Builder was available, knowledge of Apex and Visualforce was required to automate complex business processes in Salesforce. After completion of this chapter, you will get a clear-cut idea of how to automate business processes using Process Builder and minimize the need for Apex code. Now we will discuss how to use Process Builder to automate business processes. Now onwards we will use Lightning Experience to create or manage processes using Process Builder and create or manage Visual Workflows.

# Hands on 1 - auto create a child record

It's a common business requirement to auto create a child record whenever the parent record gets created. For example, as soon as an account gets activated, we need to auto create an Opportunity for that account and set the Opportunity close date to the last date of the current quarter. To satisfy these types of business requirements, a developer normally writes an Apex trigger, but there are few other ways through which you can achieve this without writing code:

- Process Builder
- A combination of Flow and Process Builder
- A combination of Flow and Inline Visualforce page on the account detail page

We will use Process Builder to solve these types of business requirements.

A business Scenario: Joe Thompson is working as a system administrator in Universal Containers. He has received a requirement from the management to auto create a contract as soon as an account gets created in Salesforce, and auto-populate these values in the new contract:

- **Contract term (months)**: 12
- **Contract start date**: Account created date + 90 days
- **Status**: Draft
- Auto-relate it with a new account

# Creating a Process

To solve the preceding business requirement, we will use Process Builder. In the run time process will responsible to auto create a contract record whenever a new account record gets created. To do this, follow these instructions:

1. In the Lightning Experience, click on **Setup (Gear Icon)** | **Setup** | **PLATFORM TOOLS** | **Process Automation** | **Process Builder** in Lighting Experience, click on the **New** button, and enter the following details:

    - **Process Name**: Enter the name for the process. Enter `Auto create new Contract` as **Process Name**. This must be within 255 characters.

    - **API Name**: This will be auto-populated based on the name. This must be within 77 characters.

    - **Description**: Write some meaningful text so that other developers or administrators can easily understand why this process has been created.

    - **This process starts when**: It allows you to select when you want to start your process. The followings are the options:

        - **A record changes**: Select this option if you want to start your process when a record is created or edited.

        - **It's invoked by another process**: Select this option if you want to invoke your process from another process. It allows you to create an **invocable process** by selecting this option. An invocable process is a process that starts when another process invokes it. In `Chapter 6`, *Building Efficient and Performance Optimized Processes* we will discuss in detail with a few use cases.

In this case, select **A record changes**. The fields should appear as shown in the following screenshot:

2. Click on the **Save** button once you are done. It will redirect you to the process canvas, which allows you to create the process by clicking, not code.

# Adding an object and evaluation criteria

Once you are done with **Define Process Properties**, the next task is to select the object on which you want to create a process and define the **evaluation criteria**:

1. Click on **Add Object** node, as shown in the following screenshot:

2. This will open a window in right-hand side, where you have to enter the following details:

- **Object**: Start typing and then select the **Account** object.
- **Start the process**: For **Start the process**, select **only when a record is created**. This means the process will fire only at the time of record creation.
- **Recursion - Allow process to evaluate a record multiple times in a single transaction?**: Select this checkbox only when you want the process to evaluate the same record up to five times in a single transaction. It might re-examine the record because a Process, Workflow Rule, or Flow may have updated the record in the same transaction. In this case, leave this unchecked. This window should appear as shown in the following screenshot:

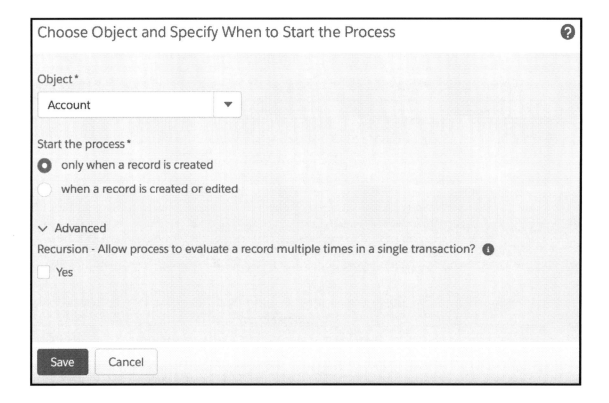

3. Once you are done, click on the **Save** button. Just as in Workflow Rule, once you save the panel, it doesn't allow you to change the selected object.

# Adding process criteria

After defining the **evaluation criteria**, the next step is to define the process criteria. This is similar to the rule criteria in Workflow Rule. Once the process criteria are true, only then will the process execute with the associated actions:

1. To define the process criteria click on the **Add Criteria** node, as shown in this screenshot:

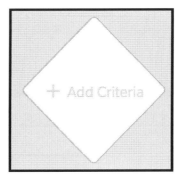

2. Now enter the following details:

   - **Criteria Name**: Enter a name for the criteria node. Enter `Always` in **Criteria Name**.

   - **Criteria for Executing Actions**: Select the type of criteria you want to define. You can either select **Formula evaluates to true** or **Conditions are met** (A filter to define the process criteria) or **No criteria-just execute the actions!**. In this case, select **No criteria-just execute the actions!**. This means the process will fire for every condition. This window should look like what is shown in the following screenshot:

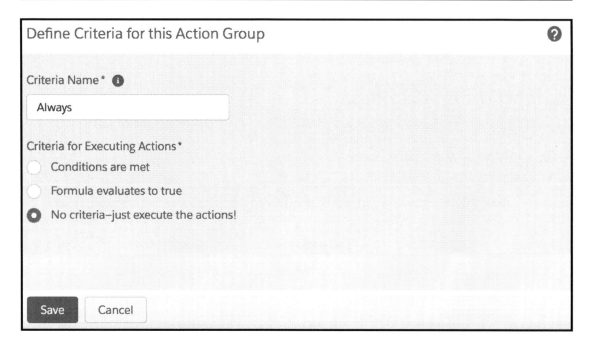

3. Once you are done, click on the **Save** button.

# Adding an action to a Process

Once you are done with the **process criteria** node, the next step is to add an immediate action to create a contract. For this, we will use the **Create a Record** action available in Process Builder. You can add multiple immediate and scheduled actions for a particular criteria node. The only limitation is the maximum number of criteria nodes that you can add in one process, which is 200. Immediate actions are executed as soon as the evaluation criteria are met.

Scheduled actions are executed at a specified time. We will add an immediate action with the following steps:

1. The next step is to add one immediate action to auto create a record. For this, we will use the **Create a Record** action available in Process Builder. Click on **Add Action** available under **IMMEDIATE ACTIONS**, as shown in the following screenshot:

2. Now enter the following details:
   - **Action Type**: Select the type of action. In this case, select **Create a Record**.
   - **Action Name**: Enter a name for this action. Enter `Create Contract record` in **Action Name**.
   - **Record Type**: Select the object that you want to create a record for. Start typing and then select the **Contract** object. In this case, select **Contract**.
   - **Set Field Values**: Certain fields are required when you create a record. When you select the object that you want to create a record for, the Process Builder automatically displays required fields for that record in each row. In this case, a row for **Account ID** and **Status** shows automatically. When setting a value for a given field or field you have added, the available value types are filtered based on the field that you have selected. The available value types are:
     - **Currency**: You can manually enter a currency value.
     - **Boolean**: This allows you to choose a true or false Boolean value.
     - **DateTime or Date**: You can manually enter a DateTime or Date value.
     - **Formula**: You can easily create a formula using functions and fields.

- **Global Constant**: It allows you to choose a global constant to set a value to null or an empty string. For example, choose $GlobalConstant.Null or $GlobalConstant.EmptyString
- **ID**: You can manually enter a Salesforce ID.
- **MultiPicklist**: This allows you to choose one or more multi-select picklist values.
- **Number**: You can manually enter a number value.
- **Picklist**: This allows you to choose a picklist value.
- **Reference**: This allows you to choose a value based on a field on the record or on a related record.
- **String**: You can manually enter a string value.

To select the fields, you can use **field picker**. To enter the values, use the **text entry** field and map the fields according to the following screenshot:

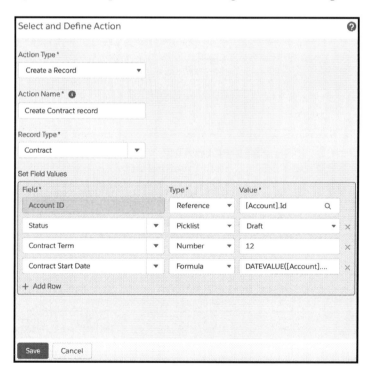

Use the formula to set the **Contract Start Date** dynamically based on the preceding requirement, in this case the account created date + 90 days. Use function to select **DATEVALUE** (returns a date value for a dateTime), use field picker to select the **Created Date** field, use operator to select **+** and then enter 90, as shown in the following screenshot:

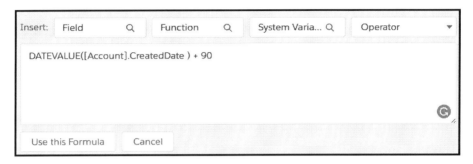

The new record's Created By field is set to the user who started the process by creating or editing a record.

3. Once you are done, click on the **Save** button to save process immediate action. Finally, the Process will appear as shown in this screenshot:

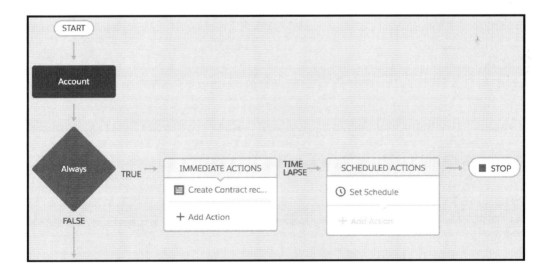

# Activating a Process

As soon as you are done with the process creation, the next step is to activate it:

1. To activate a process, click on the **Activate** button available on the button bar, as shown in the following screenshot:

2. A warning message will appear on the screen. Read it carefully and then click on the **Confirm** button, as shown in this screenshot:

3. Once you click on the **Confirm** button, it will activate the Process.

For activation, a process must have an action added to it. If a process doesn't have any action added to it, the activate button won't be clickable. After activation of a process, it's impossible to make any changes to it. If you want to do that, you have to clone it and save it as either **New Version** or a **New Process**, which we will discuss later:

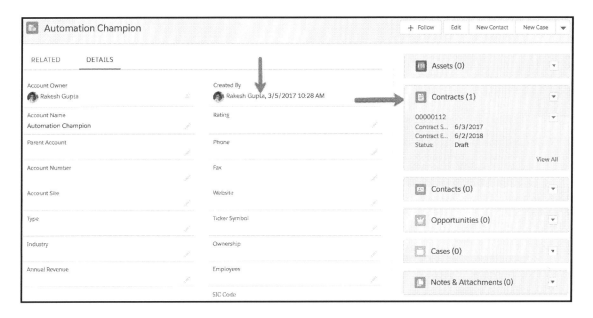

From now on, if you try to create a new account, after successful attempts, you can see a contract getting created for the account by the process you have created, as shown in the preceding screenshot.

# Deactivating a Process

If some active processes are no longer required by the business, you can deactivate them. To deactivate an activated process, open the process and click on the **Deactivate** button, as shown in the following screenshot:

After deactivation, Salesforce stops using the process to evaluate when an account record is created or edited. After you deactivate a process, any scheduled actions will still be there in a queue for execution.

# Deleting a Process version

If a process version is no longer in use, then you can delete it. You can delete only those process versions that are in the **Draft**, **Inactive**, or **Invalid Draft** status. This means that you can't delete an active process. If you want to delete an active process version, you must deactivate it first and then delete it. If a process version has scheduled actions, then you can't delete it; in such a case, you must wait until those pending actions have been completed or deleted. To delete a Process, follow these instructions:

1. Navigate to **Setup (Gear Icon)** | **Setup** | **PLATFORM TOOLS** | **Process Automation** | **Process Builder**.

2. This will redirect you to the Process Management page. Click on the name of the process whose version you want to delete.

3. Identify the process version that you want to delete and click on **Delete**, as shown in the following screenshot:

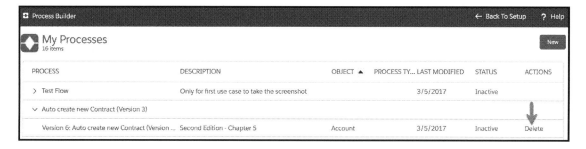

If your process has only one version and you delete that version, the whole process will be removed from the Process Management page.

# Hands on 2 - auto update child records

There are several business use cases where a customer wants to update child records based on some criteria, for example, auto-updating all related opportunity to Closed Lost if an account is updated to **Inactive**. To achieve these types of business requirements, you can use an Apex trigger. You can also achieve these types of requirements using the following methods:

- Process Builder

- A combination of Flow and Process Builder

- A combination of Flow and the Inline Visualforce page on the account detail page

We will use Process Builder to solve these types of problems. Let's start with a business requirement.

Let's look at a business scenario. Alice Atwood is working as a system administrator with Universal Containers. She has received a requirement that once an account gets activated, the account **Phone** must be synced with the related contact **Asst. Phone** field. This means that whenever an account **Phone** field gets updated, the same phone number will be copied to the related contacts **Asst. Phone** field.

Follow these instructions to achieve the preceding requirement using Process Builder:

1. First of all, navigate to **Setup (Gear Icon)** | **Setup** | **PLATFORM TOOLS** | **Objects and Fields** | **Object manager** | **Fields & Relationships** and make sure that the **Active** picklist is available in your Salesforce organization. If it's not available, create a custom Picklist field with the name as **Active**, and enter the `Yes` and `No` values.

2. To create a process, navigate to **Setup (Gear Icon)** | **Setup** | **PLATFORM TOOLS** | **Process Automation** | **Process Builder**, click on **New Button**, and enter the following details:

   - **Process Name**: Enter the name of the Process. Enter `Update Contacts Asst Phone` in **Process Name**

   - **API Name**: This will be autopopulated based on the name

   - **Description**: Write some meaningful text so that other developers or can easily understand why this process has been created

   - **This process starts when**: Configure the process to start when a record is created or edited. In this case, select **A record changes**

The properties window will appear as shown in the following screenshot:

3. Once you are done, click on the **Save** button. It will redirect you to the process canvas, which allows you to create or modify the process.
4. After **Define Process Properties**, the next task is to select the object on which you want to create a process and define the **evaluation criteria**. For this, click on the **Add Object** node. It will open an additional window on the right-hand side of the process canvas screen, where you have to enter the following details:
   - **Object**: Start typing and then select the **Account** object.
   - **Start the process**: For **Start the process**, select **when a record is created or edited**. This means that the process will fire every time irrespective of record creation or updating.

- **Recursion - Allow process to evaluate a record multiple times in a single transaction?**: Select this checkbox only when you want the process to evaluate the same record up to five times in a single transaction. In this case, leave this unchecked. This window will appear as shown in the following screenshot:

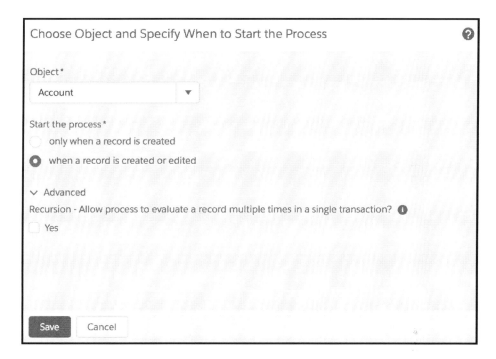

5. Once you are done, click on the Save button.
6. After defining the **evaluation criteria,** the next step is to add the process criteria. Once the process criteria are true, only then will the Process execute the associated actions. To define the process criteria, click on the Add Criteria node. It will open an additional window on the right-hand side of the process canvas screen, where you have to enter the following details:
    - **Criteria Name**: Enter a name for the criteria node. Enter Update Contacts in **Criteria Name**.

- **Criteria for Executing Actions**: Select the type of criteria you want to define. You can select either **Formula evaluates to true** or **Conditions are met** (a filter to define the process criteria) or **No criteria-just execute the actions!**. In this case, select **Conditions are met.**

- **Set Conditions**: This field lets you specify which combination of the filter conditions must be true for the process to execute the associated actions. In this case, select **Active** equals to **Yes**. This means that the process will fire only when the account is active.

- **Conditions**: In the conditions section, select **All of the conditions are met (AND)**. This field lets you specify which combination of the filter conditions must be true for the process to execute the associated actions.

- Under **Advanced**, select **Yes** to execute the actions only when specified changes are made. This means that the actions are executed only if the record meets the criteria now but the values that the record had immediately before it was saved didn't meet criteria. This means that these actions won't be executed when irrelevant changes are made. For example, if the account status is **Active** and a user updates the record by adding a **Shipping Address**, the process won't execute the associated actions. This setting isn't available if:

  - Your process starts only when a record is created

  - Your process starts when a record is created or edited and the criteria node doesn't evaluate any criteria

  - The criteria node evaluates a formula but the formula doesn't include a reference to the record that started the process

  - Your process uses the Is changed operator in a filter condition

In this case, leave this unchecked. At the end process criteria, a window will appear, as shown in the following screenshot:

7. Once you are done, click on the **Save** button.

8. Once you are done with the **process criteria** node, the next step is to add an immediate action to update the related contact's **Asst. Phone** field. For this, we will use the **Update Records** action available in Process Builder. Click on **Add Action** available under **IMMEDIATE ACTIONS**. It will open an additional window on the right-hand side of the process canvas screen, where you have to enter the following details:

- **Action Type**: Select the type of action. In this case, select **Update Records**.

- **Action Name**: Enter a name for this action. Enter `Update Asst. Phone` in **Action Name**.

- **Record Type**: Select the record or records that you need to update. Click on the **Record type**, it will pop up a window, where you will get the following options:

  - **Select the Account record that started your process**

  - **Select a record related to the Account**

  - These are radio buttons and only one can be selected and to update the child record. In this case, choose **Select a record related to the Account**. Then, in **Type to filter list**, look for the child object, **Contacts**, as shown in the following screenshot:

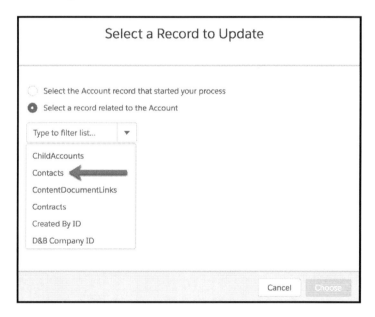

- **Criteria for Updating Records**: Optionally, you can specify conditions to filter the records you are updating. Select **No criteria—just update the records!**. There are cool use cases around it, which we will discuss in `Chapter 6`, *Building Efficient and Performance Optimized Processes*.

- **Field**: Map the **Asst. Phone** field with the **[Account].Phone** field.

Select the **Contacts** object, and then click the on **Choose** button. To select the fields, you can use **field picker**. To enter the value, use the **text entry** field. It will appear as shown in the following screenshot:

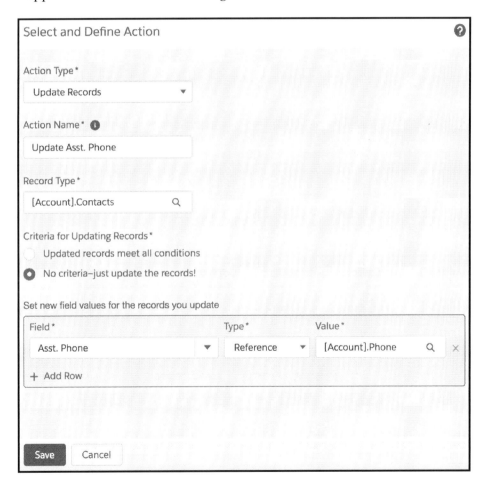

9. Once you are done, click on the **Save** button.

10. The final step is to activate it. To activate a process, click on the **Activate** button available on the button bar. Finally, the process will appear as shown in this screenshot:

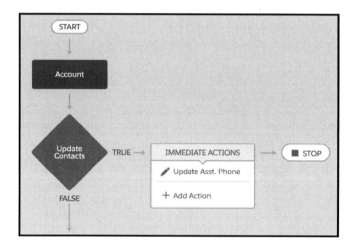

From now on, if users try to update the **Phone** field of an active account, the process will automatically update the related contact's **Asst. Phone** field with the value available in the account **Phone** field, as shown in the following screenshot:

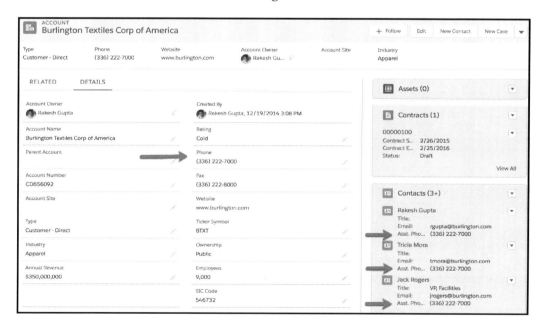

Before testing the process, make sure that you have activated your process.

# Hands on 3 - cloning a Process

Once you have activated a process, it doesn't allow you to make any changes to it. If you want to make any changes to the active process, then you have to clone it and save it as either a **New Version** or a **New Process**.

A business Scenario: Alice Atwood is working as a system administrator in Universal Containers and she has created a Process (`Update_Contacts_Asst_Phone`) to update the related contact **Asst. Phone** field from the account **Phone** field once an account gets activated and after that related contacts **Asst. Phone** field must be synced with account **Asst. Phone** field. She has received another request from a business saying that they want to add one more condition to the process. The entry criteria are such that it will work only for accounts wherein the billing country is the USA.

To meet this business requirement, you have to add one more condition to the existing process. For this, you have to modify your process. As the process is already activated, the only possibility is to clone it. To clone a process, follow these instructions:

1. Click on the **Clone** button available on the button bar. It will open a popup for you. Under **Save As**, select the appropriate options:
2. From the Process Management page, click on the Process that you want to modify. It will redirect you to the Process canvas page:

    - **Version of current process**: This allows you to create a new version of an existing process

    - **A new process**: If you want to create a new process, select this option

In this case, select **Version of current process** to create a new version of an existing process, as shown in the following screenshot:

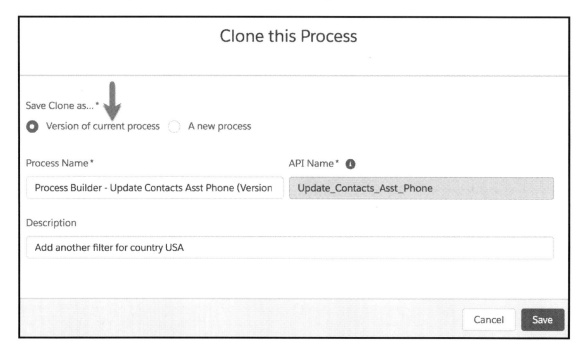

3. Click on the **Save** button once you are done.

4. Now you can modify the process as per the preceding business requirement, as follows:

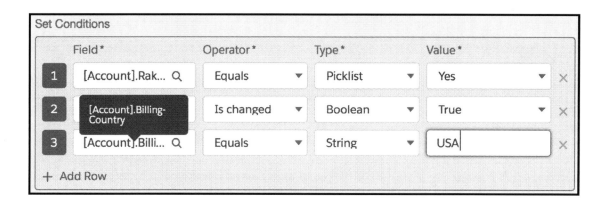

Business requiements will appear as shown in the preceding screenshot. Once you are done, click on the **Activate** button to activate the current version of a Process. Salesforce automatically deactivates others active versions of the current process, if any exist.

## Adding an Apex plugin to your Process

Process Builder allows you to call an Apex class that includes methods annotated with @InvocableMethod. You can also pass the required value in Apex class variables.

To do this, select the **Apex** action in the process. In Chapter 6, *Building Efficient and Performance Optimized Processes,* we will discuss a use case where the system can auto-delete open cases when an account is out of business using an Apex class and by calling it from Process Builder.

# Hands on 4 - posting opportunity details to the Chatter group

Often, the business wants to auto-post details of records to Chatter groups. This is possible through the Apex code, but there is another way you can achieve it without code, that is, Process Builder. Process Builder has a specific action for this called **Post to Chatter**. You can auto-post record details to a Chatter group using the following methods:

- Process Builder
- Combination of Flow and Process Builder
- Flow and Inline Visualforce page

Let's look at a business scenario. Helina Jolly is working as a system administrator at Universal Containers. She has received a requirement to post Opportunity details to the `Sales Executive` Chatter group whenever an Opportunity gets created with an amount greater than $1,000,000.

Follow these instructions to achieve this using Process Builder:

1. Create a public Chatter group named `Sales Executive`.

 Go to `https://help.salesforce.com/HTViewHelpDoc?id=collab_group _creating.htm&language=en_US` to know how to create a Chatter group.

2. To create a process, navigate to **Setup (Gear Icon)** | **Setup** | **PLATFORM TOOLS** | **Process Automation** | **Process Builder**, click on the **New** button, and enter the following details:

    - **Name**: Enter the name for the Process. Enter `Post Opportunity Information to Chatter Group` in **Name**

    - **API Name**: This will be autopopulated based on the name

    - **Description**: Write some meaningful text so that other developers or administrators can easily understand why this process has been created

3. Once you are done, click on the **Save** button. This will redirect you to the process canvas, which allows you to create or modify the process.

4. After **Define Process Properties**, the next task is to select the object on which you want to create a process and define the **evaluation criteria**. For this, click on the **Add Object** node. It will open an additional window on the right-hand side of the process canvas screen, where you have to enter the following details:

- **Object**: Start typing and then select the **Opportunity** object.

- **Start the process**: For **Start the process**, select **only when a record is created**. This means Process will fire only at the time of record creation.

- **Recursion - Allow process to evaluate a record multiple times in a single transaction**: Select this checkbox only when you want Process to evaluate the same record up to five times in a single transaction. In this case, leave this box unchecked.

- Once you are done, click on the **Save** button.

- After defining the **evaluation criteria**, the next step is to add the **process criteria**. Once the process criteria are true, only then will the Process execute the associated actions. To define the process criteria, click on the **Add Criteria** node. It will open an additional window on the right-hand side of the process canvas screen, where you have to enter the following details:

    - **Criteria Name**: Enter a name for the criteria node. Enter `Only when amount > $1M` in **Criteria Name**.

    - **Criteria for Executing Actions**: Select the type of criteria you want to define. You can select either **Formula evaluates to true** or **Conditions are met** (a filter to define the process criteria) or **No criteria-just execute the actions!**. In this case, select **Conditions are met.**

    - **Set Conditions**: This field lets you specify which combination of the filter conditions must be true for the process to execute the associated actions. In this case, select **Value** greater than $1,000,000.

    - **Conditions**: In the conditions section, select **All of the conditions are met (AND)**. This field lets you specify which combination of the filter conditions must be true for the process to execute the associated actions.

The dollar sign is not required while entering the amount. What we enter in as criteria could just be the raw number, that is, 10,000,000. The system will add the currency for us.

Process criteria will look like what is shown in the following screenshot:

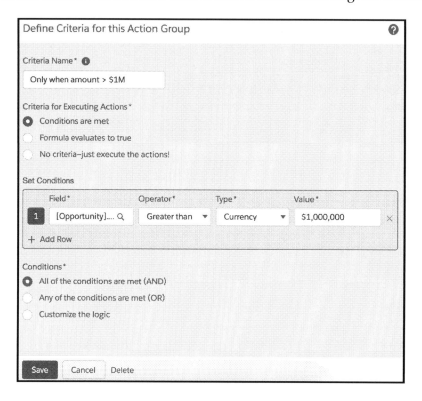

5. Once you are done, click on the **Save** button.
6. Once you are done with the **process criteria** node, the next step is to add an immediate action to post Opportunity details to the Chatter group. For this, we will use the **Post to Chatter** action available in Process Builder. Click on **Add Action** available under **IMMEDIATE ACTIONS**. This will open an additional window on the right-hand side of the process canvas screen, where you have to enter the following details:

   - **Action Type**: Select the type of action. In this case, select **Post to Chatter**.

- **Action Name**: Enter a name for this action. Enter `Post to Sales Executive Chatter group` in **Action Name**.

- **Post to**: This allows you to select the **Chatter Group** or **User** or **Current Record,** where you want to post the Opportunity details. From the dropdown, select **Chatter Group**. Then, start typing the name of the Chatter group in the textbox and select **Sales Executive**.

- **Message**: Enter the message that you want to post. You can also use the fields above the textbox to mention a user or group, add a topic, or insert a merge field into the message.

Immediate actions will appear as shown in this screenshot:

7. To insert fields, click on **Insert Field**. To mention a User or Chatter group, use the **Mention a user or group** textbox. Finally, to add the topic, use the **Add topic** textbox. Once you are done, click on the **Save** button.

8. Once you are done, the final step is to activate it. To activate a process, click on the **Activate** button available on the button bar. Finally, the process will appear as shown in this screenshot:

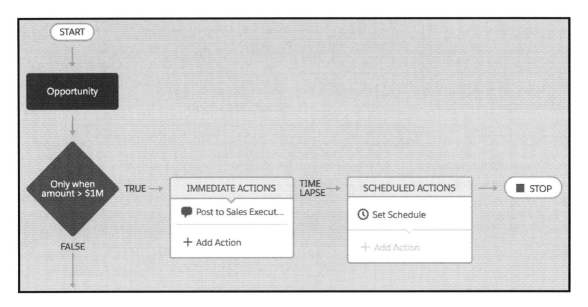

From now on, if users create an Opportunity with an amount more than $1,000,000, it will auto-post a textpost to the Chatter Group Sales Executive, which will appear as shown in the following screenshot:

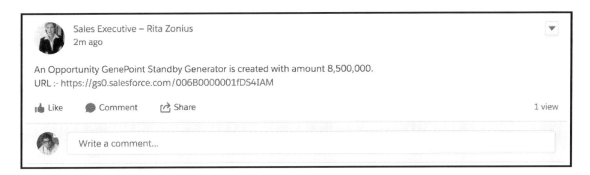

You can also achieve this through a combination of Flow and Process Builder. If you use Process Builder, you can post only textpost, whereas if you use Flow, it allows you to post as linkpost, textpost, and so on. It also allows you set **CreatedById**. For this, use the **Record Create** element and the **FeedItem** object.

 You can achieve the preceding requirement using the **Post to Chatter** static action or the **FeedItem** object available in Flow and Process Builder. To learn more about this, refer to `https://rakeshistom.wordpress.com/2014/06/14/post-opportunity-de tails-to-a-chatter-group/`.

If you have embedded the Flow in a Visualforce page, you need to use the Inline Visualforce page on the Opportunity object in order to achieve it.

# Hands on 5 - sending an e-mail to the opportunity owner

Process Builder also allows you to send e-mails to users, for example, sending out an e-mail alert to the account owner as soon as an opportunity is successfully closed.

Let's look at a business scenario. Helina Jolly is working as a system administrator at Universal Containers. She has created a process (`Post Opportunity Information to Chatter Group`) to post Opportunity details to a Chatter group if the amount is greater than $1,000,000. She receives another requirement to send an e-mail to the Opportunity's Account owner after 5 days of its creation.

Follow these instructions to achieve this using Process Builder:

1. Process Builder doesn't allow you to create a new e-mail alert, but it allows you to use an existing e-mail alert that you have created in past for the same object on which you created a process. First of all, create an e-mail template `Account owner notification` by navigating to **Setup (Gear Icon)** | **Setup** | **ADMINISTRATION** | **Email** | **Email Templates**, as shown in the following screenshot:

| **Subject** | New opportunity gets created for your account - {!Account.Name} |
|---|---|
| **HTML Preview** | |

Dear {!Account.OwnerFullName},

A new opportunity gets created for your account {!Account.Name}. Below is some key information of new opportunity

Name :- {!Opportunity.Name}
Stage:- {!Opportunity.StageName}
Amount:- {!Opportunity.Amount}
Close Date:- {!Opportunity.CloseDate}
Owner:- {!Opportunity.OwnerFullName}

Best Regards,
Universal Containers Sales Team

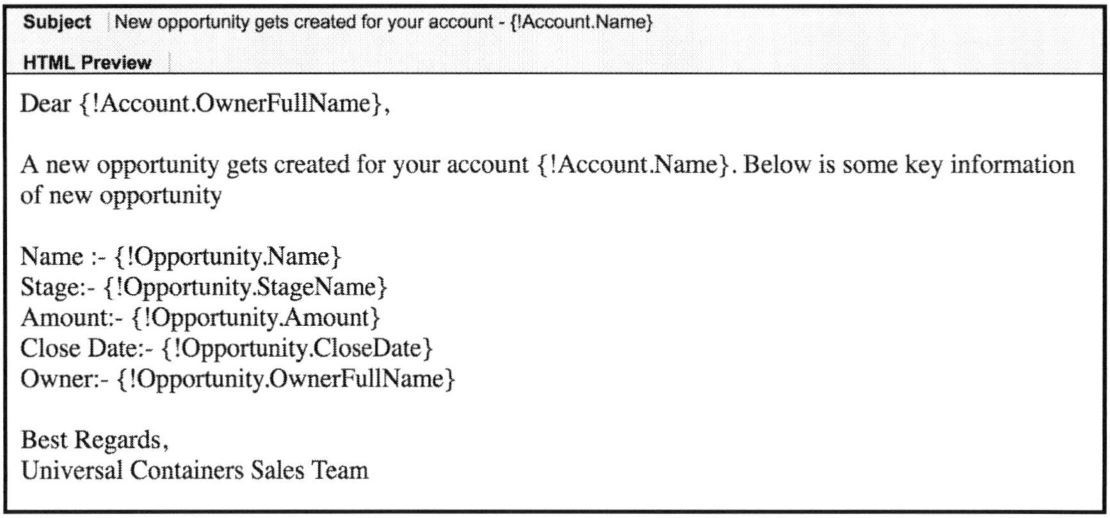

2. The second step is to create an e-mail alert on the **Opportunity** object by navigating to **Setup (Gear Icon)** | **Setup** | **PLATFORM TOOLS** | **Process Automation** | **Process Builder** | **Workflow Actions** | **Email Alerts.** Click on the **New Email Alert** button and save it with the name `Email to Opportunity Owner`. It should look like what is shown in the following screenshot:

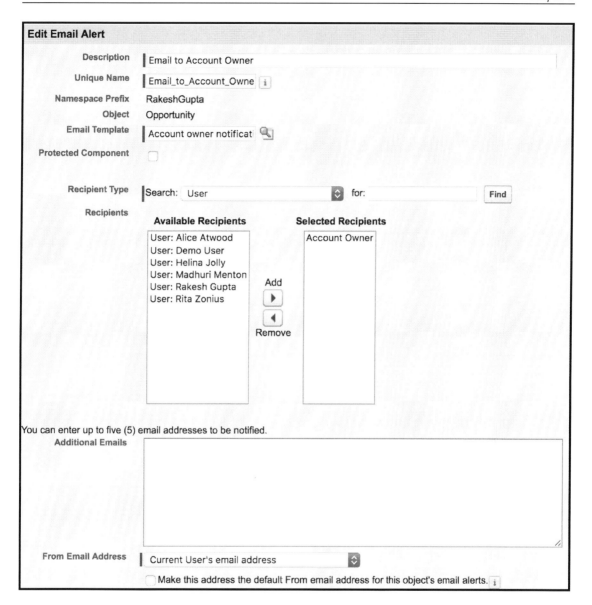

3. To add this e-mail alert to the existing process, navigate to **Setup (Gear Icon)** | **Setup** | **PLATFORM TOOLS** | **Process Automation** | **Process Builder**. Open the `Post Opportunity Information to Chatter Group` process that you created to post the Opportunity details to the Chatter group. Save it as **New Version** because you can't modify an activated process.

4. Now we have to modify the process entry criteria to make sure that the process will fire only when a new opportunity is related to an account record. To do that, add an entry criterion in your process, as shown in the following screenshot:

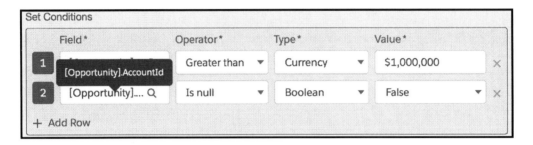

5. To add the scheduled time, click on **Set Schedule** available under **SCHEDULED ACTIONS**, and set **Set Time for Action to Execute** to five days after the Opportunity created Date, as shown in the following screenshot:

6. Once you are done, click on the **Save** button.

7. The next step is to add a scheduled action to send an e-mail. For this, we will use the **Send an Email** action available in Process Builder. To add schedule actions, click on **Add Action** available under **SCHEDULED ACTIONS**. This will open an additional window on the right-hand side of the Process canvas screen, where you have to enter the following details:

- **Action Type**: Select the type of action. In this case, select **Email Alerts**.

- **Action Name**: Enter a name for this action. Enter `Email to Account Owner` in **Action Name**.

- **Email Alert**: Select the existing e-mail alert. In this case, select the e-mail alert **Email to Account Owner** that you created in step two.

Scheduled actions will appear as shown in this screenshot:

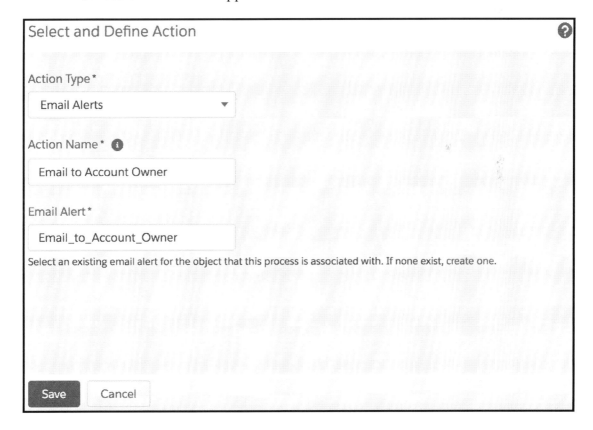

8. Once you are done, click on the **Save** button.

9. Once you are done with the process creation, don't forget to activate the process by clicking on the **Activate** button. Finally, the process will appear as shown in this screenshot:

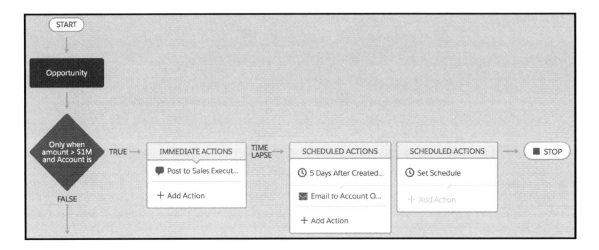

Now, for this process will do both the jobs: posting the Opportunity details to a Chatter group and sending an e-mail to the Opportunity's account owner after 5 days of record creation. The e-mail will look like what is shown in the following screenshot:

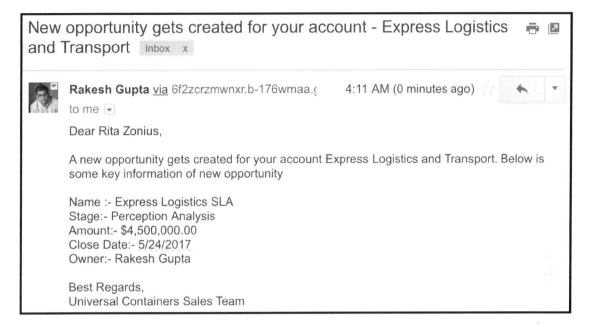

New opportunity gets created for your account - Express Logistics and Transport  Inbox  x

Rakesh Gupta via 6f2zcrzmwnxr.b-176wmaa.(          4:11 AM (0 minutes ago)
to me

Dear Rita Zonius,

A new opportunity gets created for your account Express Logistics and Transport. Below is some key information of new opportunity

Name :- Express Logistics SLA
Stage:- Perception Analysis
Amount:- $4,500,000.00
Close Date:- 5/24/2017
Owner:- Rakesh Gupta

Best Regards,
Universal Containers Sales Team

 Flow also allows you to send e-mails. For this, you have to use the **Send Email** static action available inside it. To learn more about this, go to `https://rakeshistom.wordpress.com/2014/09/08/reminder-email-to-upload-chatter-profile-photo/`.

If you have embedded the Flow in a Visualforce page, you need to use an Inline Visualforce page on the Opportunity object to achieve the preceding business use case.

# Hands on 6 - checking time-dependent actions from Process Builder

To monitor a time-dependent actions queue for Process Builder, follow these instructions:

1. Navigate to **Setup (Gear Icon)** | **Setup** | **PLATFORM TOOLS** | **Process Automation** | **Flows**.

2. Go to the **Paused and Waiting Interviews** section, and from there, you can check out the time-dependent action queue for Process Builder, as shown in the following screenshot:

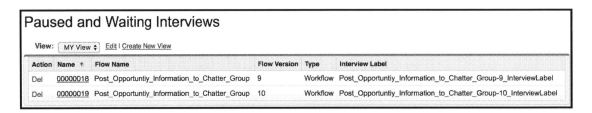

3. To remove a record from the time-based queue, use the **Del** link, as shown in the preceding screenshot.

This is because Process Builder is using a Flow **Wait** element to create a time-dependent action.

# Hands on 7 - submitting a record to an Approval Process

Process Builder also allows you to auto-submit a record to an Approval Process. Currently, the user has to manually submit a record for the Approval Process. You can achieve these types of requirements using the following methods:

- Process Builder
- A combination of Flow (submit for the Approval-static action) and Process Builder
- A combination of Flow and the Inline Visualforce page on the object's detail page

Let's look at a business scenario. Helina Jolly is working as a system administrator at Universal Containers. She has created a process (Post Opportunity Information to Chatter Group) to post Opportunity details to a Chatter group if the amount is greater than $1,000,000 and send an e-mail to the Opportunity's owner. She receives another requirement to auto-submit new Opportunity records to the Approval if the amount is greater than $1,000,000. She has already created a one-step Approval Process for this. It will send an approval request to the CEO.

Follow these instructions to achieve this using Process Builder:

1. If you haven't created an Approval Process yet, create an Approval Process on the Opportunity object, set the entry criteria Opportunity amount greater than 1,000,000, and save it with the name `Opportunity amount greater than 1M`. Add one step to it and send the Approval request to the CEO role. Make sure that you have activated the Approval Process.

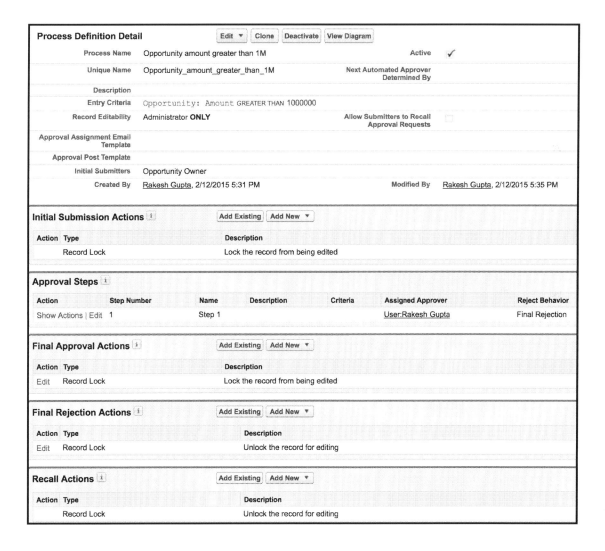

If you want to learn how to create an Approval Process, then refer to
https://help.salesforce.com/HTViewHelpDoc?id=approvals_creating_
approval_processes.htm&language=en_US.

The process (Process Builder) will fail at runtime if it allows the initial submitter
to manually select the next approver.

2. To auto-submit records to an Approval Process, you have to use Process Builder.
   Navigate to **Setup (Gear Icon)** | **Setup** | **PLATFORM TOOLS** | **Process
   Automation** | **Process Builder**. Open the Post Opportunity Information to
   Chatter Group process that you have created in order to post the Opportunity
   details to Chatter group. Save it as **New Version** because you can't modify the
   activate Process.

3. The next step is to add an immediate action to auto-submit a record to the
   Approval Process. For this, we will use the **Submit for Approval** action available
   in Process Builder. Click on **Add Action** available under **IMMEDIATE
   ACTIONS**. This will open an additional window on the right-hand side of the
   process canvas screen, where you have to enter the following details:

   - **Action Type**: Select the type of action. In this case, select **Submit for
     Approval**.

   - **Action Name**: Enter a name for this action. Enter Auto submit
     record into approval in **Action Name**.

   - **Object**: This will automatically populate from the object on which you
     have created the Process.

   - **Approval Process**: You can select **Default approval process**, or if the
     object contains more than one Approval Process, you can use the
     **Specific approval process** option from the dropdown. Select **Default
     approval process**.

   - **Submitter**: This allows you to choose a user to auto-submit a record to
     the Approval Process, and it receives all related notifications. In this
     case, select **Current User**.

- **Submission Comments**: Optionally, you can enter submission comments. They will appear in the Approval history for the specified record. Enter `Auto submit` in this case.

Immediate actions will look like what is shown in the following screenshot:

4. Once you are done, click on the **Save** button.

5. Once you are done with the process creation, don't forget to activate the process by clicking on the **Activate** button. Finally, the process will appear as shown in this screenshot:

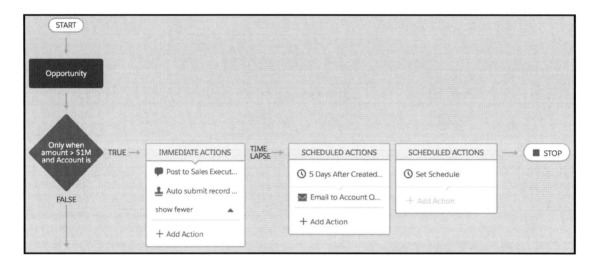

 You can achieve the preceding requirement using the **Submit for Approval** static action available in Flow and Process Builder. To learn more about this, go to `https://rakeshistom.wordpress.com/2014/06/27/auto-submit-record-into-approval-process-with-flow/`.

It is not possible to submit any related records to the Approval Process using Process Builder.

# Hands on 8 - calling a Flow from Process Builder

Process Builder allows you to launch a Flow. In `Chapter 3`, *Manipulating Records in Visual Workflow* and `Chapter 4`, *Debugging and New Ways to Call a Flow*, we saw various ways to invoke or launch a Flow. Process Builder is another way to auto-launch a Flow. For example, there is a Flow that allows the removal of followers from closed Opportunity records. If you want this Flow to automatically execute whenever the Opportunity status gets closed, you should use Process Builder.

Some Flows don't require any user interaction to start, that is, a Flow of the type **Autolaunched Flow**. An Autolaunched Flow can be launched without user interaction, such as from Process Builder or the Apex `interview.start` method.

Let's look at a business scenario. Sara Bareilles, who is working as a system administrator at Universal Containers, has created a Flow to create a new Opportunity using the **Record Create** element, as shown in the following screenshot:

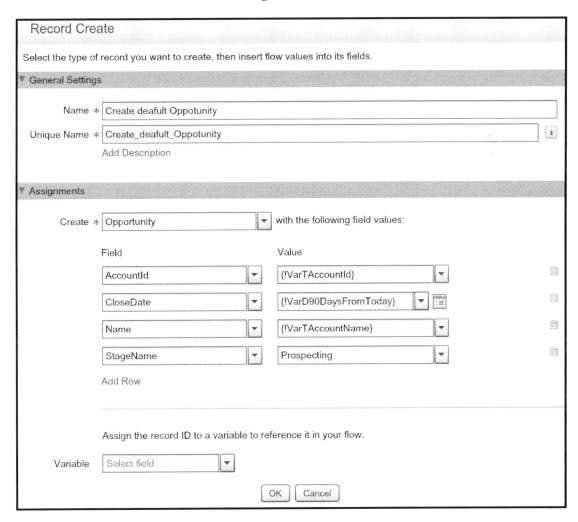

Currently, she is using a custom button on the Account Page Layout to call the Flow. She wants to use Process Builder to automatically fire Flow whenever an account gets created. The VarD90DaysFromToday is a date variable, and the VarTAccountId and VarTAccountName variables used in the preceding example are nothing but text variables. We will use Process Builder to pass the value in these variables.

Follow these instructions to call a Flow from the process:

1. Create a Flow similar to what is shown in the preceding screenshot, save it with the name Create an Opportunity, and **Type** as **Autolaunched Flow** and then click on the **Close** button to close the canvas. Don't forget to activate the Flow.

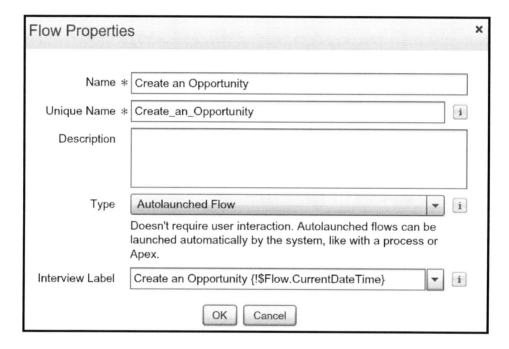

2. To create a process, navigate to **Setup (Gear Icon)** | **Setup** | **PLATFORM TOOLS** | **Process Automation** | **Process Builder**, click on the **New Button**, and enter the following details:
   - **Name**: Enter the name for the Process. Enter Auto create an Opportunity in **Name**

- **API Name**: This will be autopopulated based on the **Name** field
- **Description**: Write some meaningful text so that other developers or administrators can easily understand why this process has been created

3. Once you are done, click on the **Save** button. It will redirect you to the Process canvas, which allows you to create the Process.

4. After **Define Process Properties**, the next task is to select the object on which you want to create a process and define the evaluation criteria. For this, click on the Add Object node. This will open an additional window on the right-hand side of the Process canvas screen, where you have to enter the following details:

   - **Object**: Start typing the name and then select the **Account** object.
   - **Start the process**: For **Start the process**, select **only when a record is created**. This means Process will fire only at the time of record creation.
   - **Recursion**: Allow process to evaluate a record multiple times in a single transaction?: Select this checkbox only when you want the Process to evaluate the same record up to five times in a single transaction. In this case, leave this box unchecked.

5. Once you are done, click on the **Save** button.

6. After defining the **evaluation criteria**, the next step is to add the **process criteria**. To define the process criteria, click on the **Add Criteria** node. This will open an additional window on the right-hand side of the process canvas screen, where you have to enter the following details:

   - **Criteria Name**: Enter a name for the criteria node. Enter `Always` as the criteria name.

- **Criteria for Executing Actions**: Select the type of criteria you want to define. You can select either **Formula evaluates to true** or **Conditions are met** (a filter to define the process criteria) or **No criteria-just execute the actions!**. In this case, select **No criteria-just execute the actions!**. This means that the Process will fire in every condition.

7. Click on the **Save** button.

8. Once you are done with the **process criteria** node, the next step is to add an immediate action to launch a Flow. For this, we will use the **Flows** action available in Process Builder. Click on **Add Action** available under **IMMEDIATE ACTIONS**. This will open an additional window on the right-hand side of the Process canvas screen, where you have to enter the following details:

   - **Action Type**: Select the type of action. In this case, select **Flows**.
   - **Action Name**: Enter a name for this action. Enter `Auto create new Opportunity` in **Action Name**.
   - **Flow**: Select the Flow that you want to execute. In this case, select **Create an Opportunity** Flow.
   - **Set Flow Variables**: Use this to pass the value in your Flow variables. For the current use case, map the `VarD90DaysFromToday` variable with formula `TODAY() + 90`, `VarTAccountId` variable with **[Account].Id**, and the `VarTAccountName` variable with **[Account].Name**.

   Immediate actions will look like what is shown in the following screenshot:

9. To assign the value to multiple variables, click on the **Add Row** link. Once you are done, click on the **Save** button.

10. The final step is to activate it. To activate a process, click on the **Activate** button available on the button bar. Finally, the process will appear as shown in this screenshot:

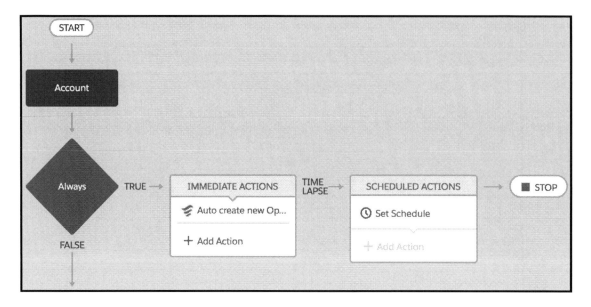

From now on, if an account gets created, Flow will automatically get executed by Process Builder, and a new Opportunity will be created.

# A few points to remember

The following are some noteworthy points regarding Process Builder:

1. A Process's API name must be less than, or equal to, 77 characters, and it's always associated with a single object.
2. Using Process Builder, you can't delete records. If you want to do that, you have to use Flow with Process Builder.
3. To set **Text** data field to blank, you can use `{!$GlobalConstant.EmptyString}`.
4. The Process owner will receive an e-mail from Salesforce. If the Process failed at runtime or if any fault occurs, the error or warning messages might refer to a Flow instead of a Process.

5. The process follows all the governor limits that apply to Apex.

6. You can have a maximum of 50 active rules and processes on any object. Rules include Workflow Rules, Escalation Rules, Assignment Rules, and Auto-assignment Rules.

7. Process actions are executed in the same order in which they appear in the Process Builder.

8. You can't delete an active process; first, you have to deactivate it. Once you have deactivated a Process, you can immediately delete it.

9. If a custom field is referenced in a Process/Flow, you can't delete that field.

10. Before you change a custom field's type or name, make sure that it isn't referenced in a process that would be invalidated by the change.

11. An immediate action on a record update obeys validation rules.

12. A scheduled action on a record update skips validation rules.

13. If any of the actions fail, the entire transaction fails and an error message is displayed.

14. File type custom fields aren't supported in Process Builder.

15. External objects and deprecated custom objects aren't supported in the Process Builder.

16. If a single action group includes multiple **Update Records** actions that apply different values to the same field, then the last action's value is used.

17. The total number of process criteria nodes that are evaluated and actions that are executed at runtime is 2,000.

# Exercises

1. Create a one-step Approval Process for the account to get an approval from the CEO once an account becomes active. Use Process Builder to automatically submit an account for approval once it gets activated.

2. Automatically update the lead rating to **Warm** whenever the lead status gets updated to **Working—Contacted**.

3. Develop an application using Flow and Process Builder. It will automatically remove all the followers except the opportunity owner from an Opportunity once its stage is updated to Closed-Won or Closed-Lost.

4. Automatically create a child case whenever a case is created with the **High** priority. Use the following information to create the child case:
    - **Status**: New
    - **Priority**: Medium
    - **Case Origin**: Phone
    - Associate it with a high priority case

5. Create a one-step Approval Process for the account to get an approval from the CEO once an account becomes active. Use Process Builder to automatically submit an account for approval once it gets activated.

6. Develop an application using Flow and Process Builder that will automatically add a new user who has the role of Sales Executive to the `Sales Executive` Chatter group.

> If the Sales Executive Chatter group does not exist in your Salesforce organization, create a new one.

7. Once the account gets created, auto-post the account details to a Chatter group (`Sales Executive`).

8. Once the Opportunity is successfully closed, auto-post a linkpost on a Chatter group (`Sales Executive`). The output should look similar to what is shown in the following screenshot:

9. Auto-create a child case whenever the case's **Type** field changes to `Mechanical` and assign it to the `Mechanical Engineers` queue.

> If the Mechanical Engineers queue does not exist in your Salesforce organization, create a new one.

10. Whenever a case gets created, automatically add the user Helina Jolly to the case team members.

> Create a new user named Helina Jolly in your organization.

11. First, set OWD for Lead to Private. Now develop an application using Flow and Process Builder that will automatically share new lead records with user Helina Jolly and grant her read/write access.

12. Once the account becomes inactive, send an e-mail notification to all Opportunity owners related to that account. Also, update any related open Opportunities status to Closed Lost.

> Use the Active field to decide the account status.

13. Once an Opportunity is successfully closed, auto-create a new Opportunity by copying the data from closed Opportunity. Set the Opportunity closed date as the new Opportunity created date plus 100 days.

> Copy only the field that is required to create an Opportunity.

14. Create a process that will automatically add new users who have the profile APAC Support Agent to a Queue (High Priority Accounts).

> If the High Priority Accounts **queue and the** APAC Support Agent profile do not exist in your Salesforce organization, create new ones.

# Summary

In this chapter, we went through various concepts and actions available in Process Builder. We looked at a way to auto-create and update a record. We also covered various ways to call a Flow from Process Builder. Then, we moved on to discussing ways to auto-submit a record to the Approval Process and send e-mails to users. We also discussed a way to call Apex from Process Builder. Finally, we discussed the key points of Process Builder. In the next chapter, we will discuss concepts related to how you can create efficient and performance-optimized processes. We will also cover concepts such as executing multiple criteria of a process.

# 6
# Building Efficient and Performance Optimized Processes

In the previous chapter, we discussed an overview of Process Builder. We learned the difference between automation tools such as Flow, Process Builder, and Workflow Rule. We also discussed various actions available in Process Builder. In this chapter, we will discuss some advanced concepts of Process Builder, such as how to apply a filter while updating related records and how to execute multiple groups of actions in Process Builder. We will also discuss how you can use one process to implement multiple business requirements.

The following topics will be covered in this chapter:

- Using Workbench to get complete details for a process
- Defining additional conditions when updating records
- Executing multiple criteria of a process
- Scheduling multiple groups of actions
- Creating reusable processes using an invocable process

# An overview of process management

Now that you have an understanding of Process Builder, you know that it is a tool that allows you to streamline business processes without writing code. You can also view your process visually. The process management page allows you to see all the processes created in the current Salesforce organization. The process management page has the following features:

- Creating a new process
- Editing a process
- Deleting an inactive process or its version
- Checking the status of processes created in the current organization
- Sorting your process by name, description, object, last modified date, or status

Your process management page should look like what is shown in the following screenshot:

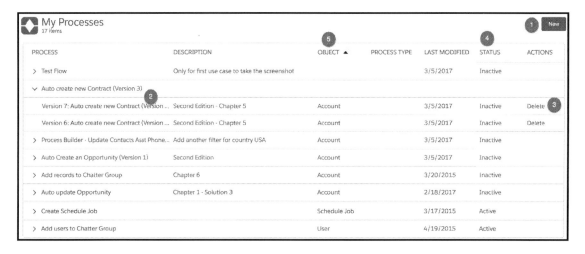

The process management page displays fields such as **PROCESS**, **DESCRIPTION**, **OBJECT**, **PROCESS TYPE**, **LAST MODIFIED**, **STATUS**, and **ACTIONS**. As of the **Spring'17** release, Process Builder does not display **Created By, Created Date**, or **Last Modified By** on the process management page.

Let's look at a business scenario. Alice Atwood is working as a system administrator at Universal Containers. In Chapter 5, *Developing Applications with Process Builder*, she developed a process, that is, Update Contacts Asst Phone, to fulfill the requirement that once an account gets activated, the related contact **Asst. Phone** field must be synced with the account's **Phone**.

She received a few messages from business users saying that the process stops when she tries to sync the contact **Asst. Phone** field with the account **Phone** field. While looking at the process version, she sees that someone has deactivated the process. Now she wants to identify who deactivated the process.

Here are the ways that you can track the user who activated, deactivated, created, or deleted a Flow or Process:

- View the Setup Audit Trail
- Metadata component (Flow and FlowDefinition)

# Using Audit Trail to track setup changes in a Process or a Flow

Setup Audit Trail tracks the recent configuration changes that you and other system administrators have made to your Salesforce organization. Audit history is especially useful in organizations with multiple system administrators. You can use Audit Trail to track the user who activated, deactivated, created, or deleted a Flow or Process.

**View Setup Audit Trail**

| Date | User | Action | Section | Delegate User ⑦ |
|------|------|--------|---------|----------------|
| 3/6/2017 6:32:36 PM PST | sarikahojonojno@gmail.com | Deleted Flow Trigger RakeshGupta_Update_Contacts_Asst_Phone301B0000000CfPs for Object: Account | Workflow Rule | |
| 3/6/2017 6:32:36 PM PST | sarikahojonojno@gmail.com | Deleted workflow rule RakeshGupta_Update_Contacts_Asst_Phone301B0000000CfPs for Object: Account | Workflow Rule | |
| 3/6/2017 6:32:36 PM PST | sarikahojonojno@gmail.com | Deactivated workflow rule RakeshGupta_Update_Contacts_Asst_Phone301B0000000CfPs for Object: Account | Workflow Rule | |
| 3/6/2017 6:32:36 PM PST | sarikahojonojno@gmail.com | Deactivated flow version #4 "Process Builder - Update Contacts Asst Phone (Version 2)" for flow with Unique Name "Update_Contacts_Asst_Phone" | Flows | |
| 3/6/2017 6:01:54 PM PST | alice.atwood@book.com | Created Flow Trigger RakeshGupta_Update_Contacts_Asst_Phone301B0000000CfPs for Object: Account | Workflow Rule | |
| 3/6/2017 6:01:54 PM PST | alice.atwood@book.com | Created workflow rule RakeshGupta_Update_Contacts_Asst_Phone301B0000000CfPs for Object: Account | Workflow Rule | |
| 3/6/2017 6:01:54 PM PST | alice.atwood@book.com | Activated flow version #4 "Process Builder - Update Contacts Asst Phone (Version 2)" for flow with Unique Name "Update_Contacts_Asst_Phone" | Flows | |

In Chapter 5, *Developing Applications with Process Builder*, we discussed that Process Builder is nothing but a combination of **Flow** (type: **Workflow**) and **Flow Trigger** (deprecated). Process Builder always generates a Flow and Flow Trigger for all processes. This happens behind the scenes, and the user doesn't need to interact with these shadow Flows. The Audit trail only stores the data for the past 180 days. So it is helpful to track recent setup changes in Flows or Processes.

 Go to https://help.salesforce.com/articleView?id=admin_monitors etup.htm&language=en_US to learn more about Audit Trail.

# Hands on 1 - using Workbench to get all the details of a process

If you want to know details about the version of a process or a process that someone created a few months or a year back, then the metadata component is the right option for you.

Let's look at a business scenario. Alice Atwood is working as a system administrator at Universal Containers. In Chapter 5, *Developing Applications with Process Builder*, she developed a process, **Update Contacts Asst Phone.** Now she wants to identify the user who created version 1 of this process.

Before going ahead, let's understand the metadata components that stores Flow and its versions in Salesforce, which are as follows:

- **Flow**: This represents the metadata that is associated with a Flow
- **FlowDefinition**: This represents the Flow definition's description and active Flow version number

The following screenshot displays Flow and Flow Definition:

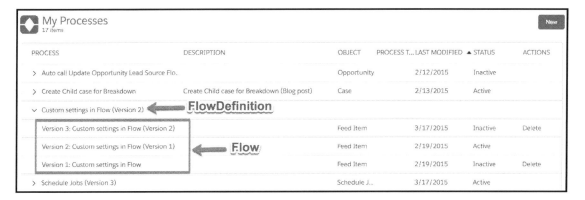

To view the metadata components, you can use either the Force.com IDE, the Force.com Migration Tool, or any third-party tool that supports the viewing of the metadata components of your Salesforce organization. **Workbench** is a powerful, web-based tool that's designed for administrators and developers to interact with their Salesforce organizations via the Force.com APIs. It also offers support for the Bulk API, Rest API, Streaming API, Metadata API, and Apex APIs, which let users describe things, query the objects, and manipulate the data in a Salesforce organization directly in their web browser.

Follow these instructions to achieve the preceding requirement using Workbench:

1. Log in to Workbench by going to `https://workbench.developerforce.com/log in.php`.

2. For **Environment**, select **Production** (if you are using developer or live org); otherwise, select **Sandbox** (if you are using sandbox). For API Version, select **37.0**, or the highest number. Make sure that you have selected the **I agree to the terms of service** checkbox.

3. Once you're done, click on the **Login with Salesforce** button, as shown in the following screenshot:

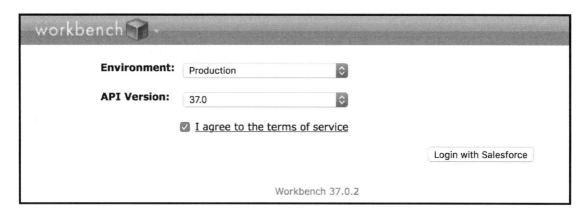

4. After successful login, under the **Jump to** dropdown, select **Metadata Types & Components**, and then click on the **Select** button, as shown in the following screenshot:

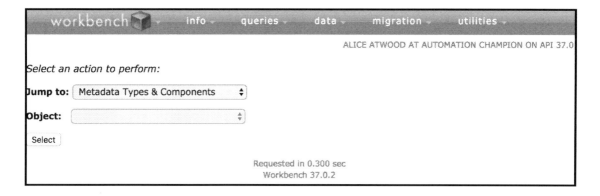

5. The next step is to choose the **Metadata Types & Components.** In this case, select **Flow**, and then click on `Components` to see versions of all Flows and Processes, as shown in the following screenshot:

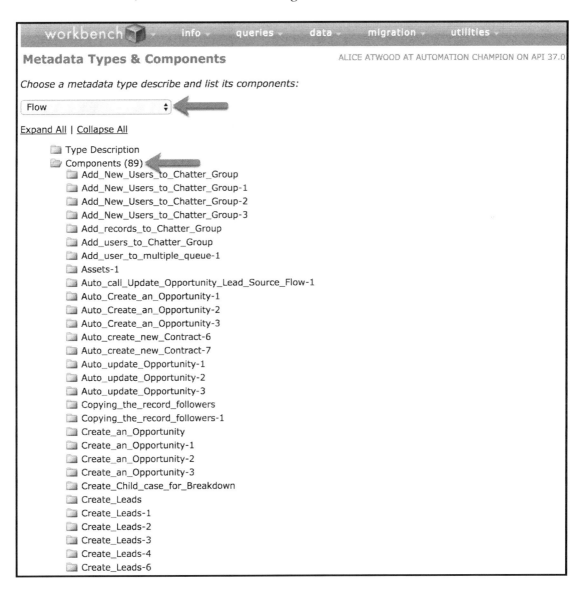

6. Now identify the `Update_Contacts_Asset_Phone-1` Flow (behind the scene process is nothing but a combination of Flow and Flow Trigger). It will display **createdByName**, **createdDate**, **lastModifiedByName**, **lastModifiedDate**, **fullName**, **id**, **type**, and so on, as shown in the following screenshot:

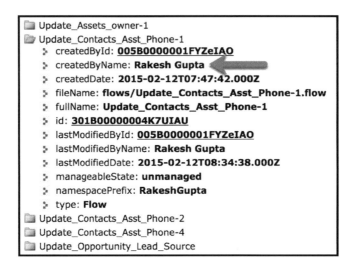

For the current business use case, the answer is that system administrator **Rakesh Gupta** created the first version of the `Update_Contacts_Asst_Phone-1` process on **2015-02-12**.

 Salesforce appends 1, 2, 3, and so on with **API Name** to manage the versions of a Flow or Process. For the preceding business scenario, it is `Update_Contacts_Asset_Phone-1` (**Version 1**) and `Update_Contacts_Asset_Phone-2` (**Version 2**).

# Hands on 2 – using custom labels in Process Builder

Custom labels are custom text values that can be accessed from Apex, Visual Workflow, Process Builder, and so on. The values can be translated into any language that Salesforce supports. You can create up to 5,000 custom labels in an organization, and they can be up to 1,000 characters in length. Custom labels are not only used for translation, but they can also be used to store the username, password, and endpoint URL in the case of invoking API calls for a third-party system.

For example, if you are integrating two systems, Salesforce and SAP, to sync the account information, to start the API calls, you have to pass SAP integration user credentials and an endpoint URL. You have three options to store these values:

1. Hardcoding credentials and endpoint URL in an Apex class.
2. Using multiple custom labels to save the username, password, and endpoint URL.
3. Custom metadata type to store this information.

The benefits of using custom labels compared to hardcoding the username and password in Apex are that if the password changes in future, then you don't have to update the Apex class; instead, you can update the custom labels. This can easily be done in the production org itself. On the other hand, to update the Apex class, you have to do this in a Sandbox and then migrate the changes into your production org. Using this approach, you can save time and hassle. You can also take the approach of using custom metadata type, which is totally fine, but remember that Salesforce has put a limitation on everything. So, before starting the implementation, you should carefully design your complete process. I would suggest that you use custom labels if you want to save credentials and the endpoint URL as we don't want to save this information in the cache. In `Chapter 7`, *Building Applications without Code*, we will look at an example of how to use custom metadata type with Visual Workflow.

Let's look at a business scenario. Alice Atwood is working as a system administrator at Universal Containers. She has received a requirement from the management to auto-add an activated **Campaign** to the **Sales Executive** Chatter group.

# Creating a custom label

We will now create a custom label to store the **Sales Executive** Chatter group ID. Perform the following steps to create a custom label to store the Chatter group ID:

1. First of all, navigate to the Chatter group Sales Executive and copy the group Id from the URL. It will look like this: `0F9B0000000CyPe`
2. Navigate to **Setup (Gear Icon)** | **Setup** | **PLATFORM TOOLS** | **User Interface** | **Custom Labels** and click on the **New Custom Label** button; it will redirect you to a new window, where you have to enter following details:

   - **Short Description**: Enter an easily identifiable term to recognize this custom label. In this case, use **Sales Executive Id**.

- **Name**: This will be autopopulated based on the **Short Description**.
- **Categories**: Enter the text to categorize the label. You can use this field in the filter criteria when creating custom label list views.
- **Value**: Enter text up to 1,000 characters. In this case, enter the Sales Executive Chatter Group ID, 0F9B0000000CyPe.

It will look like what is shown in the following screenshot:

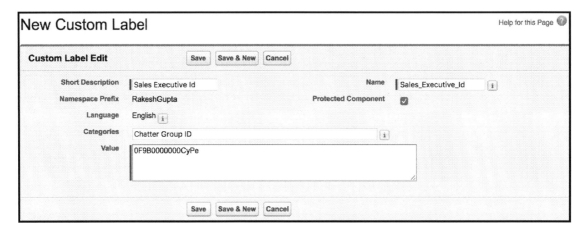

3. Once you are done, click on the **Save** button.

# Hands on 3 – using a Quick action to add a record to a Chatter group

Quick actions can be object-specific or global actions. To use a quick action from Process Builder, the action must exist in your organization. If your organization is using quick actions that allow your users to create and update records easily, you can also use these actions in Process Builder. When you use these quick actions in Process Builder, you are only allowed to set values for fields that are part of the action's layout. Now we will create a process to fulfill the preceding business scenario and use our custom label:

1. In Lightning Experience, navigate to **Setup (Gear Icon)** | **Setup** | **PLATFORM TOOLS** | **Feature Settings** | **Chatter** | **Chatter Settings** and make sure that the **Allow Records in Groups** checkbox is selected.

2. To create a process, navigate to **Setup (Gear Icon)** | **Setup** | **PLATFORM TOOLS** | **Process Automation** | **Process Builder**, click on the **New** button, and enter the following details:

- **Name**: Enter the name of the process. Enter `Add campaign to Sales Executive group` in **Name**.
- **API Name**: This will be autopopulated based on the name.
- **Description**: Write some meaningful text so that other developers or administrators can easily understand why this process was created.
- **This process starts when**: Configure the process to start when a record is created or edited. In this case, select **A record changes**.

3. Once you are done, click on the **Save** button.

4. After **Define Process Properties**, the next task is to select the object on which you want to create a process and define the **evaluation criteria**. For this, click on the **Add Object** node. This will open an additional window on the right-hand side of the process canvas screen, where you have to enter the following details:

- **Object**: Start typing and then select the **Campaign** object.
- **Start the process**: For **Start the process**, select **when a record is created or edited**. This means that the process will fire whenever a record gets created or edited.
- **Recursion - Allow process to evaluate a record multiple times in a single transaction?**: Select this checkbox only when you want process to evaluate the same record up to five times in a single transaction. In this case, leave this box unchecked.

The additional window will look like what is shown in the following screenshot:

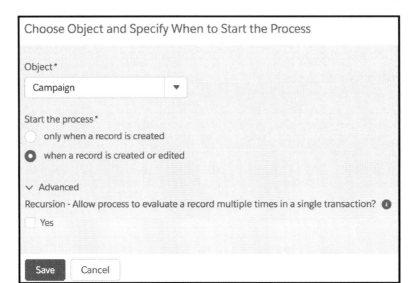

5. Once you are done, click on the **Save** button.
6. After defining the **evaluation criteria**, the next step is to add the **process criteria**. Once the process criteria are true, only then will the process execute the associated actions. To define the process criteria, click on the **Add Criteria** node. It will open an additional window on the right-hand side of the process canvas screen, where you have to enter the following details:

- **Criteria Name**: Enter a name for the criteria node. Enter `Only for active campaigns` as the criteria name.
- **Criteria for Executing Actions**: Select the type of criteria you want to define. You can select either **Formula evaluates to true** or **Conditions are met** (a filter to define the process criteria) or **No criteria-just execute the actions!**. In this case, select **Conditions are met.**
- **Set Conditions**: This field lets you specify which combination of the filter conditions must be true for the process to execute the associated actions. Set **[Campaign].IsActive** to **True.**
- **Conditions**: In the **Conditions** section, select **All of the conditions are met (AND)**. This field lets you specify which combination of the filter conditions must be true for the process to execute the associated actions.
- Under **Advanced**, select **Yes** to execute the actions only when specified changes are made.

It will look like what is shown in the following screenshot:

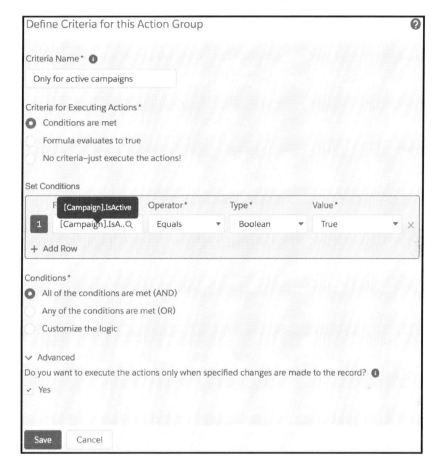

7. Once you are done, click on the **Save** button.
8. Once you are done with the **process criteria** node, the next step is to add an immediate action to add a campaign to the Sales Executive Chatter group. For this, we will use the **Quick Actions** action available in Process Builder. Click on the **Add Action** available under **IMMEDIATE ACTIONS**; it will open an additional window on the right-hand side of the process canvas screen, where you have to enter the following details:

- **Action Type**: Select the type of action; in this case, select **Quick Actions**.
- **Action Name**: Enter a name for this action. Enter `Add record to Chatter group` as the action name.

- **Filter Search By**: It allows you to specify the kind of action you want to execute. In this case, select **Type** and then for **Type**; select **Create a Record**; and for **Action**, select **NewGroupRecord.**
- **Set Quick Action Field Values**: Use this to set values for the action's fields. For the current use case, to map the `Related Record ID` field, select the **formula**, and then select **System Variable**. It will open a popup, from where you can select the **Custom Label** that you have created.

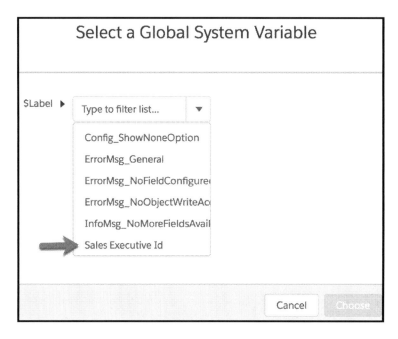

Likewise, map the `Record ID` field to **[Campaign].Id**.

It will look like what is shown in the following screenshot:

9. Once you are done, click on the **Save** button.

10. The final step is to activate it. To activate a process, click on the **Activate** button on the button bar. Finally, the process will appear, as shown in this screenshot:

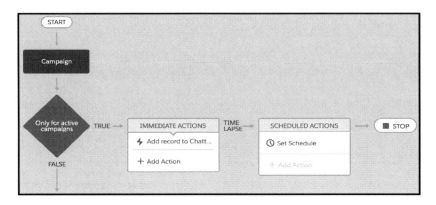

Now, if a campaign gets created or updated with the Active status, the record will be added to the **Sales Executive** Chatter group by this process, as shown in the following screenshot:

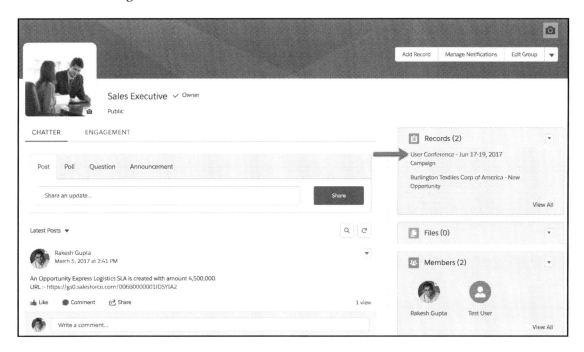

Likewise, you can create another process to add new users to a Chatter group.

# Hands on 4 – calling an Apex class from Process Builder

Process Builder allows you to call an Apex class that includes methods annotated with @InvocableMethod. By calling an Apex class from Process Builder, you can add customized functionality such as, auto-converting leads, deleting records, or running lead assignment rules from Process Builder. You can also pass the required value into Apex class variables.

When no other process actions can get your job done, by calling an Apex method, you add customized functionality to your users. You can only call an Apex class from Process Builder or Visual Workflow that have the @InvocableMethod annotation. This means that it is possible to extend the Process Builder functionality by writing an Apex class that executes your business logic and then invoking the Apex from your process. If the class contains one or more invocable variables, then you have to manually enter values or reference field values from a related record.

Let's look at a business scenario. Alice Atwood is working as a system administrator at Universal Containers. She has received a requirement from the management to auto-delete open cases if the **out of business** checkbox is checked on the account record.

The following is the approach that we are going to use in order to solve the preceding business requirement:

1. First of all, create a custom **out of business** checkbox field on the **account** object and make sure that you set the field-level security for the respective profiles.
2. The next step is to write an Apex class that will delete open cases for accounts whose IDs we are going to pass through the process. To create an Apex class, navigate to **Setup (Gear Icon)** | **Setup** | **PLATFORM TOOLS** | **Custom Code** | **Apex Classes** and then click on the **New** button. The following is the sample code where AccountIds is the record ID of accounts where out of business is updated as **true**:

```
public class DeleteOpenCases
{
    @InvocableMethod
    public static void CaseDelete(List<Id> AccountIds)
    {
        List<Case> Cases =[select id from case
                           where Account.id in :AccountIds
                           and Status != 'Closed'];
        delete Cases;
```

```
      }
    }
```

3. The next step is to create a process to call the Apex class you have just created only when the **out of business** checkbox is checked on the account record. To create a process, navigate to **Setup (Gear Icon)** | **Setup** | **PLATFORM TOOLS** | **Process Automation** | **Process Builder**, click on the **New** button, and enter the following details:

   - **Name**: Enter the name of the process. Enter `Delete open cases - Out of business accounts` in **Name**.
   - **API Name**: This will be autopopulated based on the name.
   - **Description**: Write some meaningful text so that other developers or administrators can easily understand why this process has been created.
   - **This process starts when**: Configure the process to start when a record is created or edited. In this case, select **A record changes.**

4. Once you are done, click on the **Save** button.
5. After **Define Process Properties**, the next task is to select the object on which you want to create a process and define the **Evaluation Criteria**. For this, click on the **Add Object** node. It will open an additional window on the right-hand side of the process canvas screen, where you have to enter the following details:

   - **Object**: Start typing and then select the **Account** object.
   - **Start the process**: For **Start the process**, select **when a record is created or edited**. This means that process will fire whenever a record gets created or edited.
   - **Recursion - Allow process to evaluate a record multiple times in a single transaction?**: Select this checkbox only when you want the process to evaluate the same record up to five times in a single transaction. In this case, leave this box unchecked.

It will look like what is shown in the following screenshot:

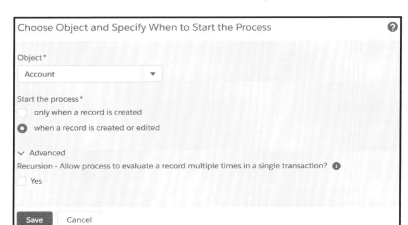

6. Once you are done, click on the **Save** button.

7. After defining the **Evaluation Criteria**, the next step is to add the **Process Criteria**. Once the process criteria are true, only then will the Process execute the associated actions. To define the process criteria, click on the **Add Criteria** node. It will open an additional window on the right-hand side of the process canvas screen, where you have to enter the following details:

- **Criteria Name**: Enter a name for the criteria node. Enter `Only for out of business accounts` as the criteria name.

- **Criteria for Executing Actions**: Select the type of criteria you want to define. You can select either **Formula evaluates to true** or **Conditions are met** (a filter to define the process criteria) or **No criteria-just execute the actions!**. In this case, select **Conditions are met.**

- **Set Conditions**: This field lets you specify which combination of the filter conditions must be true for the process to execute the associated actions. In this case, set **[Account].RakeshGupta__out_of_business__c** to **True.**

- **Conditions**: In the conditions section, select **All of the conditions are met (AND)**. This field lets you specify which combination of the filter conditions must be true for the process to execute the associated actions.

- Under **Advanced**, select **Yes** to execute the actions only when specified changes are made.

The additional window will look like what is shown in the following screenshot:

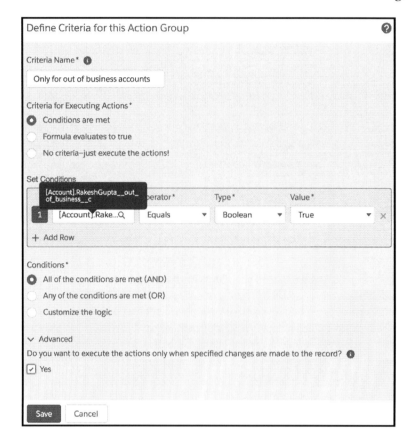

8. Once you are done, click on the **Save** button.

9. Once you are done with the process criteria node, the next step is to add an immediate action to delete open cases when the account is out of business. For this, we will use the **Apex** action available in Process Builder. Click on the **Add Action** available under **IMMEDIATE ACTIONS**; it will open an additional window on the right-hand side of the process canvas screen, where you have to enter the following details:

- **Action Type**: Select the type of action; in this case, select **Apex**.
- **Action Name**: Enter a name for this action. Enter `Delete open cases` as the action name.

- **Apex Class**: Select the Apex class that you want to execute; in this case, select **RakeshGupta__DeleteOpenCases**.
- **Set Apex Variables**: Use this to set values for sObject variables and sObject list values. For the current use case, map the `AccountIds` field to **[Account].Id**.

The window will look like what is shown in the following screenshot:

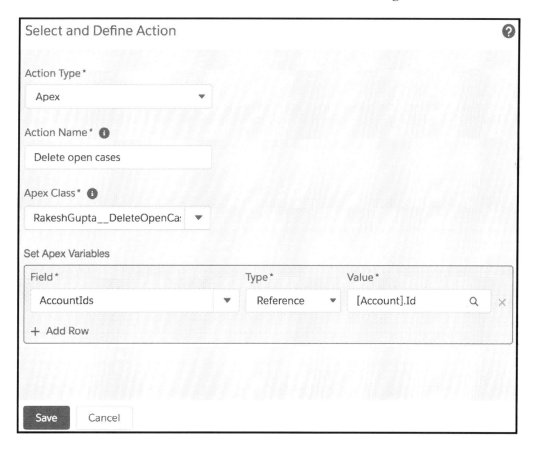

To assign values to multiple variables, click on the **Add Row** link.

10. Once you are done, click on the **Save** button.

11. The final step is to activate it. To activate a process, click on the **Activate** button on the button bar. Finally, the process will appear as shown in this screenshot:

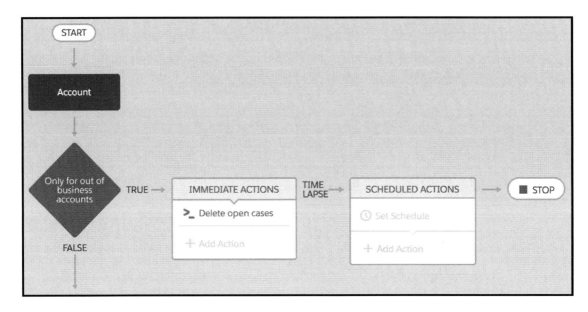

12. Go ahead and identify an account where there are a few open cases, as shown in the following screenshot:

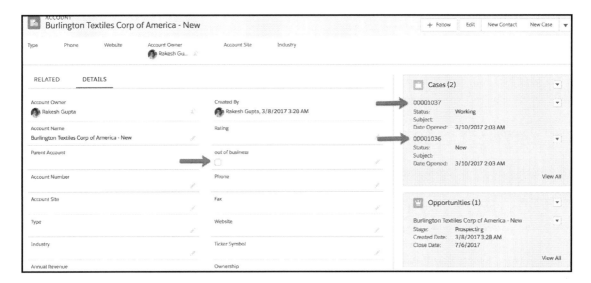

13. Now update the **out of business** checkbox to True and then reload the page. It will look like the following screenshot:

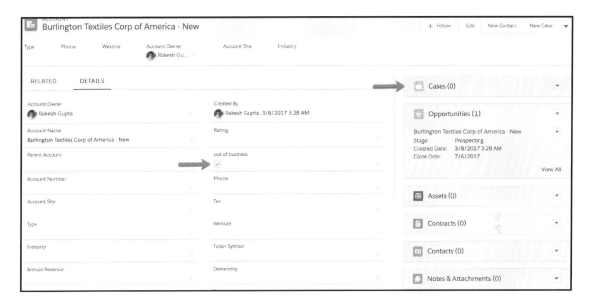

Before testing the process, make sure that you have activated the process.

# Hands on 5 – bypass processes using Custom Permission

Until now, we have created many processes using Process Builder. It is a quite easy and fun experience to create processes. These processes will execute as soon as they meet the criteria. There are some situations where a business may want to bypass these processes.

Let's take one example. Helina Jolly is working as a system administrator at Universal Containers. She developed the **Post Opportunity Information to Chatter Group** process in `Chapter 5`, *Developing Applications with Process Builder*. She has now received a requirement to bypass this process for the system administrator.

It is quite easy to bypass it for the system administrator by adding an additional condition in your process, as shown in the following screenshot:

But if the business came back after 2 months and asked her to bypass it from one more profile and one user (belonging to a different profile), then the situation is going to be worse, because the question is how many times you are going to modify a process to bypass it for different profiles or users? After a few weeks, you may get another requirement to bypass the process for a few more users who belong to different profiles; then, this is going to be a nightmare for you. This is the right place to learn Process Builder best practices.

# Creating a custom permission

Let's look at a business scenario. Helina Jolly is working as a system administrator at Universal Containers. She has received a requirement from the management to auto-update related open opportunities status to Closed Lost if the **out of business** checkbox is checked on the account record. They also want to make sure that this process must not work for the System Administrator and Supply Chain User profiles.

Using custom permissions, you can grant users access to custom apps. In Salesforce, you can use custom permissions to check which users can access a certain functionality. Custom permissions let you define access checks that can be assigned to users via permission sets or profiles, similar to how you assign user permissions and other access settings. We will now create a custom permission to bypass processes. Perform the following steps to create a custom permission:

1. Navigate to **Setup (Gear Icon)** | **Setup** | **PLATFORM TOOLS** | **Custom Code** | **Custom Permission** and click on the **New** button; it will redirect you to a new window, where you have to enter following details:

- **Label**: Enter an easily identifiable term to recognize this custom permission. In this case, use `By Pass Process Builder`.
- **Name**: This will be autopopulated based on the **Label**.
- **Description**: Write some meaningful text so that other developers or administrators can easily understand why this custom permission has been created.

The **Custom Permission** page will look like what is shown in the following screenshot:

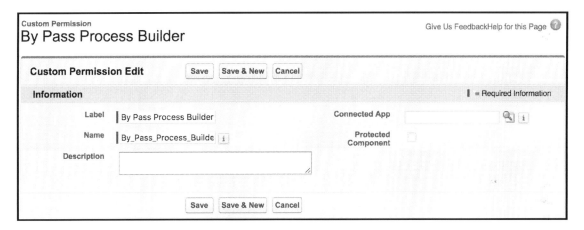

2. Once you are done, click on the **Save** button.
3. To assign a custom permission to a profile (you can also assign it to Permission Set), navigate to **Setup (Gear Icon)** | **Setup** | **Users** | **Profiles** and open the **Supply Chain User** profile (create one profile using the Salesforce license type with the name **Supply Chain User** if you haven't created it yet):
4. Navigate to **Apps** | **Custom Permission**.
5. Open the custom permission and click on the **Edit** button.

6. Then, assign the **By Pass Process Builder** custom permission to the profile, as shown in the following screenshot:

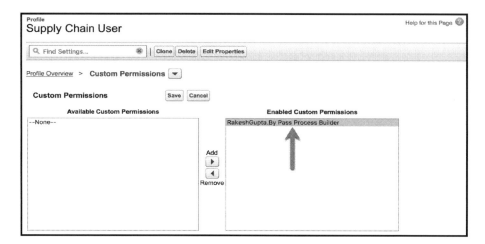

7. Once you are done, click on the **Save** button.
8. Repeat *step 3* to assign the custom permission to the system administrator profile.

You can learn more about custom permissions
at https://help.salesforce.com/HTViewHelpDoc?id=changesets.htm&language=en_US.

# Hands on 6 - defining additional conditions when updating records

When you update records using Process Builder, you can filter the records you are updating using conditions. To add filter conditions to an update records action, there are two steps, as follows:

1. Select the **updated records meet all conditions** option.
2. Set the conditions that you want to use to filter **updated records**.

Now we will create a process to fulfill the preceding business scenario and use custom permission to bypass the process for the **System Administrator** and **Supply Chain User** profiles:

1. To create a process, navigate to **Setup (Gear Icon)** | **Setup** | **PLATFORM TOOLS** | **Process Automation** | **Process Builder,** and click on the **New** button and enter the following details:

- **Name**: Enter the name of the process. Enter `Update open opps - out of business accounts` in **Name**.
- **API Name**: This will be autopopulated based on the name.
- **Description**: Write some meaningful text so that other developers or administrators can easily understand why this process was created.
- **This process starts when**: Configure the process to start when a record is created or edited. In this case, select **A record changes**.

2. Once you are done, click on the **Save** button; it will redirect you to the process canvas, which allows you to create the process.

3. After **Define Process Properties**, the next task is to select the object on which you want to create a process and define the **Evaluation Criteria**. For this, click on the **Add Object** node. It will open an additional window on the right-hand side of the process canvas screen, where you have to enter the following details:

- **Object**: Start typing and then select the **Account** object.
- **Start the process**: For **Start the process**, select **when a record is created or edited**. This means that the process will fire whenever a record gets created or edited.
- **Recursion - Allow process to evaluate a record multiple times in a single transaction?**: Select this checkbox only when you want process to evaluate the same record up to five times in a single transaction. In this case, leave this box unchecked.

The evaluation criteria page will look like what is shown in the following screenshot:

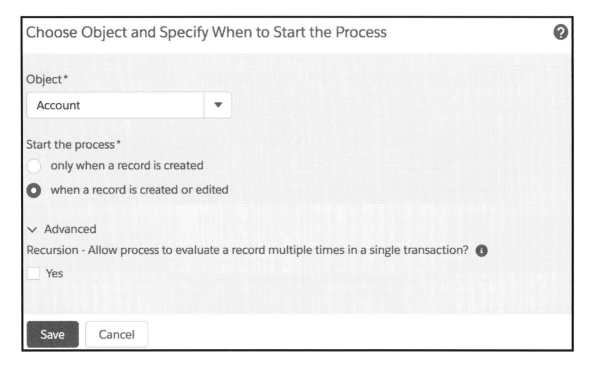

4. Once you are done, click on the **Save** button.
5. After defining the Evaluation Criteria, the next step is to add the **Process Criteria**. Once the process criteria are true, only then will the process execute the associated actions. To define the **Process Criteria**, click on the **Add Criteria** node. It will open an additional window on the right-hand side of the process canvas screen, where you have to enter the following details:

- **Criteria Name**: Enter a name for the criteria node. Enter `Only for out of business accounts` as the criteria name.
- **Criteria for Executing Actions**: Select the type of criteria you want to define. You can select either **Formula evaluates to true** or **Conditions are met** (a filter to define the process criteria) or **No criteria-just execute the actions!**. In this case, select **Formula evaluates to true.**

- **Build Formula**: Use this to define the formula using functions and fields. Select **System Variable**. It will open a popup from where you can select the custom permission that you have created:

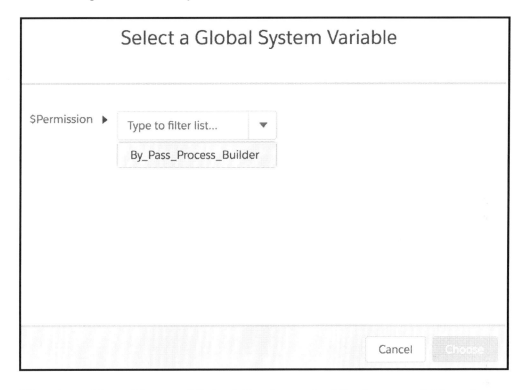

Select a Global System Variable

$Permission ▶

Type to filter list... ▼

By_Pass_Process_Builder

Cancel    Choose

Likewise, add one **[Account].RakeshGupta__out_of_business__c** field, as shown in the preceding screenshot.

- Under **Advanced**, select **Yes** to execute the actions only when specified changes are made.

The process criteria will look like what is shown in the following screenshot:

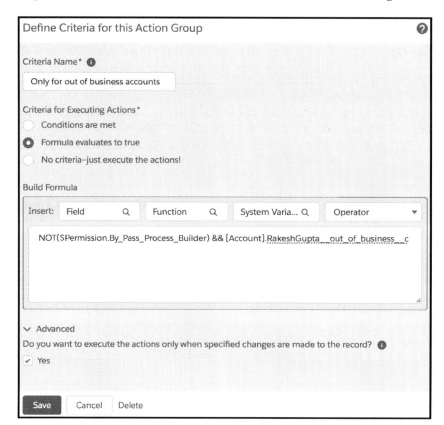

6. Once you are done, click on the **Save** button.
7. Once you are done with the **Process Criteria** node, the next step is to add an **Immediate Action** to update open opportunities to Closed Lost. For this, we will use the **Update Records** action available in Process Builder. Click on **Add Action** under **IMMEDIATE ACTIONS**; it will open an additional window on the right-hand side of the process canvas screen, where you have to enter the following details:

- **Action Type**: Select the type of action; in this case, select **Update Records**.
- **Action Name**: Enter a name for this action. Enter Update open Opportunities as the action name.

- **Record Type**: Select the record or records that you need to update. Click on the **Record Type.** It will open a window where you will get two options: **Select the Account record that started your process** and **Select a record related to the Account.** These are radio buttons and only one can be selected to update child record. In this case, choose to **Select a record related to the Account**. Then, in the **Type to filter list**, look for the **Opportunities** child object.
- **Criteria for Updating Records**: Optionally, you can specify conditions to filter the records you are updating. Select **Updated records meet all conditions** to filter out the related opportunities records. Then, set the **Stage** field value from **Does not equal** to **Closed Won**.
- **Set new field values for the records you update**: Select the field whose value you want to set. In this case, set the **Stage** field to **Closed Lost**.

It will look like what is shown in the following screenshot:

8. Once you are done, click on the **Save** button.

9. The final step is to activate it. To activate a process, click on the **Activate** button on the button bar. Finally, the process will appear as shown in this screenshot:

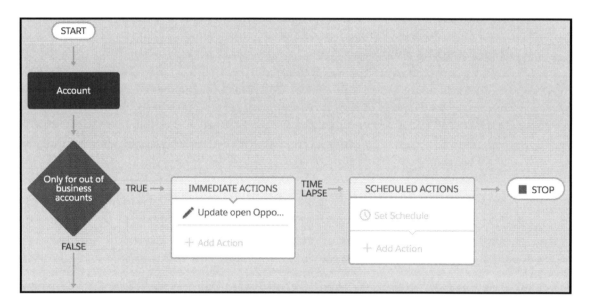

Now onwards, if an account gets **out of business,** then the process will update the related open opportunities stage to Closed Lost. This process will only work when an account is updated by users whose profile does not equal the system administrator and supply chain user (because we have assigned a custom permission to these profiles). If you want to bypass a process for a single user, then consider using a permission set instead of using the profile.

# Hands on 7 - scheduling multiple groups of actions

With multiple schedules, you can easily optimize sales or support processes, automate follow-up on outstanding cases and reminder notifications for a task, and incorporate all your business requirements within a single process. For example, when case **origin** is **Phone** and **priority** is **high**, then you can execute multiple groups of scheduled actions, such as the following:

- Sending a reminder e-mail after 1 day to the case owner if a case is not closed
- Sending a reminder e-mail to the case owner and account owner after 2 days if a case is still open
- Sending a satisfaction survey e-mail to case contacts 2 days after the case closure

Let's look at a business scenario. Alice Atwood is working as a system administrator at Universal Containers. She has received a requirement to send out e-mail reminders to the task assignee 1 day and 2 days before the task's due date if the task has not yet been completed.

Follow these instructions to achieve this using Process Builder:

1. Process Builder doesn't allow you to create a new e-mail alert, but it allows you to use an existing e-mail alert that you have created in the past for the same object on which you created a process. First of all, create an `Task reminder notification` e-mail template by navigating to **Setup (Gear Icon)** | **Setup** | **ADMINISTRATION** | **Email** | **Email Templates**, as shown in the following screenshot:

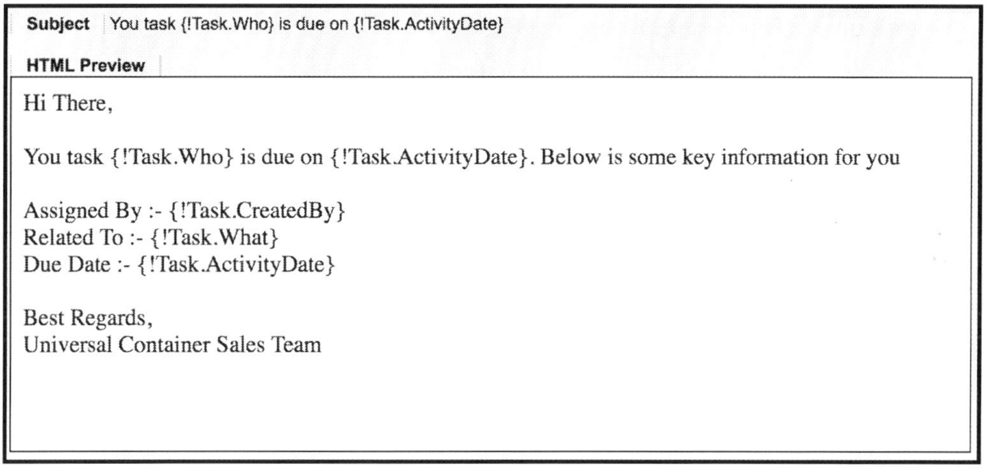

---

**Subject** | You task {!Task.Who} is due on {!Task.ActivityDate}

**HTML Preview**

Hi There,

You task {!Task.Who} is due on {!Task.ActivityDate}. Below is some key information for you

Assigned By :- {!Task.CreatedBy}
Related To :- {!Task.What}
Due Date :- {!Task.ActivityDate}

Best Regards,
Universal Container Sales Team

---

2. The second step is to create an e-mail alert on the **Opportunity** object by navigating to **Setup (Gear Icon)** | **Setup** | **PLATFORM TOOLS** | **Process Automation** | **Process Builder** | **Workflow Actions** | **Email Alerts.** Click on the **New Email Alert** button and save it with the name `Email to Task assignee`. It should look like what is shown the following screenshot:

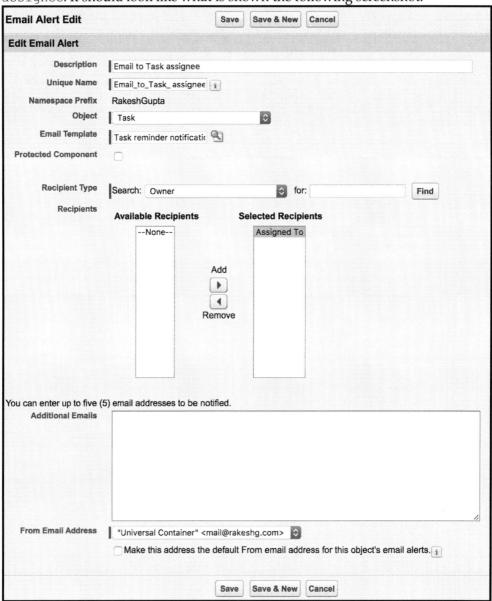

3. To create a process, navigate to **Setup (Gear Icon) | Setup | PLATFORM TOOLS | Process Automation | Process Builder**, click on the **New** button, and enter the following details:
   - **Name**: Enter the name of the process. Enter `Task reminders` in **Name**.
   - **API Name**: This will be autopopulated based on the name.
   - **Description**: Write some meaningful text so that other developers or administrators can easily understand why this process has been created.
   - **This process starts when**: Configure the process to start when a record is created or edited. In this case, select **A record changes.**

4. Once you are done, click on the **Save** button; it will redirect you to the process canvas that allows you to create the process.

5. After **Define Process Properties**, the next task is to select the object on which you want to create a process and define the **Evaluation Criteria**. For this, click on the **Add Object** node. It will open an additional window on the right-hand side of the process canvas screen, where you have to enter the following details:
   - **Object**: Start typing and then select the **Task** object.
   - **Start the process**: For **Start the process**, select **when a record is created or edited**. This means that Process will fire whenever a record gets created or edited.
   - **Recursion - Allow process to evaluate a record multiple times in a single transaction?**: Select this checkbox only when you want the process to evaluate the same record up to five times in a single transaction. In this case, leave this box unchecked.

6. Once you are done, click on the **Save** button.

7. After defining the **Evaluation Criteria**, the next step is to add the **Process Criteria**. Once the process criteria are true, only then will the process execute the associated actions. To define the process criteria, click on the **Add Criteria** node. It will open an additional window on the right-hand side of the process canvas screen, where you have to enter the following details:
   - **Criteria Name**: Enter a name for the criteria node. Enter `Only for open tasks` as the criteria name.
   - **Criteria for Executing Actions**: Select the type of criteria you want to define. You can select either **Formula evaluates to true** or **Conditions are met** (a filter to define the process criteria) or **No criteria-just execute the actions!**. In this case, select **Conditions are met.**

- **Set Conditions**: This field lets you specify which combination of the filter conditions must be true for the process to execute the associated actions. In this case, select **[Task].Status Does not equal Completed.**
- **Conditions**: In the conditions section, select **All of the conditions are met (AND)**. This field lets you specify which combination of the filter conditions must be true for the process to execute the associated actions.
- Under **Advanced**, select **Yes** to execute the actions only when specified changes are made.

It will look like what is shown in the following screenshot:

In the very first step, we have selected **when a record is created or edited**; if you want to create scheduled actions, then make sure to select the **Do you want to execute the actions only when specified changes are made to the record?** checkbox. This is similar to **Evaluate the rule when a record is created, and any time it's edited to subsequently meet criteria** in Workflow Rule.

8. Once you are done, click on the **Save** button.
9. To add the scheduled time, click on **Set Schedule** available under **SCHEDULED ACTIONS**, and set **Set Time for Action to Execute** to **2 Days Before ActivityDate** (the Task Due Date), as shown in the following screenshot:

10. The next step is to add a scheduled action to send an e-mail. For this, we will use the **Send an Email** action available under the process. To add schedule actions, click on **Add Action** under **SCHEDULED ACTIONS**. This will open an additional window on the right-hand side of the process canvas screen, where you have to enter the following details:

    - **Action Type**: Select the type of action. In this case, select **Email Alerts**.
    - **Action Name**: Enter a name for this action. Enter `Email to Task Assignee- 2 Days` in **Action Name**.
    - **Email Alert**: Select the existing e-mail alert. In this case, select the e-mail alert (**Email_to_Task_assignee**) that you created in *step 2*.

It will appear as shown in this screenshot:

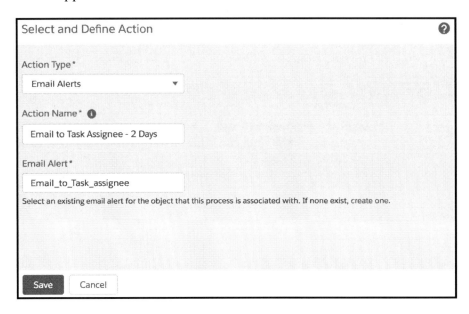

11. Once you are done, click on the **Save** button.

12. Repeat *steps 9*, *10*, and *11* to add one more scheduled action for 1 day before.

13. Once you are done with the process creation, the final step is to activate it. To activate a process, click on the **Activate** button on the button bar. Finally, the process will appear as shown in this screenshot:

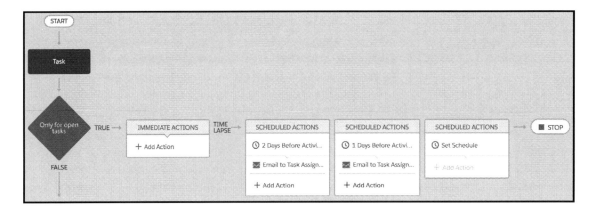

Now onward, this process will send reminder e-mails to the task assignee 1 and 2 days prior to the task completion date, and the e-mail alert will look like what is shown in the following screenshot:

These time-dependent actions will automatically be removed from the queue if the assignee closes a task before the due date.

# Hands on 8 - executing multiple criteria of a process

After the **Summer'16** release, it has become possible to choose what happens after your process executes a specific action group. Should the process stop, or should it continue to evaluate the next criteria in the process? Use this option to better manage your multiple business requirements in one process.

It easy to manage all of your processes for a given object, like a Lead, in one place.

Let's look at a business scenario. Alice Atwood is working as a system administrator at Universal Containers. She has received a requirement from the management; once a task is successfully closed 5 days before its due date, then auto-update the **Eligible for bonus** checkbox to true.

There are two possible solutions for the preceding business requirement:

- Create a new process to solve the business requierment
- Use an existing process and add one more criteria to it

We will use the second approach to solve the preceding business requirement. Follow these instructions to achieve this using Process Builder and execute multiple criteria in one transaction:

1. First of all, create a **Eligible for bonus** custom checkbox field on the **Activity** object and make sure that you set the field level security for the respective profiles.

2. Navigate to **Setup (Gear Icon)** | **Setup** | **PLATFORM TOOLS** | **Process Automation** | **Process Builder**. Open the `Task reminders` process that you created to send an an e-mail to the assignee. Save it as **New Version** because you can't modify the activate Process.

3. The next step is to add one more process criteria to the process. To define the **Process Criteria**, click on the **Add Criteria** node; it will open an additional window on the right-hand side of the process canvas screen, where you have to enter the following details:

- **Criteria Name**: Enter a name for the criteria node. Enter `Update eligible for bonus` as the criteria name.

- **Criteria for Executing Actions**: Select the type of criteria you want to define. You can select either **Formula evaluates to true** or **Conditions are met** (a filter to define the process criteria) or **No criteria-just execute the actions!**. In this case, select **Formula evaluates to true.**

- **Build Formula**: Use this to define the formula using functions and fields. At the end, your formula should look like this: `[Task].ActivityDate - TODAY() >=5 && [Task].IsClosed`.

- Under **Advanced**, select **Yes** to execute the actions only when specified changes are made.

It will look like what is shown in the following screenshot:

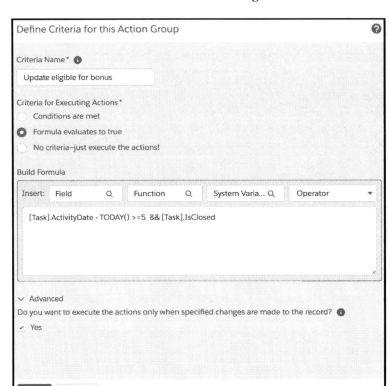

4. Once you are done, click on the Save button.

5. Once you are done with the process criteria node, the next step is to add an immediate action to update task field **eligible for bonus** to true if the task is closed 5 days before the due date. For this, we will use the **Update Records** action that is available in Process. Click on **Add Action** available under **IMMEDIATE ACTIONS**; it will open an additional window on the right-hand side of the process canvas screen, where you have to enter the following details:

- **Action Type**: Select the type of action; in this case, select **Update Records**.
- **Action Name**: Enter a name for this action. Enter `Update Eligible for bonus to true` as the action name.
- **Record Type**: Select the record or records that you need to update. In this case, select **Select the Task record that started your process option.**

- **Criteria for Updating Records**: Optionally, you can specify conditions to filter the records you are updating. Select **No criteria—just update the records!**.
- **Set new field values for the records you update**: Select the field whose value you want to set. In this case, select **Eligible for bonus** field to **True.**

It will look like what is shown in the following screenshot:

6. Once you are done, click on the **Save** button.
7. The final step is to activate it. To activate a process, click on the **Activate** button available on the button bar. Finally, the process will appear, as shown in this screenshot:

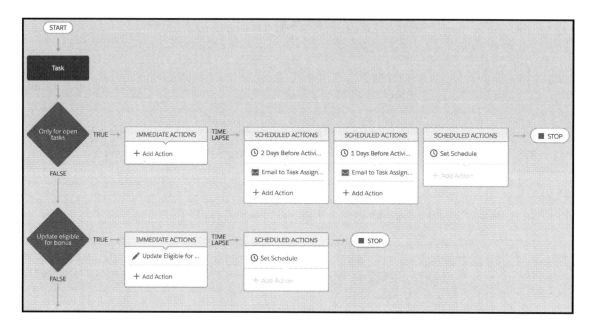

Still, only one criteria node will execute in one transaction because the process works on the if...else statement. This means that only one criteria node can be true in a transaction.

# Reordering the criteria node in Process Builder

Before executing both the criteria in a transaction, first, let's look at how to reorder the criteria nodes. You can reorder the criteria nodes by just dragging and dropping them, but it is not possible to change the order of actions. Drag and drop the first process criteria node, **Only for open tasks**, as shown in the following screenshot:

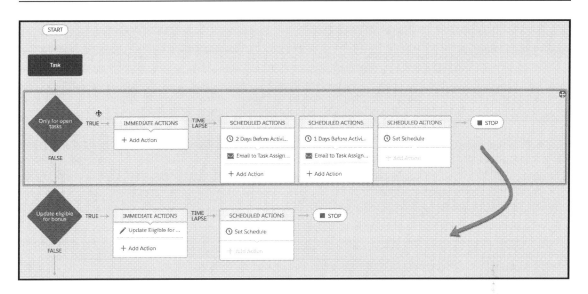

Criteria are evaluated in the order in which they shown on the process canvas. When the criteria are true, the process executes the associated action group and stops evaluating additional criteria. After reordering your process, it should look like what is shown in the following screenshot:

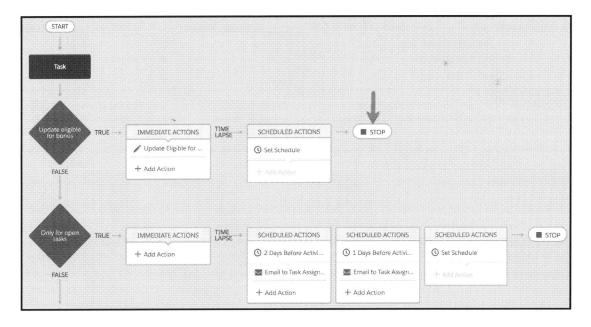

If you want to execute multiple criteria nodes in one transaction, then you have to connect both the criteria. To do that, click on **STOP**, as shown in the preceding screenshot. It will open an additional window on the right-hand side of the process canvas screen, where you will find following options:

- **Stop the process**: You will be able to stop the process after executing the actions. By default, each action group is set to stop after executing actions.
- **Evaluate the next criteria**: Select this if you want to continue evaluating the next defined criteria in the same transaction.

In this case, select **Evaluate the next criteria**, as shown in the following screenshot:

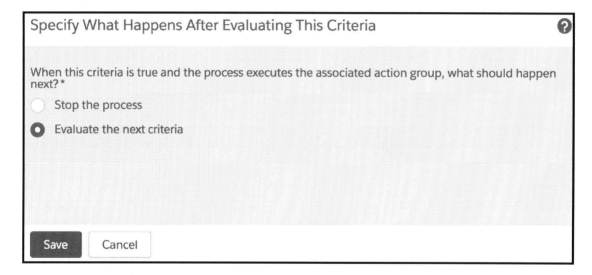

Once you are done, the final step is to activate it. To activate a process, click on the Activate button on the button bar. Finally, the process will appear as shown in this screenshot:

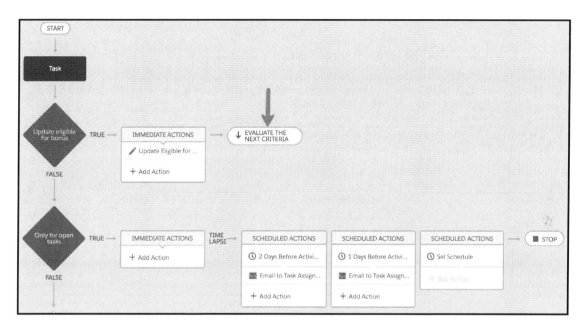

From now on, the process will send reminder e-mails to the assignee 1 and 2 days prior to the task's due date and update **Eligible for bonus** to **True** if a task is successfully closed 5 days before the due date.

# Hands on 9 - creating reusable processes using invocable process

Invocable processes are a way to call one process from another process. Using invocable processes, you can reuse sections of your processes. Create an invocable process, and call it from multiple processes or from multiple action groups in the same process. You can invoke processes with objects that share at least one unique ID.

For example, in the Opportunity and Quote objects, the OpportunityID field is unique to Opportunity and is also used by Quote. You can create an invocable process that updates an Opportunity record. Then, you can invoke it from the following:

- A process that updates an Opportunity record
- A process that updates a Quote record

When you create a process, make sure that you start it when another process invokes it by selecting **It's invoked by another process**.

Let's look at a business scenario. Alice Atwood is working as a system administrator at Universal Containers. She has received a requirement from the management to automate the sales process a bit; that is, if a quote is denied by the customer, then auto-update the opportunity to Closed Lost.

There are numerous ways in which you can solve the preceding business requirement, such as the following:

- Process Builder
- Visual Workflow and Process Builder
- Visual Workflow and inline Visualforce page
- Apex trigger

We will use the invocable process to solve this business requirement. We have to create two processes for this, as follows:

- The first process (**It's invoked by another process**) is placed on the **Opportunity** object to update **Stage** to **Closed Lost**
- Another process (**A record changes**) is placed on the **Quote** object, and it will fire only when quote **status** is updated to **Denied**

The benefit of using this approach is that if you get a requirement in the future to update the opportunities stage to Closed Lost when the account Active field is updated to false, then you call this process from your account process without adding another Record Update on the account process.

Perform the following steps to solve the preceding business requirement:

1. Navigate to **Setup (Gear Icon)** | **Setup** | **PLATFORM TOOLS** | **Process Automation** | **Process Builder**, click on **New Button**, and enter the following details:

   - **Name**: Enter the name of the Process. Enter `Update Opportunity Stage` in **Name**.
   - **API Name**: This will be autopopulated based on the name.
   - **Description**: Write some meaningful text so that other developers or administrators can easily understand why this process has been created.
   - **This process starts when**: Configure the process to start when a record is created or edited. In this case, select **It's invoked by another process**.

2. Once you are done, click on the **Save** button. It will redirect you to the process canvas, which allows you to create or modify the process.
3. After **Define Process Properties**, the next task is to select the object on which you want to create a process and define **Evaluation Criteria**. For this, click on the **Add Object** node. It will open an additional window on the right-hand side of the process canvas screen, where you have to enter the **Object**. Start typing and then select the **Opportunity** object. A window will appear, as shown in the following screenshot:

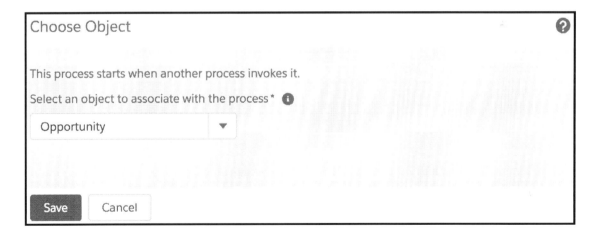

4. Once you are done, click on the **Save** button.

5. After defining the **Evaluation Criteria**, the next step is to add the **Process Criteria**. Once the process criteria are true, only then iwill the process execute the associated actions. To define the process criteria, click on the **Add Criteria** node. It will open an additional window on the right-hand side of the process canvas screen, where you have to enter the following details:

- **Criteria Name**: Enter a name for the criteria node. Enter `Only for open opportunity` in **Criteria Name**.

- **Criteria for Executing Actions**: Select the type of criteria you want to define. You can select **Formula evaluates to true**, **Conditions are met** (a filter to define the process criteria), or **No criteria-just execute the actions!**. In this case, select **Conditions are met.**

- **Set Conditions**: This field lets you specify which combination of the filter conditions must be true for the process to execute the associated actions. In this case, select **[Opportunity].StageName Does not equal Closed Won.**

- **Conditions**: In the conditions section, select **All of the conditions are met (AND)**. This field lets you specify which combination of the filter conditions must be true for the process to execute the associated actions.

It will appear as shown in the following screenshot:

6. Once you are done, click on the Save button.

7. Once you are done with the **Process Criteria** node, the next step is to add an **Immediate Action** to update the opportunity stage to Closed Lost. For this, we will use the **Update Records** action in process. Click on **Add Action** available under **IMMEDIATE ACTIONS**; it will open an additional window on the right-hand side of process canvas screen, where you have to enter the following details:

- **Action Type**: Select the type of action; in this case, select **Update Records**.
- **Action Name**: Enter a name for this action. Enter Stage to Closed Lost as the **Action Name**.

- **Record Type**: Select the record or records that you need to update. Click on the **Record type**, and it will open a window where you have to select **Select the Opportunity record that started your process.**
- **Criteria for Updating Records**: Optionally, you can specify conditions to filter the records you are updating. In this case, select **No criteria—just update the records!**.
- **Set new field values for the records you update**: Select the field whose value you want to set. In this case, set the **Stage** field to **Closed Lost**.

It will look like what is shown in the following screenshot:

8. Once you are done with the process creation, the final step is to activate it. To activate a process, click on the **Activate** button on the button bar. Finally, the process will appear, as shown in this screenshot:

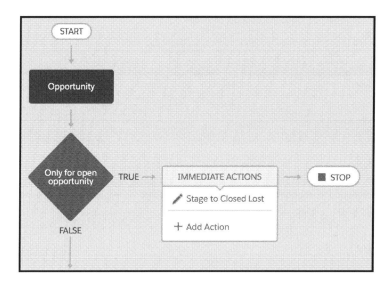

The next step is to create another process (**A record changes**) on the **Quote** object; it will fire only when quote **status** is updated to **Denied** and call the process we have just created.

# Creating a master process to call a invocable process

Perform the following steps to create a master process to call the process we just created:

1. Navigate to **Setup (Gear Icon)** | **Setup** | **PLATFORM TOOLS** | **Process Automation** | **Process Builder**, click on **New Button**, and enter the following details:

- **Name**: Enter the name of the Process. Enter `Master process to call invocable process` in **Name**.
- **API Name**: This will be autopopulated based on the name.
- **Description**: Write some meaningful text so that other developers or administrators can easily understand why this process has been created.

- **This process starts when**: Configure the process to start when a record is created or edited. In this case, select **A record changes.**

2. Once you are done, click on the **Save** button; it will redirect you to the process canvas that allows you to create the Process.
3. After **Define Process Properties,** the next task is to select the object on which you want to create a process and define the **Evaluation Criteria.** For this, click on the **Add Object** node. It will open an additional window on the right-hand side of the process canvas screen, where you have to enter the following details:

- **Object**: Start typing and then select the **Quote** object.
- **Start the process**: For **Start the process,** select **when a record is created or edited**. This means that the process will fire whenever a record gets created or edited.
- **Recursion - Allow process to evaluate a record multiple times in a single transaction?**: Select this checkbox only when you want the process to evaluate the same record up to five times in a single transaction. In this case, leave this box unchecked.

4. Once you are done, click on the **Save** button.
5. After defining the **Evaluation Criteria,** the next step is to add the **Process Criteria.** To define the process criteria, click on the **Add Criteria** node; it will open an additional window on the right-hand side of the process canvas screen, where you have to enter the following details:

- **Criteria Name**: Enter a name for the criteria node. Enter `Only for denied quotes` as the **Criteria Name**.
- **Criteria for Executing Actions**: Select the type of criteria you want to define. You can select either **Formula evaluates to true, Conditions are met** (a filter to define the process criteria), or **No criteria-just execute the actions!**. In this case, select **Conditions are met.**
- **Set Conditions**: This field lets you specify which combination of the filter conditions must be true for the process to execute the associated actions. In this case, select **[Quotes].Status** equals **Denied.**
- **Conditions**: In the conditions section, select **All of the conditions are met (AND)**. This field lets you specify which combination of the filter conditions must be true for the process to execute the associated actions.
- Under **Advanced,** select **Yes** to execute the actions only when specified changes are made.

It will look like what is shown in the following screenshot:

6. Once you are done, click on the **Save** button.
7. The next step is to add an immediate action to update opportunities to Closed Lost. For this, we will use the **Processes** action available in Process. Click on **Add Action** available under **IMMEDIATE ACTIONS**; it will open an additional window on the right-hand side of process canvas screen, where you have to enter the following details:

- **Action Type**: Select the type of action; in this case, select **Processes**.
- **Action Name**: Enter a name for this action. Enter `Launch opportunity invocable process` as the **Action Name**.
- **Process**: Select the process that you want to execute. In this case, select **Update Opportunity Stage**. You can only select active invocable processes.

- **Set Process Variables**: Select your **Process Variable**. In this case, map the `SObject` variable with **Opportunity ID.**

It will look like what is shown in the following screenshot:

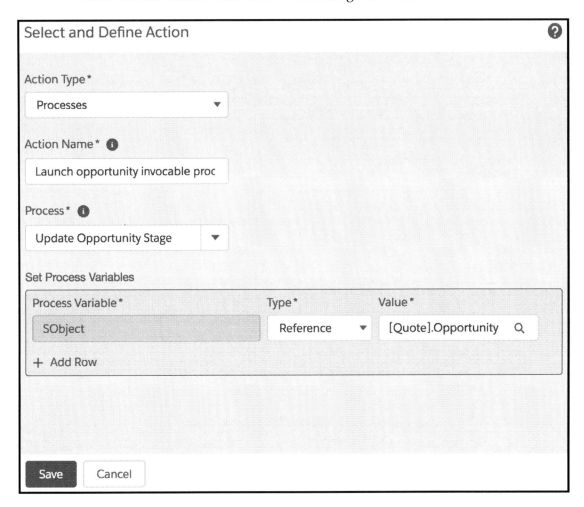

8. Once you are done with the process creation, the final step is to activate it. To activate a process, click on the **Activate** button on the button bar. Finally, the process will appear as shown in this screenshot:

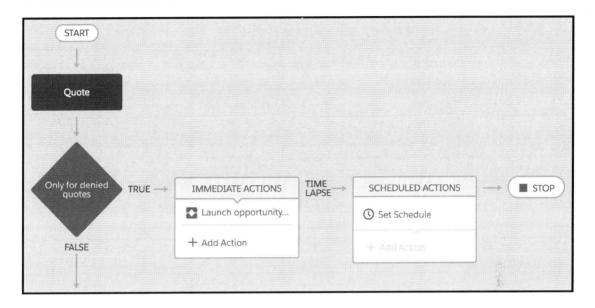

From the next time, when a user updates the quote **status** to Denied, both the processes will fire and update the Opportunity Stage to Closed Lost, as shown in the following screenshot:

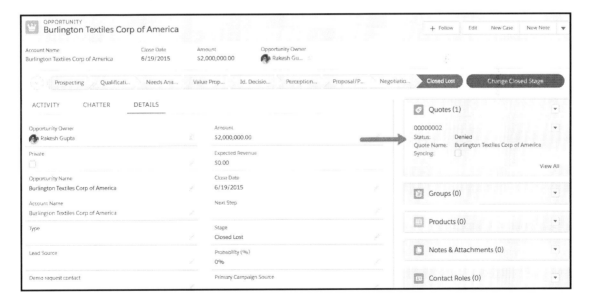

Before testing the process, make sure that you have activated the process.

# A few points to remember

The following are some noteworthy points to remember:

- You can't evaluate the next criteria if a criteria group contains scheduled actions.
- DML operation on a setup object is not permitted after you have updated a non-setup object (or vice versa). If you want to do that, then use time-dependent action. Here, you can find the list of setup objects in Salesforce at `https://devel oper.salesforce.com/docs/atlas.en-us.api_tooling.meta/api_tooling/re ference_objects_setup.htm`.
- Activating this process automatically deactivates any other active version. The deactivated version will be available in your version history.
- Actions are executed in the order in which they appear in Process Builder.
- Only active invocable processes are available to select under action processes.
- Avoid creating an infinite loop when allowing your process to reevaluate records multiple times in a transaction. For example, if your process checks whether an opportunity description changes and then updates an opportunity description and creates a Chatter post every time an opportunity record is created or edited, the process will evaluate and trigger actions resulting in six Chatter posts.
- You can have up to 200 criteria nodes in a process.
- After you deactivate a process, any scheduled actions will still be there in a queue for execution.
- An organization can have up to 30,000 pending schedules and waiting flow interviews at one time.
- If a user deletes the record or the object that the schedule is associated with, the schedule is never processed.
- The formula returns true or false. If the formula returns true, the associated actions will be executed.

# Exercises

1. Create a process that auto-adds new users to the `Sales Best Practices` Chatter group.

First, create a Chatter group called `Sales Best Practices`. Use Quick Actions to complete it.

2. Create a process that will automatically delete open opportunities when an account is **out of business.**

Use the Apex class and invoke it from the process.

3. Modify the previous process in such a way that it will not work for the **System Administrator** and **Supply Chain User** profiles.
4. Create a process that will automatically count related contacts in the account and update the value in a **Number of contacts** field. This process will fire whenever the account is updated by all users except the System Administrator profile.

You may need to use Flow to get the counts of contacts in an account.

5. Create a process that will auto-remove all followers from a case when it is successfully closed.
6. Create a process that will do the following tasks:
    1. Send out an e-mail to the owner 10, 15, and 20 days before the Opportunity close date.
    2. After three reminder e-mails, if the Opportunity is still open, then send an e-mail to the account owner.
    3. Once an opportunity is successfully closed, auto-create the contract from it. Use the following values to create a new contract:
        - **Name**: The same as the account name
        - **Status**: Active
        - **Contrat Start Date**: Today
        - **Contract Term (Months)**: 12
7. Create a process that will do the following tasks:

1. Update the opportunity stage to Closed Lost if the opportunity is still open 30 days after the close date.
2. Remove all members from the opportunity team.
3. Create a case from the lost opportunity to find the cause. Use the following values to create the new contract:
   - **Subject**: The same as the opportunity name
   - **Status**: New
   - **Priority**: High
   - **Case Origin**: Lost opportunity (add one value in the picklist)
   - **Owner**: Assign it to the account owner
8. Once an order is successfully completed, send out an e-mail to the order owner after 10 and 20 days for payment confirmation.
9. Create a process that will send a private message to new users with the Chatter best practices link.

You may need to use Flow to send a Chat message.

10. Automatically create a Chatter group for each campaign as soon as the campaign is activated by a user. Set yourself as the Chatter group owner and the campaign owner as the Chatter group manager. For the Chatter group name, use the campaign name.
11. Create a process that will auto-update account information to **Automation Champion** in an opportunity if the opportunity gets created with no account.

First, create an account with the name Automation Champion. Use the custom label to store the account ID.

12. Once an opportunity is successfully closed, auto-create assets from opportunity products.

Use Flow to create assets from opportunity products.

13. Create a process that will auto-remove users from public groups once a user's account gets deactivated by the system administrator.

Use both Flow and Process Builder to remove users.

14. Once an account is updated to **out of buisness**, update all open opportunities to Closed Lost.

Use the invocable process that you created in the Creating reusable processes using invocable process section.

15. Create a process that auto-converts leads once **Rating** is updated to **Hot**.

# Summary

In this chapter, we went through some advanced concepts of Process Builder, starting with Workbench and audit trail to get more information about Flows and Processes. Then, we moved ahead and discussed how to define an additional condition using record updates. We discussed how you can execute multiple criteria of a process. Finally, we discussed the way through which you can schedule multiple groups of actions and create reusable processes using an invocable process. In the next chapter, we will discuss concepts related to deploying and distributing Flows and Processes. We will also look at concepts such as login flow and subflow.

# 7
# Building Applications without Code

In the previous chapter, we discussed some advanced concepts of Process Builder. We learned how to apply additional conditions when updating records, how to use a custom label, and how to create custom permissions in Process Builder. We also discussed how you can create invocable processes using Process Builder. In this chapter, we will discuss the various ways to distribute Flows and Processes. We will also discuss how you can use a combination of Flow and Process Builder to solve complex business scenarios. The following topics will be covered in this chapter:

- Distributing or deploying Flows and Processes
- Displaying messages after login
- Understanding **Subflow** and the **Wait** element
- Using custom settings in a Flow
- Creating schedule jobs using a Flow

## Distributing or deploying Flows and Processes

Once you are done with Flow or Process development, the next step is to deploy it. There are a couple of ways through which you can deploy or distribute it. They are as follows:

- Change Sets
- Packages

# Deploying using Change Sets

Change Sets allow you to deploy the Flows and Processes to a connected Salesforce organization such as your production environment.

Let's look at a business scenario. Alice Atwood is working as a system administrator at Universal Containers. She has developed a process in a Sandbox (Full Sandbox) and is done with the testing. She wants to migrate the newly created process to the production organization.

For the preceding business scenario, when both the Salesforce organizations are connected like a Full Sandbox and Production, it's a best practice to use Change Sets to deploy the components. In this chapter, we are going to focus on the alternative: using a package.

 You can learn more about deploying Flows or Processes using Change Sets at `https://help.salesforce.com/HTViewHelpDoc?id=changesets.htm&language=en_US`.

Change Sets allow you to add active Flows or Processes to outbound Change Sets. Active Processes and Flows are available under the component type **Flow Definition**.

# Hands on 1 - creating an unmanaged package

Packages give you the flexibility to deploy Flows or Processes in any Salesforce organization, which means that if you have developed a Flow in a free developer organization and want to share it with your colleagues, they can install it in their Salesforce developer organization. In this case, the two Salesforce organizations are not connected.

 To learn more about packages in Salesforce, visit `https://help.salesforce.com/HTViewHelpDoc?id=sharing_apps.htm&language=en_US`.

Let's look at a business scenario. Joe Thompson is working as a system administrator at Universal Containers. He has developed the `Auto create new Contract` process in `Chapter 5`, *Developing Applications with Process Builder*, in his personal developer organization. Now he wants to install this process to his organization's Full Sandbox.

When the organizations are not connected, you can use a package to migrate application, code, or any changes. If a package (**Managed - Released**) contains Apex code, Flows, or Processes, then you can only install the packages into Developer Edition, Lightning Enterprise Edition or higher, if the package doesn't pass the AppExchange security review. If a package that contains Apex code passes the security review, then you can install this type of application in any of the Salesforce Editions, even in Lightning Professional Edition or below. To solve the preceding business requirement, we will create an unmanaged package. Perform the following steps to create a package:

1. In the Lightning Experience, navigate to **Setup (Gear Icon)** | **Setup** | **PLATFORM TOOLS** | **Apps** | **Package Manager**, click on the **Packages** section, and then click on the **New** button.

2. It will redirect you to a new window, where you have to enter **Package Name**, **Language**, **Configure Custom Link**, **Notify on Apex Error**, and **Description**, as shown in the following screenshot:

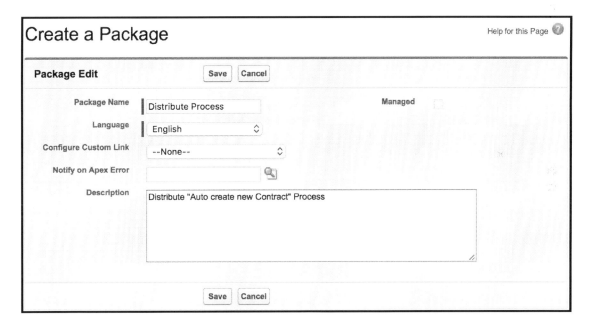

3. Once you are done, click on the **Save** button; it will redirect you to the package detail page.

4. The next task is to add components to the package. To do that, click on the **Components** tab, and then click on the **Add** button, as shown in the following screenshot:

It will redirect you to the **Add To Package** page, from where you can add different components to it.

5. From the **Component Type** dropdown, choose the **Flow Definition** option, and then select the **Auto create new Contract** process, as shown in the following screenshot:

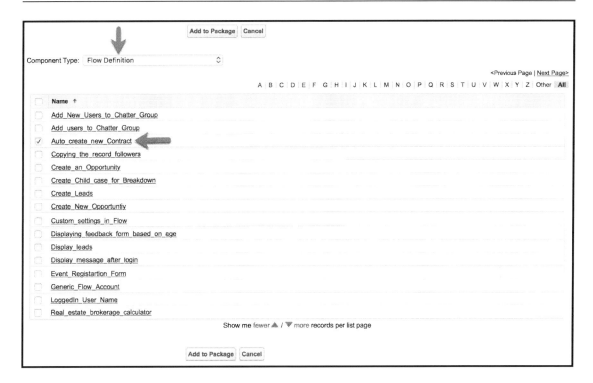

6. Once you are done, click on the **Add To Package** button. It will redirect you to the package detail page. Make sure that you have added all the dependent components that are used in Process Builder.

7. Once you are done, the next step is to upload the package. To do that, click on the **Upload** button; it will redirect you to the **Upload Package** page, where you have to enter the version name as Spring2017, 1.0 for the version number, and the requirements to install a package. Once you are done, click on the **Upload** button.

8. After the successful upload, you will get an e-mail from Salesforce with a link to install the package in any organization, as shown in the following screenshot:

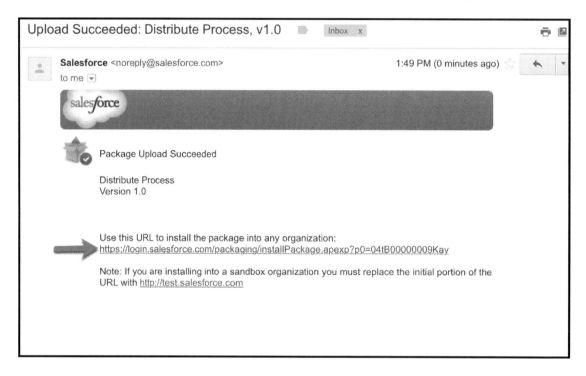

If you're planning to install this package in a developer organization, use the link as it is. To install this package in Sandbox, replace `login` with `test`; it will then look like the following URL:

```
https://test.salesforce.com/packaging/installPackage.apexp?p0=04tB00000009Kay
```

We have created an unmanaged package to distribute the Processes or Flows. Using this URL, anyone will be able to install the package in their organization. You can make it secure by adding a password at the time of package creation.

# Hands on 2 - displaying messages after login

Often, businesses have a requirement to display a message to users after a successful login. With the help of Flow and Login Flow, we can achieve that. Login Flow allows us to provide a custom login experience to users, which means that you can collect data, enhance security, and display custom messages as per your business needs.

Let's look at a business scenario. Helina Jolly is working as a system administrator at Universal Containers. She has received a requirement to display the internal event details to users who have a **Standard User** profile after successful login.

To solve this requirement, we will use Flow to display a message using the **Screen** element and Login Flow to launch the Flow after successful login. Perform the following steps to solve the preceding business requirement:

1. In the Lightning Experience, navigate to **Setup (Gear Icon)** | **Setup** | **PLATFORM TOOLS** | **Process Automation** | **Flows**.
2. Click on the **New Flow** button; it will open the Flow canvas for you.
3. Then, click on the **Palette** tab, and drag and drop the **Screen** element onto the canvas; it will open a **Screen** element window for you.
4. Enter `Display event details` in the **Name** field, and you can also add a description. Under the **Navigation Options** section, select **Don't show Previous button** from the dropdown. Optionally, you can also add **Help Text** to guide your users.

5. The next step is to configure the display message. For this, we will use **Display Text**. Click on the **Add a Field** tab available under the **Screen** element. Double-click on **Display Text** available under the **OUTPUTS** section. In the **Screen** overlays preview pane, click on the **Display Text** field to configure its settings by entering **Unique Name**; for **Display Text**, and enter the message you want to display. It will look like what is shown in the following screenshot:

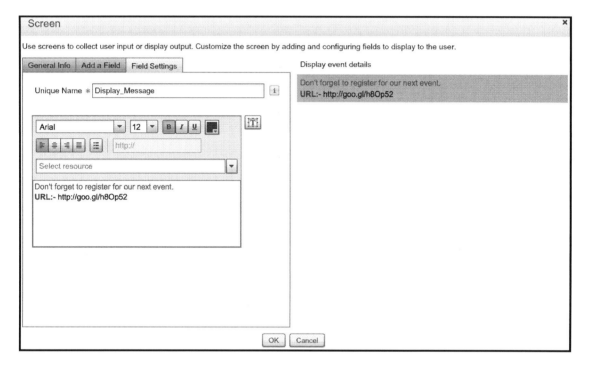

6. Once you are done, click on the **OK** button.
7. Set the **Screen** element **Display event details** as the **Start** element, as shown in the following screenshot:

8. Save the Flow with the name `Display message after login` and **Type** as **Flow** and then click on the **Close** button. It will redirect you to Flow detail page. Don't forget to activate the Flow.

# Connecting a Login Flow to a profile

Login flows allow the system administrator to build post-authentication processes to fulfill their business requirement and then associate the Flow with a user profile and redirect the user to that Flow after successful login. You can use Login Flow to collect information from users, provide a terms-of-service acceptance form, prompt the user for a second-factor authentication, and so on.

We are now done with the Flow development. The next step is to configure a Login Flow so that it will display Flow to users after the successful login attempt:

1. In Lightning Experience, navigate to **Setup (Gear Icon)** | **Setup** | **SETTINGS** | **Identity** | **Login Flows**.
2. Click on the **New** button available under the **Flows for User Interface Logins** section; it will redirect you to Login Flow edit page, where you have to enter the following details:
    * **Name**: Enter the name for the Login Flow. Enter `Display message after login` as the name. It must be within 64 characters.
    * **Flow**: From the dropdown, select the Flow that you want to execute after successful login. It will list all the Flows saved in the Flow Designer. Select the **Display_message_after_login** Flow from the dropdown.
    * **User License**: Select the user license for which you want to implement Login Flow; in this case, select the **Salesforce** license from the dropdown.
    * **Profile**: From the dropdown, select the profile to connect to the Login Flow; in this case, select **Standard User**.

It will look like what is shown in the following screenshot:

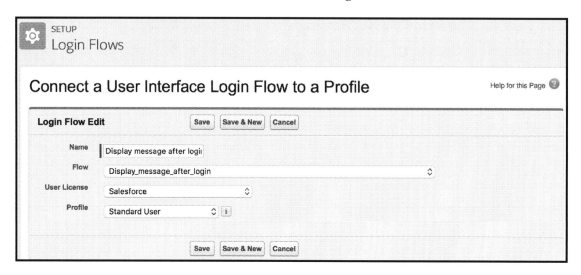

After you connect the Login Flow, you can edit or delete the Flows listed on this login Flows page. You can only connect a Login Flow with one or more profiles. However, a profile cannot be connected to more than one Login Flow.

3. Once you are done, click on the **Save** button.

 If the selected Flow doesn't have an active version, you will get an error. The selected Flow must have an active version after clicking on the Save button.

4. Now, try to log in from a user account to which you have assigned a standard user profile. After successful login, it will look like what is shown in the following screenshot:

5.  Click on the **Finish** button; it will redirect users to their respective landing page.

# Hands on 3 - setting the Login Flow finish behavior

Just as Salesforce allows us to set **finish** or **redirect URL** for the Flow whenever we embed it in a custom button/link or a Visualforce page, likewise, Login Flows allow us to set the finish location and the force logout URL.

Let's look at a business scenario. Helina Jolly is working as a system administrator at Universal Containers and she has created a Login Flow to display the event detail to users after successful login. She has received another requirement to set the finish location. Currently, after clicking on the **Finish** button, it redirects users to their respective landing page, but the business wants to redirect these users to the **Sales Executive** Chatter group, which we created in Chapter 5, *Developing Applications with Process Builder*.

It's very easy to set the finish location and force logout URL. Perform the following steps to set this in motion:

1. First of all, navigate to the `Sales Executive` Chatter group and copy the URL; it will look like the following URL:

   ```
   https://gs0.salesforce.com/_ui/core/chatter/groups/GroupProfileP
   age?g=0F9B0000000CyPe
   ```

2. In the Lightning Experience, navigate to **Setup (Gear Icon)** | **Setup** | **PLATFORM TOOLS** | **Process Automation** | **Flows** and open the `Display message after login` Flow that we just created for the previous use case.

3. To set the finish location, create a **Text** variable, `LoginFlow_FinishLocation`, set **Input/Output Type** as **Input and Output**, and for **Default Value**, use the `Sales Executive` Chatter group's URL, as shown in the following screenshot:

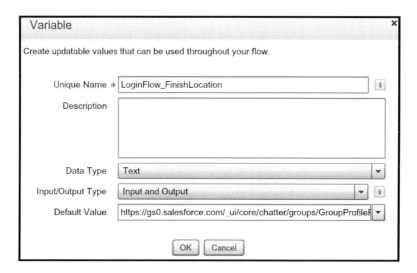

The variable name is very important because this is a "reserved" name, or a "special" variable name, that has built-in functionality. Make sure that you have used the same variable name as the one shown in the preceding screenshot.

4. Once you are done, click on the **OK** button.

5. The next step is to save the changes; as Flow is already activated, save it as **New Version**. Once you are done, close the canvas and activate the latest version.

Now, after clicking on the **Finish** button in Login Flow, it will redirect the users to the `Sales Executive` **Chatter** group.

 For force logout, users create a Boolean variable with the name `LoginFlow_ForceLogout` and set it to true.

You can't redirect your users to a URL that is external to your Salesforce organization.

# Hands on 4 - understanding Subflow and the Wait element

Subflow allows us to embed an existing Flow into another Flow. You can use Subflow input and output assignments to transfer data between the master Flow and the referenced Flow, whereas the **Wait** element can only be used in an auto-launched Flow to create a time-dependent action, for example, to send an e-mail to the Opportunity owner 10 days after the Opportunity close date. To understand Subflow, we have to create a master Flow first.

## Creating a master Flow

Let's look at a business scenario. Sara Bareilles is working as a system administrator at Universal Containers. She wants to use Flow to create an Opportunity and set the Opportunity fields according to the following requirements:

- **Close Date**: Today plus 120 days
- **Opportunity Name**: The same as the account name
- **Account**: Map with the account record that started this Flow
- **Stage**: Prospecting

She wants to launch the Flow using Process Builder whenever an account gets created. Perform the following steps to solve the preceding business requirement:

1. In the Lightning Experience, navigate to **Setup (Gear Icon)** | **Setup** | **PLATFORM TOOLS** | **Process Automation** | **Flows**.
2. Click on the **New Flow** button; it will open the Flow canvas for you.
3. Create three **Text** variables: `VarTAccount_Id`, `VarTAccount_Name`, and `VarTOpp_Id`. Set **Input/Output Type** as **Input and Output**.
4. Then, create a **Formula** resource to generate a dynamic date, that is, 120 days from today, as shown in the following screenshot:

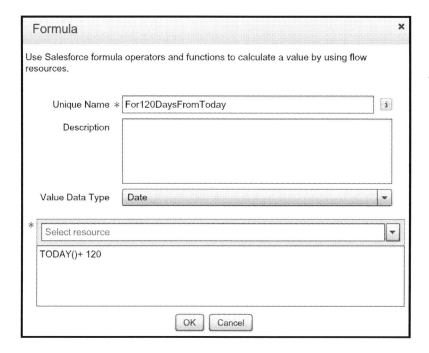

5. Once you are done, click on the **OK** button.
6. Then, click on the **Palette** tab, and drag and drop the **Record Create** element onto the canvas; it will open a window for you, where you have to enter the name `Create new Opportunity`. Map the fields according to the following screenshot and then save the newly created Opportunity ID in the `VarTOpp_Id` variable:

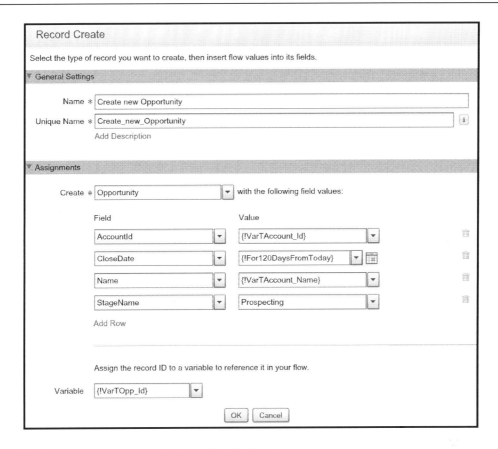

7. Once you are done, click on the **OK** button.

8. Set the **Record Create** element as the start point. Save the Flow with the name `Create new Opportunity` and **Type** as **Autolaunched Flow**, and then click on the **Close** button to close the canvas. Don't forget to activate the Flow.

# Adding a Subflow element to a Flow

Subflow is a way to call an existing Flow from another Flow. In other words, you can say that Subflow is based on reusable component concepts; for example, you can use components in any Visualforce page. The benefits of components are that you only have to create it once and you can use and refer to it in multiple places.

Let's look at a business scenario. Sara Bareilles is working as a system administrator at Universal Containers. She has created a Flow for Opportunity creation in the previous example. She received an additional requirement (keep the previous requirement in your mind; at the end, we will use Process Builder to complete it) to auto-add the new Opportunity to `Sales Executive` Chatter group 1 hour after Opportunity creation.

You can now share records with Chatter groups. There are numerous ways in which you can solve the preceding business requirement, such as the following:

- Process Builder
- Modifying the existing Flow and embedding it into a Visualforce page
- Apex trigger

We will use Subflow and Process Builder to resolve the preceding business scenario. Perform the following steps to solve the preceding business requirement:

1. In the Lightning Experience, navigate to **Setup (Gear Icon)** | **Setup** | **PLATFORM TOOLS** | **Feature Settings** | **Chatter** | **Chatter Settings** and make sure that the **Allow Records in Groups** checkbox is selected, as shown in the following screenshot:

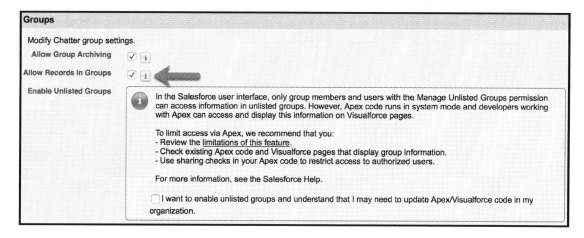

2. Navigate to **Setup (Gear Icon)** | **Setup** | **PLATFORM TOOLS** | **Process Automation** | **Flows**.
3. Click on the **New Flow** button; it will open the Flow canvas for you.
4. Create three **Text** variables: `VarTNew_AccountId`, `VarTNew_AccountName`, and `VarTNew_OppId`, and set **Input/Output Type** to **Input and Output** for all the variables.

5. Click on the **Palette** tab, navigate to the **FLOWS** section, and drag and drop the **Create new Opportunity** Flow onto the canvas; it will open a window, where you have to enter the following details:

- **Name**: Enter the name for the Subflow element. In this case, enter `Create an Opportunity` as the name.
- **Unique Name**: This will be autopopulated based on the name.
- **Description**: Write some meaningful text so that another developer or administrator can easily understand why this Subflow was used.
- **Input/Output Variable Assignments**: Use this section to set values for input and output elements.
  - **Input**: Click on the **Inputs** tab to assign values or elements from the master Flow to the variables in the current or referenced Flow. In this case, we will use the `VarTNew_AccountId` and `VarTNew_AccountName` variables to pass the values in the referenced Flow variables, as shown in the following screenshot:

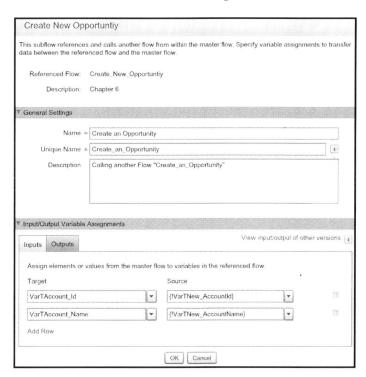

- In the referenced Flow, we have to pass the account ID and the account name to create an Opportunity.

- **Outputs**: Click on the **Outputs** tab to assign variables from the referenced Flow to the variables in the master Flow. Here, we will save the ID of newly the created Opportunity in the `VarTNew_OppId` variable, so you can use it later in the Flow. It will look like what is shown in the following screenshot:

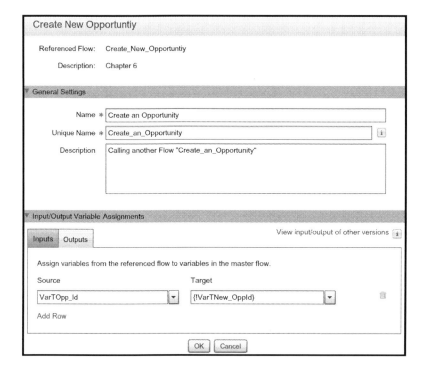

6. Once you are done, click on the **OK** button.

# Hands on 5 - adding a Wait element to a Flow

The next step is to add a **Wait** element into the Flow. The **Wait** element allows you to set the time interval, so before executing the next step, it will wait for a defined time period:

1. Click on the **Palette** tab, then click on the **LOGIC** section, and drag and drop the **Wait** element onto the canvas; it will open a new window, where you have to enter the following details:

   - **Name**: Enter the name for the Subflow element. In this case, enter `Wait for 1 hrs` as the name.
   - **Unique Name**: This will be autopopulated based on the name.
   - **Description**: Write some meaningful text so that another developer or administrator can easily understand why this Wait element was used.
   - **Events**: Click on **Add Event** available on the left-hand side of the overlay to define each additional event that you need. For each event, you have to define the following things:
     - **Name**: Enter the name for the event. In this case, enter `After 1 hrs` as the name.
     - **Unique Name**: This will be autopopulated based on the name.
     - **Event Type**: Select the event type based on which different input parameters are available:
       - **Alarm: Absolute Time**: This waits for a defined time that is based upon an absolute date/time value. For example, send an e-mail to the system administrator 1 day after starting the Flow interview.
       - **Alarm: Relative time**: This waits for a defined time that is based upon a date/time field on a record. For example, send an e-mail to the Opportunity owner 3 days after closing ofthe Opportunity. In this case, select **Alarm: Relative time**.
   - **Event Conditions**: Based on the event type that you have selected, different input parameters are available. Parameters that appear automatically are required. Map **Record ID** with the `VarTNew_OppId` variable. For **Base Date/Time Field**, you can enter the API name of any date/time field on the particular record; for **Object Type**, enter the name or ID of the object that contains **Date/Time** field; for **Offset Unit**, you can only use **Hours** or **Days**, and for **Offset Number**, enter the number to offset the alarm by.

- **Waiting Conditions**: Optionally, it allows you to set the waiting condition. For example, you want your Flow to wait for the event only if additional conditions are met. In this case, leave this box unchecked.
- **Variable Assignments**: Use this to pass the event's outputs to Flow variables. In this case, remove all rows.

Finally, it will look like what is shown in the following screenshot:

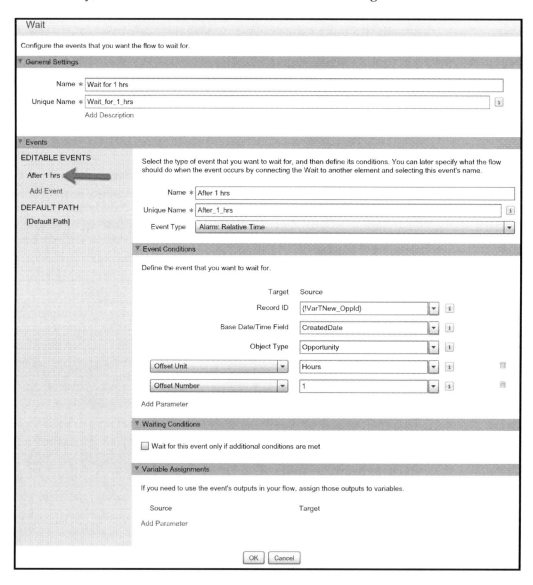

2. Once you are done, click on the **OK** button.
3. The next step is to find the ID for Sales Executive Chatter group. Click on the **Palette** tab and drag and drop the **Record Lookup** element onto the canvas; it will open a new window for you, where you have to enter following details:

    - **Name**: Enter the name for the **Record Lookup** element. In this case, enter `Find Chatter Group Sales Executive Id` as the name.
    - **Unique Name**: This will be autopopulated based on the name.
    - **Description**: Write some meaningful text so that another developer or administrator can easily understand why this **Record Lookup** element was created.
    - **Look up**: Select the object for which you want to search the record. In this case, select the **CollaborationGroup** object. The next task is to define the search criteria; for this example, we will filter by group name = Sales Exec. If you want to add multiple fields to the search criteria, then click on the **Add Row** link to add a new row.
    - **Assign the record's field value to variables**: Optionally, you can save the field's values into variables so you can use it later in the Flow. Let's create a **Text** variable with the name `VarTChatterGroupId` by expanding the **CREATE NEW** section of the drop-down list, setting **Input/Output Type** as **Input and Output**, and mapping it with the record **Id** field.

This will look like what is shown in the following screenshot:

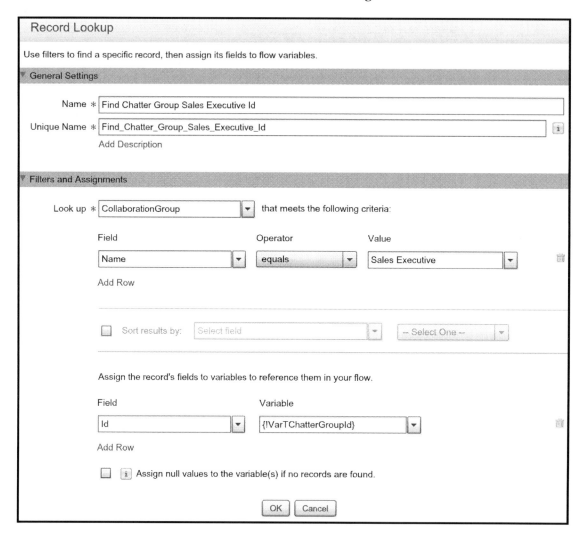

4. Once you are done, click on the **OK** button.
5. The next step is to add a **Record Create** element to auto-add a new Opportunity to the Sales Executive Chatter group. Click on the **Palette** tab and drag and drop the **Record Create** element onto the canvas; it will open a new window for you, where you have to enter following details:
   - **Name**: Enter the name for the **Record Create** element. In this case, enter Add Record to Chatter Group as the name.

- **Unique Name**: This will be autopopulated based on the name.
- **Description**: Write some meaningful text so that another developer or administrator can easily understand why this **Record Create** element was created.
- **Create**: Select the object for which you want to create the record. In this case, select the **CollaborationGroupRecord** object. The next task is to assign the value or resource to the object fields (data types must match). To assign values to multiple fields, click on the **Add Row** link.
- **Variable**: Optionally, you can save the new record's ID into a variable, so you can use it later in the Flow.

It will look like what is shown in the following screenshot:

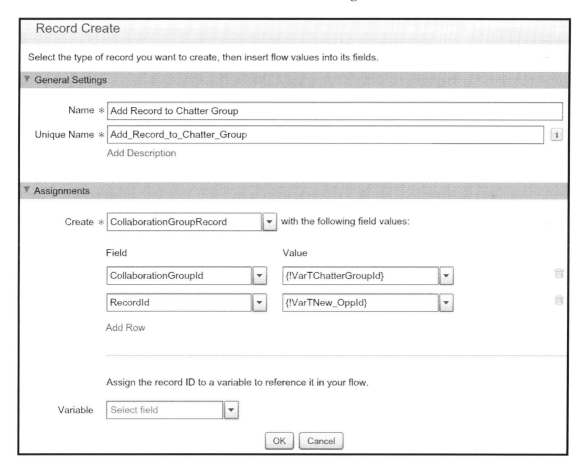

6. Once you are done, click on the **OK** button.

7. Use a connector to connect the **Subflow, Wait, Record Lookup** and **Record Create** elements. Set the referenced Flow **Create an Opportunity** as the **Start** element, as shown in the following screenshot:

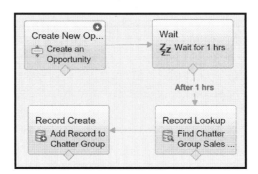

8. Save your Flow with the name Understanding Sub-flow and Wait element, **Type** set as **Autolaunched Flow**, and click on the **Close** button to close the canvas. Don't forget to activate the Flow.

# Launching the Flow from Process Builder

Now we will launch the Flow using Process Builder. Perform the following instructions to call a Flow from a process:

1. In the Lightning Experience, navigate to **Setup (Gear Icon)** | **Setup** | **PLATFORM TOOLS** | **Process Automation** | **Process Builder**, click on the **New** button, and enter the following details:
    - **Name**: Enter the name of the process. Enter Add records to Chatter Group in **Name**.
    - **API Name**: This will be autopopulated based on the name.
    - **Description**: Write some meaningful text so that other developers or administrators can easily understand why this process has been created.

- **This process starts when**: Configure the process to start when a record is created or edited. In this case, select **A record changes.**

2. Once you are done, click on the **Save** button; it will redirect you to the Process canvas that allows you to create the Process.

3. After **Define Process Properties**, the next task is to select the object on which you want to create a process and define the **evaluation criteria**. For this, click on the **Add Object** node. It will open an additional window on the right-hand side of the process canvas screen, where you have to enter the following details:

- **Object**: Start typing and then select the **Account** object.
- **Start the process**: For **Start the process**, select **only when a record is created**. This means that Process will only fire at the time of record creation.
- **Recursion - Allow process to evaluate a record multiple times in a single transaction?**: Select this checkbox only when you want Process to evaluate the same record up to five times in a single transaction. In this case, leave this box unchecked.

It will look like what is shown in the following screenshot:

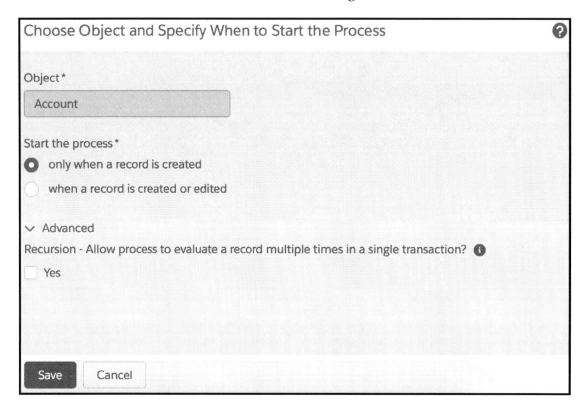

4. Once you are done, click on the **Save** button.
5. After defining the **evaluation criteria**, the next step is to add **process criteria**. Once the process criteria are true, only then will the process execute the associated actions. To define the process criteria, click on the **Add Criteria** node. It will open an additional window on the right-hand side of the process canvas screen, where you have to enter the following details:

     - **Criteria Name**: Enter a name for the criteria node. Enter Always as the criteria name.
     - **Criteria for Executing Actions**: Select the type of criteria you want to define. You can select either **Formula evaluates to true, Conditions are met** (a filter to define the process criteria), or **No criteria-just execute the actions**. In this case, select **No criteria-just execute the actions!**; this means that the Process will fire in every condition.

6. Once you are done, click on the **Save** button.

7. Once you are done with the **process criteria** node, the next step is to add an immediate action to launch a Flow so that it will add Opportunity to the `Sales Executive` Chatter group 1 hour after its creation. For this, we will use the **Flows** action available in Process. Click on **Add Action** under **IMMEDIATE ACTIONS**. This will open an additional window on the right-hand side of the Process canvas screen, where you have to enter the following details:

   - **Action Type**: Select the type of action. In this case, select **Flows**.
   - **Action Name**: Enter a name for this action. Enter `Auto add new Opportunity to Chatter Group` as the action name.
   - **Flow**: Select the Flow that you want to execute; in this case, select the **Understanding Sub-flow and Wait element** Flow.
   - **Set Flow Variables**: Use this to pass the value in your Flow variables. For the current use case, map the `VarTNew_AccountId` variable with `[Account].Id`, and the `VarTNew_AccountName` variable with `[Account].Name`.

It will look like what is shown the following screenshot:

To assign a value to multiple variables, click on the **Add Row** link.

8. The final step is to activate it. To activate a process, click on the **Activate** button on the button bar. Finally, the process will appear as shown in this screenshot:

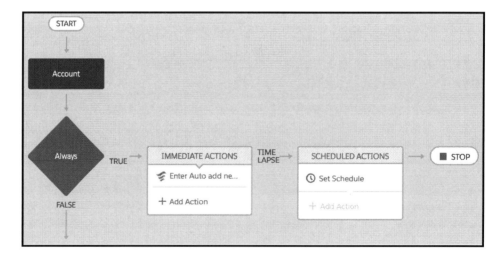

From now on, if an account gets created, Flow will automatically be executed by Process Builder and a new Opportunity will be created, and after 1 hour, it will add an Opportunity record to the `Sales Executive` Chatter group.

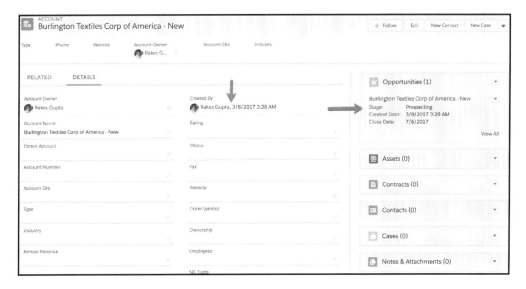

Before testing the process, make sure that you have activated your Process.

# Checking time-dependent actions from Flow

To monitor a time-dependent actions queue for Flow, follow these instructions:

1. Navigate to **Setup (Gear Icon)** | **Setup** | **PLATFORM TOOLS** | **Process Automation** | **Flows**.
2. Go to the **Paused and Waiting Interviews** section, and there you can check out the time-dependent action queue for Process Builder, as shown in the following screenshot:

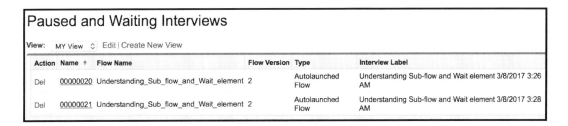

3. To remove a record from the time-based queue, use the **Del** link, as shown in the preceding screenshot.

   Come after 1 hour and navigate to the **Sales Executive** Chatter group and locate the list section related to **Records**. It should now contain the created `Burlington Textiles Corp of America - New` record, as shown in the following screenshot:

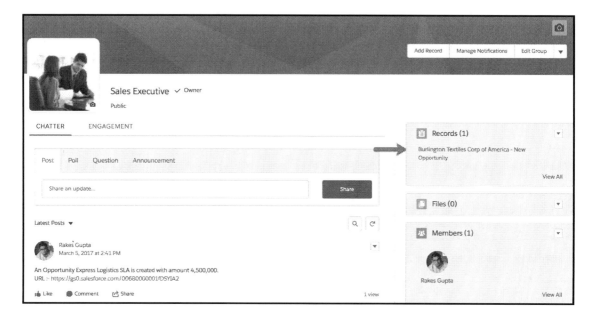

Likewise, you can create another Flow and process to remove a record from a Chatter group once an Opportunity is successfully closed.

# Hands on 6 - using custom metadata types in a Flow

Custom metadata types are similar to custom objects. They allow application developers to create custom sets of data, as well as create and associate custom data with an organization. All custom metadata type data is available in the application cache, which allows efficient access without the cost of repeated queries to the database. It is mainly used to store information that will be frequently accessed from Apex code. It will perform better than a custom object as it doesn't have to be queried. Building a custom metadata types is very similar to building a custom object. The main difference that you will notice is the __**mdt** suffix at the end of the custom metadata type, as opposed to the usual __**c** for custom objects. As of the Summer'17 release, custom metadata is not yet available in Process Builder, but is available in Flow.

Let's look at a business scenario. Helina Jolly is working as a system administrator at Universal Containers. She has received a requirement to auto-create a case whenever a new Chatter post (not a comment) contains a banned word. She also received a list of banned words (almost 50 words) from her manager. If Chatter posts contain numerous banned words, create a single case.

For the preceding business scenario, you can use all 50 words in a Process Builder criteria and use the **Create a Record** action to auto-create a case. But the problem with this approach is that if, after few days, the business wants to add/remove a few banned words, then you have to start from scratch again. Custom metadata provides the flexibility to add/remove banned words without having to change your Process definition or Flow.

To learn more about custom meta, go to `https://developer.salesforce .com/docs/atlas.en-us.api_meta.meta/api_meta/meta_custommetada tatypes.htm`.

To solve the preceding business requirement, we will use custom metadata types to store the banned words, Flow to compare the banned words with the Chatter post body, and Process Builder to launch the Flow. Perform the following steps to solve the preceding business requirement:

1. To create new custom metadata type, navigate to **Setup (Gear Icon)** | **Setup** | **PLATFORM TOOLS** | **Custom Code** | **Custom Metadata Types** and click on the **New Custom Metadata Type** button; it will redirect you to a new window, where you have to enter following details:

   - **Label**: Enter a label for the custom settings. Enter `Chatter Post` as the criteria name.
   - **Plural Label**: Enter a plural label. If you create a tab for the custom metadata type, this name will be used. Enter `Chatter Posts` as the plural name.
   - **Object Name**: Enter the unique object name; it will be used when the custom metadata type is referenced by formula fields, validation rules, Apex, or the SOAP API. This will be autopopulated based on the Label.
   - **Description**: Write some meaningful text so that another developer or administrator can easily understand why this custom metadata type has been created.
   - **Visibility**: For **Visibility**, select **All Apex code and APIs can use the type, and it is visible in Setup**.

2. Once you are done, click on the **Save** button.

3. Create a **Text** field `Banned Word` to store the words that are not allowed in the Chatter post and make this field a required field. At the end, the **Chatter Post** custom metadata type should look like what is shown in the following screenshot:

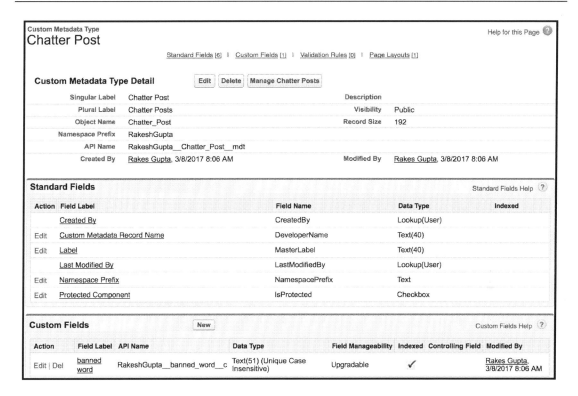

4. The next step is to insert a few records into the custom metadata type. To do that, click on the **Manage Chatter Posts** button on the custom metadata type detail page, and then click on **New** to create some custom setting records, as shown in the following screenshot:

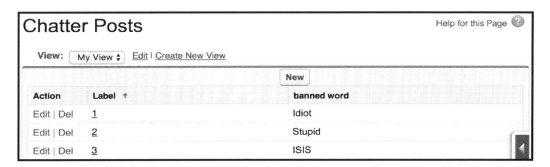

5. The next step is to create a Flow. To do that, navigate to **Setup (Gear Icon)** | **Setup** | **PLATFORM TOOLS** | **Process Automation** | **Flows**. Click on the **New Flow** button; it will open the Flow canvas for you. Create the variables in the Flow, as shown in the following table:

| Name | Variable type | Object type | Input/Output type |
|---|---|---|---|
| VarT_Feedbody | **Text** | Not applicable | **Input and Output** |
| VarT_FeedItemId | **Text** | Not applicable | **Input and Output** |
| SovBannedWord | **SObject variable** | Chatter_Post__mdt | **Input and Output** |
| SOCVBannedWords | **SObject Collection variable** | Chatter_Post__mdt | **Input and Output** |

We will use these variables in the Flow.

6. The next task is to get the Chatter post body. For this, we will use the **Record Lookup** element. Click on the **Palette** tab and drag and drop the **Record Lookup** element onto the canvas; it will open a new window for you, where you have to enter the following details:

- **Name**: Enter the name for the **Record Lookup** element. Enter Get the Feedbody as the name.
- **Unique Name**: This will be autopopulated based on the name.
- **Description**: Write some meaningful text so that another developer or administrator can easily understand why this **Record Lookup** element has been added to the Flow.
- **Look up**: Select the object for which you want to search the record. In this case, select the **FeedItem** object. The next task is to define the search criteria. For this, using **Id** equal VarT_FeedItemId.
- **Assign the record's fields to variables to reference them in your flow**: Optionally, you can save the fields' values into variables, so you can use them later in the Flow. Save **Body** into the VarT_Feedbody variable.

To map the fields, you can use the information in the following screenshot:

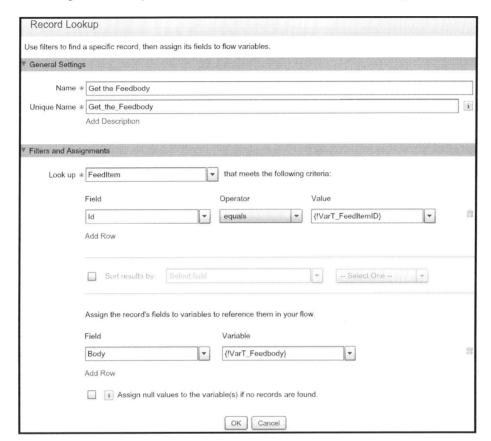

7. Once you are done, click on the **OK** button.

8. The next step is to get all the banned words from custom metadata type. For this, we will use the **Fast Lookup** element. Click on the **Palette** tab and drag and drop the **Fast Lookup** element onto the canvas; it will open a new window for you, where you have to enter the following details:

   - **Name**: Enter the name for the **Fast Lookup** element. In this case, enter `Get all banned words` as the name.

   - **Unique Name**: This will be auto-populated based on the name.

   - **Description**: Enter a meaningful description.

- **Look up**: Select the object for which you want to search the records. In this case, select `Chatter_Post_mdt`. The next task is to define the search criteria; for this, select `banned_word__c` as the field, the **does not equal** operator, and the global constant `{!$GlobalConstant.EmptyString}` as the value.
- **Variable**: Use the SObject Collection variable `SOCVBannedWords`. Don't forget to select the **Assign null to the variable if no records are found** checkbox. Finally, select the fields whose values you want to store in the SObject variable or SObject Collection variable; in this case, select `banned_word__c`.

To map the fields, you can use the information in the following screenshot:

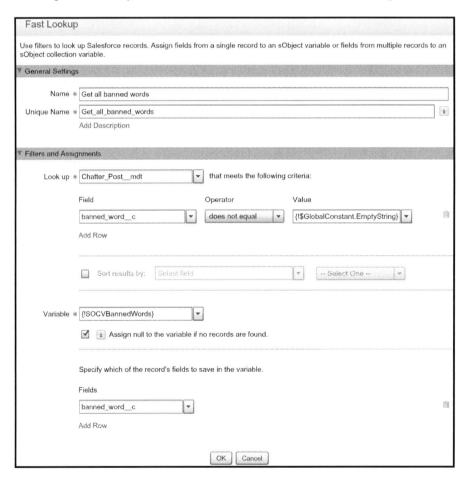

9. Once you are done, click on the **OK** button.
10. The next task is to check whether the SObject Collection variable contains any banned words or not. To check this, we will use the **Decision** element. To do that, drag and drop the **Decision** element onto the Flow canvas. Enter the name Check SObject Collection Variable Size, and **Unique Name** will be auto-populated based on the name. Optionally, you can also add **Description** for the **Decision** element. Then, create two outcomes for the **Decision** element, which are as follows:
    - **Not Exist**: Enter the name Null as **DEFAULT OUTCOME**
    - **Not Null**: Select the SObject Collection variable SOCVBannedWords, the **is null** operator, and the {!$ GlobalConstant.False} global constant as the value.

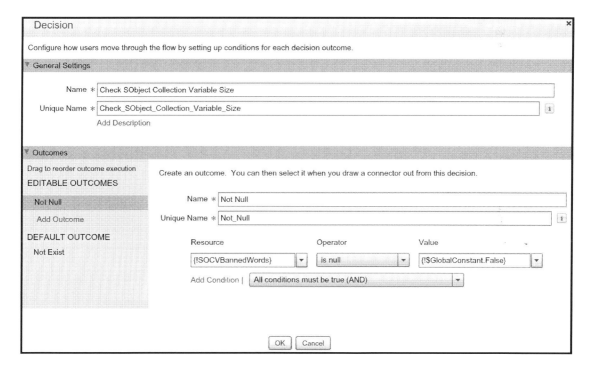

11. Once you are done, click on the **OK** button.

12. If the SObject Collection variable is not null, that means that it contains some banned words. We will use the **Loop** element to extract records from the SObject Collection variable (`SOCVBannedWords`) and store it to the SObject variable (`SovBannedWord`). Click on the **Palette** tab and drag and drop the **Loop** element onto the Flow canvas. It will open a new window for you, where you have to enter the following details:

- **Name**: Enter the name for the **Loop** element. In this case, enter `Loop over collection` as the name.
- **Unique Name**: This will be auto-populated based on the name.
- **Description**: Write some meaningful text so that another developer or administrator can easily understand why this **Loop** element was created.
- **Loop through**: Select the SObject Collection variable `SOCVBannedWords`. Select the order as **Ascending** to loop through the collection.
- **Loop Variable**: Select the SObject variable or variable as **Loop Variable**. In this case, select the SObject variable `SovBannedWord` as the loop variable.

To map the variable, you can use the information in the following screenshot:

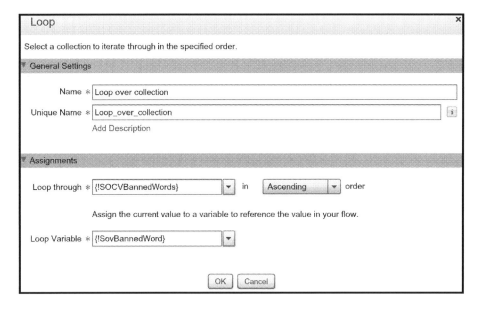

13. Once you are done, click on the **OK** button.

14. The next task is to check whether `VarT_feedbody` contains any banned words or not. To check this, we will use the **Decision** element. To do that, drag and drop the**Decision** element onto the Flow canvas. Enter the name `Lookup for banned words` and **Unique Name** will be auto-populated based on the name. Optionally, you can also add a description for the **Decision** element. Then, create two outcomes for the **Decision** element, which are as follows:
    - **Not Found**: Enter the name `Null` as **DEFAULT OUTCOME**
    - **Found**: Select the variable `VarT_Feedbody`, which contains the operator, and `{!SovBannedWord.banned_word__c}` as the value

15. Once you are done, click on the **OK** button.

16. If the `VarT_Feedbody` variable contains a banned word, then we have to create a new case. Click on the **Palette** tab and drag and drop the **Record Create** element onto the canvas; it will open a new window for you, where you have to enter following details:
    - **Name**: Enter the name for the **Record Create** element. In this case, enter `Create new case` as the name.
    - **Unique Name**: This will be auto-populated based on the name.
    - **Description**: Write some meaningful text so that another developer or administrator can easily understand why this **Record Create** element was created.
    - **Create**: Select the object for which you want to create the record. In this case, select the **Case** object. The next task is to assign the value or resource to the object fields (data types must match). To assign a value to multiple fields, click on the **Add Row** link.
    - **Variable**: Optionally, you can save the new record's ID into a variable, so you can use it later in the Flow.

To map the fields, you can use the information in the following screenshot:

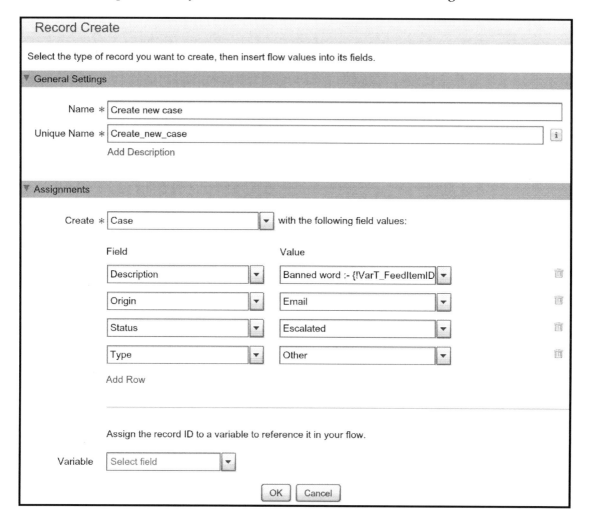

17. Once you are done, click on the **OK** button.
18. Use the connector to connect the elements used in the Flow. Set the **Record Lookup** element and **Get the Feedbody** as the Start element, as shown in the following screenshot:

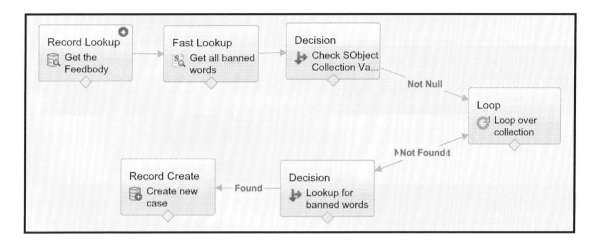

19. Save your Flow with the name `Custom metadata type in Flow`, select **Type** as **Autolaunched Flow**, and click on the **Close** button to close the canvas. Don't forget to activate the Flow.

# Launching the Flow from Process Builder

Now we will create a process to launch the Flow we have just created:

1. To create a process, navigate to **Setup (Gear Icon)** | **Setup** | **PLATFORM TOOLS** | **Process Automation** | **Process Builder** in Lighting Experience, click on the **New** button, and enter the following details:
   - **Name**: Enter the name of the Process. Enter `Custom metadata type in Flow -PB` in **Name**.
   - **API Name**: This will be auto-populated based on the name.
   - **Description**: Write some meaningful text so that other developers or administrators can easily understand why this process has been created.
   - **This process starts when**: Configure the process to start when a record is created or edited. In this case, select **A record changes**.
2. Once you are done, click on the **Save** button; it will redirect you to the Process canvas that allows you to create the Process.

3. After **Define Process Properties**, the next task is to select the object on which you want to create a process and define **evaluation criteria**. For this, click on the **Add Object** node. It will open an additional window on the right-hand side of the process canvas screen, where you have to enter the following details:

- **Object**: Start typing and then select the FeedItem object.
- **Start the process**: For **Start the process**, select **only when a record is created**. This means that Process will only fire at the time of record creation.
- **Recursion - Allow process to evaluate a record multiple times in a single transaction?**: Select this checkbox only when you want Process to evaluate the same record up to five times in a single transaction. In this case, leave this box unchecked.

It will look like what is shown in the following screenshot:

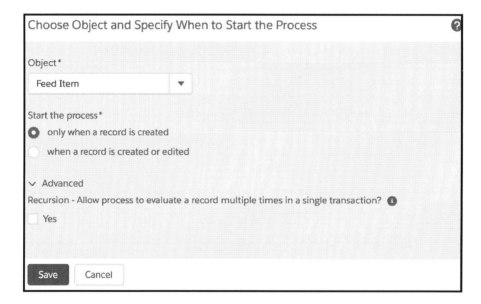

4. Once you are done, click on the **Save** button.
5. After defining the **evaluation criteria**, the next step is to add the **process criteria**. Once the process criteria are true, only then will the process execute the associated actions. To define the process criteria, click on the **Add Criteria** node. It will open an additional window on the right-hand side of the process canvas screen, where you have to enter the following details:

- **Criteria Name**: Enter a name for the criteria node. Enter `Type equals to TextPost` as the criteria name.
- **Criteria for Executing Actions**: Select the type of criteria you want to define. You can select either **Formula evaluates to true**, **Conditions are met** (a filter to define the process criteria), or **No criteria-just execute the actions**. In this case, select **Conditions are met.**
- **Set Conditions**: This field lets you specify which combination of the filter conditions must be true for the process to execute the associated actions. In this case, set **[FeedItem].Type** to **Text Post**.
- **Conditions**: In the conditions section, select **All of the conditions are met (AND)**. This field lets you specify which combination of the filter conditions must be true for the process to execute the associated actions.

It will look like what is shown in the following screenshot:

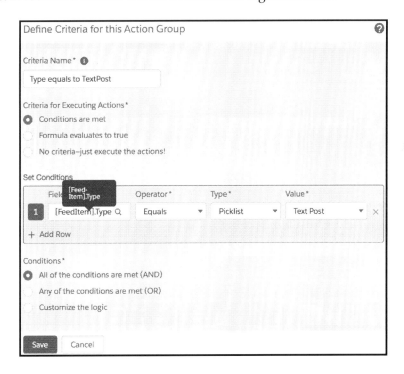

6. Once you are done, click on the **Save** button.

7. Once you are done with the **process criteria** node, the next step is to add an immediate action to launch a Flow so that it will pass the Feeditem ID to the Flow whenever any text post gets created. For this, we will use **Flows** action available in Process. Click on **Add Action** available under **IMMEDIATE ACTIONS**; it will open an additional window on the right-hand side of the Process canvas window, where you have to enter the following details:

- **Action Type**: Select the type of action; in this case, select **Flows**.
- **Action Name**: Enter a name for this action. Enter `Launch a Flow` as the action name.
- **Flow**: Select the Flow that you want to execute; in this case, select the Flow **Custom metadata type in Flow**.
- **Set Flow Variables**: Use this to pass the value in your Flow variables. For the current use case, map the variable `VarT_FeedItemId` with **[FeedItem].Id**.

It will look like what is shown in the following screenshot:

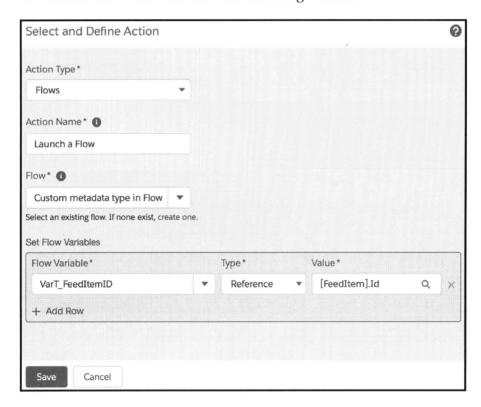

To assign values to multiple variables, click on the **Add Row** link.

8. Once you are done with the process creation, the final step is to activate it. To activate a process, click on the **Activate** button available on the button bar.

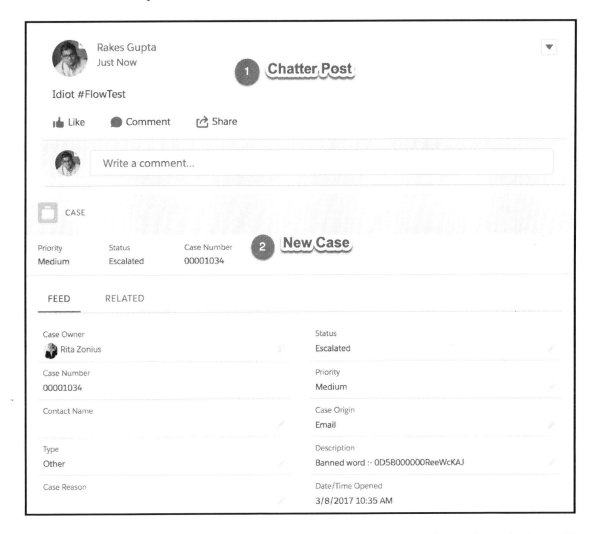

Now, if someone made a post on Chatter and it contains a banned word, Flow will auto-create a case for it, as shown in the preceding screenshot.

# Hands on 7 - creating scheduled jobs using a Flow

Scheduled jobs are automated portions of work that can be performed either at a particular time or on a recurring schedule. For example, a business wants to run a daily job at night to send out an e-mail to Opportunity owners 1 week before the Opportunity close date. You can also solve a few of them using Flow and Process Builder.

Let's look at a business scenario. Sara Bareilles is working as a system administrator at Universal Containers. She has received a requirement to create a scheduled job that will run every night at 11:00 P.M. to add all new users created on that day to the Sales Executive Chatter group. Currently, the administrator has to add new users to the Sales Executive Chatter group manually. Universal Containers grants Salesforce access to their users using the Salesforce license only.

We will use Flow and Process Builder to solve this. The following is the approach that we are going to follow in order to solve the preceding business requirement:

1. Create a custom object to save the scheduled time.
2. Create a Flow that is responsible for adding new users to the Chatter group.
3. Finally, create a Workflow Rule and Process Builder on the custom object to launch the Flow at a specified time.

Take the following steps to solve the preceding business requirement:

1. First of all, create a custom object to store the schedule job time and other information. Set the record name as **Auto Number** data type. Also, create two fields: On/Off and Scheduled Time. Make Schedule Time the required field and grant permission to the respective profiles. For more details, refer to the following screenshot:

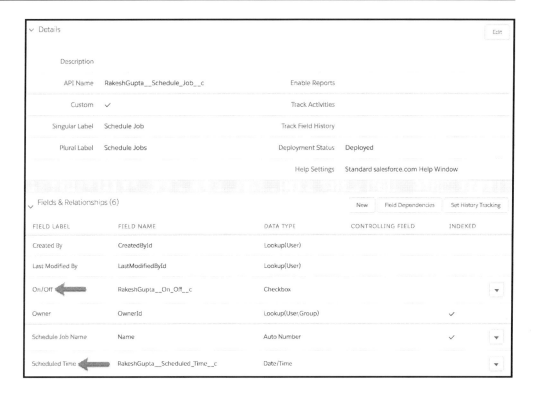

Later on, we will use this object to create schedule jobs.

2. The next step is to create a Flow. Navigate to **Setup (Gear Icon)** | **Setup** | **PLATFORM TOOLS** | **Process Automation** | **Flows** and click on the **New Flow** button; it will open the Flow canvas for you.

3. Create a few variables in the Flow as shown in the following table:

| Name | Variable type | Object type | Input/Output type |
|------|---------------|-------------|-------------------|
| SovUserId | SObject variable | User | Input and Output |
| SOCVUsersId | SObject Collection variable | User | Input and Output |
| SovNewUserId | SObject variable | Collaboration GroupMember | Input and Output |
| SOCVNewUsersId | SObject Collection variable | Collaboration GroupMember | Input and Output |

We will use these variables in the Flow.

4. First of all, we have to find the list of users that were created today. Click on the **Palette** tab and drag and drop the **Fast Lookup** element onto the Flow canvas; it will open a new window for you, where you have to enter following details:
    - **Name**: Enter the name for the **Fast Lookup** element. In this case, enter Users Created Today as the name.
    - **Unique Name**: This will be auto-populated based on the name.
    - **Description**: Enter a meaningful description.
    - **Look up**: Select the object you want to search the records for. In this case, select **User**. The next task is to define the search criteria. For this, selecting **CreatedDate** is greater than or equal to the system variable {!$Flow.CurrentDate} and **IsActive** is equal to the global constant {!$GlobalConstant.True}.

- **Variable**: Use the SObject Collection variable `SOCVUsersId`. Don't forget to select the **Assign null to the variable if no records are found** checkbox. Finally, select the fields whose values you want to store in the SObject Collection variable; in this case, select **Id**.

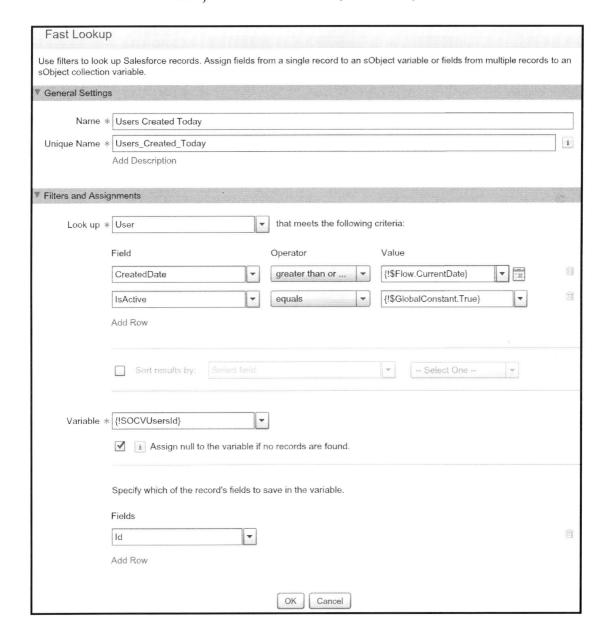

5. Once you are done, click on the **OK** button.
6. The next task is to check whether SObject Collection variables contain any users or not. To check this, we will use the **Decision** element. To do that, drag and drop the **Decision** element onto the Flow canvas. Enter the name Check SObject Collection Variable Size, and **Unique Name** will get auto-populated based on the name. Optionally, you can also add a description for the **Decision** element. Next, create two outcomes for the **Decision** element, which are as follows:
   - **User Found**: Select the SObject Collection variable SOCVUsersId, the **is null** operator, and the {!$ GlobalConstant.False} global constant as the value.
   - **User Not Found**: Enter the name Null as **DEFAULT OUTCOME**.

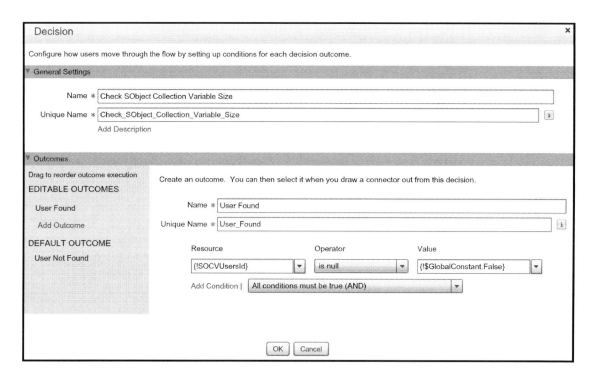

7. Once you are done, click on the **OK** button.

8. If the SObject Collection variable is `False` with the **null** operator, it means that the SObject Collection variable contains a few users. We will use the **Loop** element to extract records from the SObject Collection variable (`SOCVUsersId`) and store it to the SObject variable (`SovUserId`). Click on the **Palette** tab and drag and drop the **Loop** element onto the Flow canvas. It will open a new window for you, where you have to enter following details:

   - **Name**: Enter the name for the **Loop** element. In this case, enter `Loop over collection` as the name.
   - **Unique Name**: This will be auto-populated based on the name.
   - **Description**: Write some meaningful text so that another developer or administrator can easily understand why this **Loop** was created.
   - **Loop through**: Select the SObject Collection variable `SOCVUsersId`. Select the order as **Ascending** to loop through the collection.
   - **Loop Variable**: Select the SObject variable or variable as a **Loop** variable. In this case, select the SObject variable `SovUserId` as the loop variable.

   To map the variable, you can take help from the following screenshot:

9. Once you are done, click on the **OK** button.
10. The next step is to assign a user ID and collaboration group ID (`Sales Executive`) to the SObject variable `SovNewUserId`. Click on the **Palette** tab and drag and drop the **Assignment** element onto the Flow canvas; it will open a new window for you, where you have to enter the following details:

    - **Name**: Enter the name for the **Assignment** element. In this case, enter `Assign Details into SObject Variable` as the name.
    - **Unique Name**: This will be auto-populated based on the name.
    - **Description**: Write some meaningful text so that other developers or administrators can easily understand why this **Assignment** element was added to this Flow.

- **Assignments**: In the **Assignments** section, select **Variable** for the value you want to modify; in this case, set `{!SovNewUserId.CollaborationGroupId}` to `0F9B00000004T9e` (`Sales Executive` Chatter group's ID), and `{!SovNewUserId.MemberId}` to `{!SovUserId.Id}`. It will look like what is shown in the following screenshot:

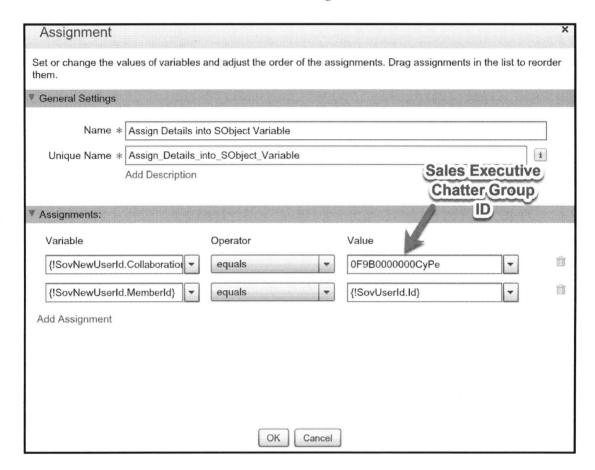

11. Once you are done, click on the **OK** button.

12. The next steps are to add all SObject variables to an SObject Collection variable, so at the end, we will create records in **CollaborationGroupMember**. If you add a record using the SObject variable for each record separately, you will easily hit the governor limit. Drag and drop the **Assignment** element onto the Flow canvas; it will open a new window for you. Enter Add SObject Variable into the SObject Collection as the name and add the SObject variable SovNewUserId to the SObject Collection variable SOCVNewUsersId. It will look like what is shown in the following screenshot:

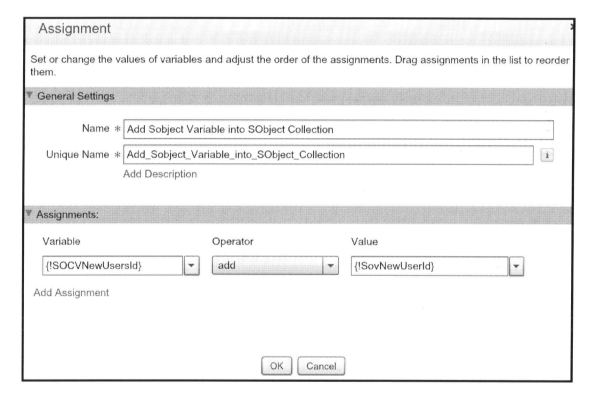

13. Once you are done, click on the **OK** button.

14. The final task is to create records in the **CollaborationGroupMember** object. For this, we will use the **Fast Create** element. Click on the **Palette** tab and drag and drop the **Fast Create** element onto the Flow canvas; it will open a new window for you, where you have to enter the following details:
    - **Name**: Enter the name for the **Fast Create** element. In this case, enter `Add Users to Chatter Group` as the name.
    - **Unique Name**: This will be auto-populated based on the name.
    - **Description**: Write some meaningful text so that other developers or administrators can easily understand why this **Fast Create** element was created.
    - **Variable**: To create a record or multiple records, you can use either the SObject variable or the SObject Collection variable. The object types must match, and each ID field must not have a value. In this case, select the SObject Collection variable `SOCVNewUsersId`.

15. Click on **OK**, and use the connector to connect the **Fast Lookup**, **Decision**, **Assignment**, **Loop**, and **Fast Create** elements. Set the **Fast Lookup** element **Users Created Today** as the **Start** element, as shown in the following screenshot:

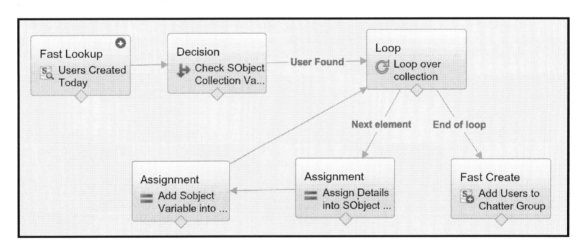

16. Save your Flow with the name `Add New Users to Chatter Group`, **Type** as **Autolaunched Flow** and close the Flow designer using the **Close** button; it will redirect you to Flow detail page. Don't forget to activate the Flow.

# Hands on 8 - creating a recurring job using a time-dependent workflow and Process Builder

Until now, we have created a Flow to add new users (user created date greater than or equal to the Flow runtime date) to the Chatter group `Sales Executive`. To fire the Flow at the same time every day, we have to create a time-dependent action. We will create Workflow Rule and Process Builder on the **Schedule Job** object; we will use this object to create a scheduler:

1. First of all, we will create a time-based workflow to update the field **On/Off** to **True**. Navigate to **Setup (Gear Icon)** | **Setup** | **PLATFORM TOOLS** | **Process Automation** | **Workflow Rules**. Next, click on the **New Rule** button, and enter the following details:
   - **Object**: Create a workflow rule on **Schedule Job**.
   - **Rule Name:** Enter the name `Create Schedule Job`.
   - **Rule Criteria**: For the rule criteria, set **On/Off** to **False.**
   - **Evaluation Criteria**: For evaluation criteria, select **created, and any time it's edited to subsequently meet criteria.**

2. Once you are done, click on the **Save & Next** button.

3. To add a time-dependent action, click on the **Add Time Trigger** button available under the **Time-Dependent Workflow Actions** section, and add 24 hours after the scheduled time, as shown in the following screenshot:

4. Once you are done, click on the **Save** button.

5. Now, add a field update action under the time-based trigger to update the **On/Off** field to **True**. For this, click on the **New Field Update** action available under time-based trigger that we defined in the previous steps and enter the following details:
   - **Name**: Enter the name `On/Off to True`.

- **Unique Name**: This will be auto-populated based on the name.
- **Field to Update**: Select **On/Off**.
- **Re-evaluate Workflow Rules after Field Change**: Don't forget to select this checkbox.
- **Checkbox Options**: Select the **True** option.

6. Once you are done, click on the **Save** button.
7. Once you are done with Workflow Rule, activate it by clicking on the **Activate** button available on Workflow Rule detail page. It should look like what is shown in the following screenshot:

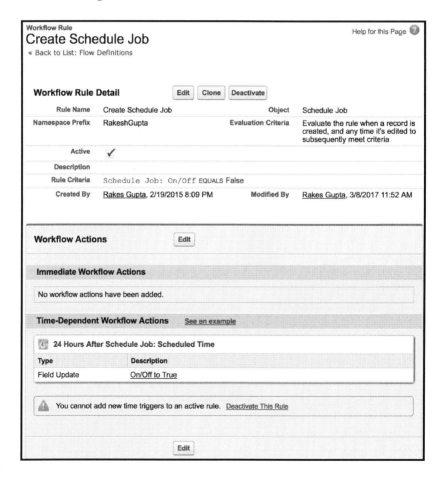

If you want to use Process Builder instead of Workflow Rule, then you have to select **Created** or **Edited** in the first step and then tick only when specified changes are made option in the criteria node. This is similar to Evaluate the rule when a record is created, and any time it's edited to subsequently meet criteria in the Workflow Rule.

8. Now we will create a process to launch the Flow. To create a Process, navigate to **Setup (Gear Icon) | Setup | PLATFORM TOOLS | Process Automation | Process Builder**, click on the **New** button, and enter the following details:
    - **Name**: Enter the name of the Process. Enter `Schedule Jobs` in **Name**.
    - **API Name**: This will be auto-populated based on the name.
    - **Description**: Write some meaningful text so that other developers or administrators can easily understand why this process has been created.
    - **This process starts when**: Configure the process to start when a record is created or edited. In this case, select **A record changes.**

9. Once you are done, click on the **Save** button; it will redirect you to the Process canvas that allows you to create the Process.

10. After **Define Process Properties**, the next task is to select the object on which you want to create a process and define the **evaluation criteria**. For this, click on the **Add Object** node. It will open an additional window on the right-hand side of the process canvas screen, where you have to enter the following details:
    - **Object**: Start typing and then select the **Schedule Job** object.
    - **Start the process**: For **Start the process**, select **when a record is created or edited**. This means that Process will fire every time a record gets created or edited.

- **Recursion - Allow process to evaluate a record multiple times in a single transaction?**: Select this checkbox only when you want Process to evaluate the same record up to five times in a single transaction. It might re-examine the record because a Process, Workflow Rule, or Flow may have updated the record in the same transaction. In this case, leave this box unchecked.

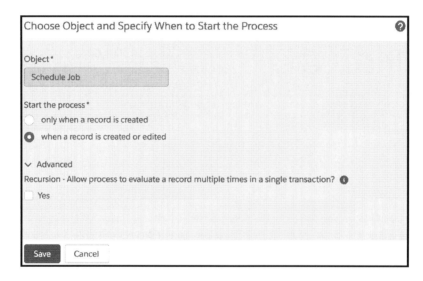

11. Once you are done, click on the **Save** button.

12. After defining the **evaluation criteria**, the next step is to add the **process criteria**. Once the process criteria are true, only then the will Process execute the associated actions. To define the Process criteria, click on the **Add Criteria** node. It will open an additional window on the right-hand side of the process canvas screen, where you have to enter the following details:

    - **Criteria Name**: Enter a name for the criteria node. Enter `On/Off equals To true` as the criteria name.

    - **Criteria for Executing Actions**: Select the type of criteria you want to define. You can select either **Formula evaluates to true**, **Conditions are met** (a filter to define the process criteria), or **No criteria-just execute the actions**. In this case, select **Conditions are met.**

- **Set Conditions**: This field lets you specify which combination of the filter conditions must be true for the process to execute the associated actions. In this case, set **[Scheduled_Job__c].On_Off__c** to **True**.
- **Conditions**: In the conditions section, select **All of the conditions are met (AND)**. This field lets you specify which combination of the filter conditions must be true for the process to execute the associated actions.
- Under **Advanced**, select **No** to executing the actions every time.

It will look like what is shown in the following screenshot:

13. Once you are done, click on the **Save** button.

14. Once you are done with the **process criteria** node, the next step is to add an immediate action to launch a Flow. For this, we will use the **Flows** action available in Process. Click on the **Add Action** available under **IMMEDIATE ACTIONS**; it will open an additional window on the right-hand side of the Process canvas screen, where you have to enter the following details:
    - **Action Type**: Select the type of action; in this case, select **Flows**.
    - **Action Name**: Enter a name for this action. Enter `Launch a Flow` as the action name.
    - **Flow**: Select the Flow that you want to execute; in this case, select the Flow **Add New Users to Chatter Group**.
    - **Set Flow Variables**: Use this to pass the value in your Flow variables. For the current case, we don't have to pass any value to any variables.

15. Once you are done, click on the **Save** button.
16. The next task is to add the **Update Records** action available under Process to update the **On/Off** field to **False**, so it will trigger the time-dependent workflow and queue a job for the next day. Also, update the scheduled time field with the last modified time of the record; it will queue a job after 24 hours from the record's modified date. Click on **Add Action** available under **IMMEDIATE ACTIONS**; it will open an additional window on the right-hand side of the Process canvas screen, where you have to enter the following details:
    - **Action Type**: Select the type of action; in this case, select **Update Records.**

- **Action Name**: Enter a name for this action. Enter `Fields Update` as the action name.
- **Record Type**: Select **Schedule Job record that started your Process**. Then, start typing and select the object; in this case, select `Schedule_Job__c` as the object.
- **Criteria for Updating Records**: Optionally, you can specify conditions to filter the records you are updating. Select **No criteria—just update the records!**.
- **Field**: Map the **On/Off** field to **False** and **Scheduled Time** to **LastModifiedDate.**

It will look like what is shown in the following screenshot:

17. Once you are done, click on the **Save** button.

Finally, your process should look like what is shown in the following screenshot:

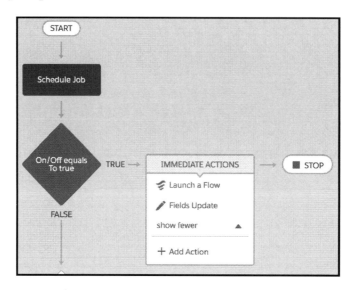

18. Once you are done with process creation, the final step is to activate it. To activate a process, click on the **Activate** button on the button bar.

# Hands on 9 - queuing a job for the next day

Until now, we have created a Flow to add new users to the Sales Executive Chatter group. We have also created time-based Workflow Rule and Process Builder to run the job every day. Finally, we will create a record on the **Schedule Job** object, as shown in the following screenshot:

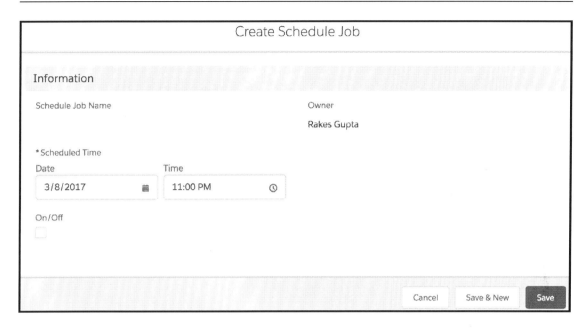

Set the time as 11:00 P.M., as seen in the preceding screenshot. Next, click on the **Save** button; it will fire the time-based workflow as it meets the rule criteria-that is, **On/Off** equals **False**-and queue a job for the next day. To verify this, navigate to **Setup (Gear Icon) | Setup | PLATFORM TOOLS |Environments | Monitoring | Time-Based Workflow** and click on the **Search** button; it will look like what is shown in the following screenshot:

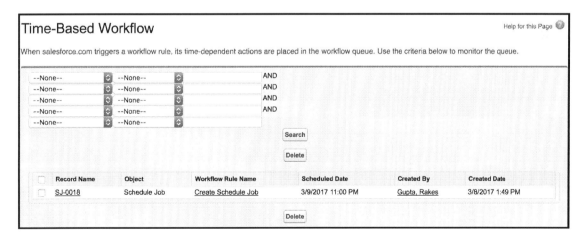

If you focus on **Schedule Date** in the preceding screenshot, it's showing **3/9/2017 11:00 PM** because in the time-dependent Workflow Rule, we have added the criteria after 24 hours of the scheduled date. The next day, the scheduled job will run and update the **On/Off** field to **True**. So, the Process Builder criteria should be met for the process to get executed. Process Builder first runs the Flow to add users to the Chatter group, as shown in the following screenshot:

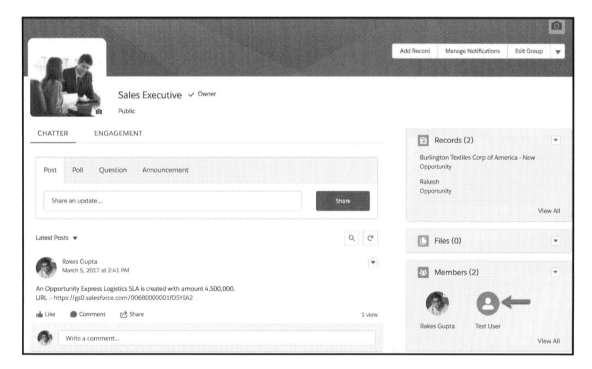

Next, your process will update the **Schedule Time** and **On/Off** fields to **False**. As soon as the **On/Off** field is updated to **False**, Workflow Rule will fire again and queue a job for the next day.

# A few points to remember

The following are some noteworthy points to remember:

- Don't perform the DML operation inside the **Loop** element. It will easily hit the governor limit, that is, **System.LimitException: Too many SOQL queries: 101**.

- You can't refer to a Flow as Subflow if both types are not the same, refer to it as either Flow or Aautolaunched.
- You can only use the **Wait** element in Autolaunched Flow.
- You can only launch Autolaunched Flow from the Process Builder.
- A Flow runs in user mode and Process Builder runs in the system mode. Let's take an example if you are trying to update Opportunity the next step field:
    - **If you use Process Builder**: If the running user doesn't have access to the next step field, Process Builder will be able to update it.
    - **If you use Flow**: If the running user doesn't have access to the next step field, they will get an error.
- If the Flow doesn't have a Start element, you won't get a link to activate the Flow.
- The DML operation on a setup object is not permitted at the same time as when you update a non-setup object (or vice versa). If you want to do that, then use a time-dependent action.
- You can display a maximum of 200 records using dynamic choices.
- The total number of records Flow can retrieve using SOQL queries is 50,000, and only 10,000 will be processed as DML operations.
- Processes on a task or the event-object support e-mail alerts.
- You can have up to 50 versions of a Process, but only one version of a Process can be active.
- When a Screen or Wait element is executed, the existing transaction ends and a new one will begin.

# Exercises

1. Create an application that auto-adds new users to the `Universal Container Employee` public group.

   First, create a public group called `Universal Container Employee`.

2. Create a Login Flow that will display the number of Opportunities successfully closed in the last 60 days by logged-in users and their subtotal (amount).
3. Create a scheduled job that will send an e-mail to all the users who don't have a profile picture on Chatter as well as a blank **About Me** section.

4. Create a scheduled job that will run at 11:30 P.M. every night to perform the following tasks:
   1. Send out an e-mail to all users who haven't logged in to Salesforce in the last 15 days.
   2. After three reminder e-mails, freeze their user account, which means that if there is no login performed in the last 45 days, then freeze those users' accounts.

5. Once an Opportunity is successfully closed, auto-create an order and copy Opportunity products to order products.

6. Create an application that will auto-create a contract three days after account creation.

 To solve the requirement, use the Flow and the **Wait** element.

7. If a post is made by the CEO on their Chatter profile, auto-post the same content to the `Sales Executive` Chatter group; set **Created by** to `CEO`.

8. Whenever a case gets created for a particular asset, auto-assign these types of cases to their respective asset owners.

9. Create scheduled jobs that will run at 11:30 P.M. every night to perform the following tasks:
   1. Delete topics if they contain banned words.
   2. Send out a warning e-mail to the user who created that topic.

 Use custom settings to store a list of banned words.

10. Once a contract is successfully activated, send out an e-mail to all contacts related to the account for which the contract is activated.

# Summary

In this chapter, we went through various concepts to automate your business processes. We started the chapter with the concept of deploying or distributing the Flows or Processes. Then, we moved on to discussing the way in which you can display the message to users after a successful login. We also covered the concepts of the Subflow and Wait elements in the Flow. We also discussed a way to use custom metadata types and custom labels in the Flow and how to create scheduled jobs. In the next chapter, we will discuss concepts related to how you can use your new Lightning skin for Flows and how you can create two-column Flows. We will also discuss the concept of controlling the behavior of a Flow when it tries to set values for inaccessible fields.

# 8
# Enabling Flows to Work with Lightning Experience

In the previous chapter, we discussed some advanced concepts of Flow and Process Builder. We learned how to apply various concepts to automate your business processes. We started the chapter with the concept of deploying or distributing the Flows or Processes. Then, we moved on to discussing the way in which you can display a message to users after a successful login. We also discussed the concepts of Subflow and the Wait element in the Flow. In the end, we discussed a way to use custom metadata types in the Flow and how to create schedule jobs. In this chapter, we will discuss the way in which you can customize the look and feel of the Flow user interface to incorporate with Lightning Experience. We will also discuss how to embed a Flow in Lightning pages. The following topics will be covered in this chapter:

- Enabling Lightning interface for Flows
- Inserting a Flow in Lightning Page
- Displaying Two Column Flow
- Controlling the behavior of Flow when it tries to access inaccessible fields

Until now, we have used classic runtime for Flows. This means that depending on how a Flow is configured for org level, your users see either the Classic runtime or the Lightning runtime user interface when they run the Flow. As the name suggests, Lightning runtime looks and feels like Lightning Experience. In this chapter, we will discuss how quickly you can convert existing classic runtime Flows to display in the Lightning runtime instead. Once you have enabled Lightning runtime for Flows, then you can embed a Flow in Lightning Page--**App pages**, **Home Pages**, and **Record Pages** similar to lighting components. You can even create two column Flows and much more. The Lightning Pages are available in Lightning Experience and the Salesforce1 mobile app.

# Lightning runtime experience for Flows

When you build a Flow that collects information using the screen elements, it can render as a never-ending skinny column of fields. How about creating two-column Flows by breaking up the layout of those screens? In another use case, if you have enabled Lightning Experience in your Salesforce organization and you wish your Flows to look better, similar to Salesforce Lightning Experience instead of showing classic Flow screen, then Lightning runtime can help.

Let's start with an example; Robby Williams is working as a system administrator at Universal Containers. In November 2016, they enabled Lightning Experience for all users. Their users are now comfortable with the new Lightning Experience user interface. At Universal Containers, they are using custom buttons or links to call Flows, and the interface still displays old classic screen for Flows. He has developed the `Real estate commission calculator` Flow, as mentioned in Chapter 2, *Creating Flow through Point and Click*. Now he is looking for a solution so that the Flow looks better, similar to Salesforce Lightning Experience, as shown in the following screenshot:

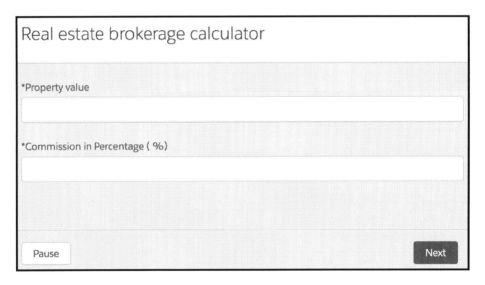

Salesforce offers two flavors of runtime experience for your Flow users. **Classic runtime** looks more like a standard Visualforce page. **Lightning runtime** fits right in with Lightning Experience. It is possible that all of your URL-based Flows render using the Lightning runtime instead of the Classic runtime. To do that, the system administrator has to enable a setting at the organization level.

# Hands on 1 - enabling a Flow in Lightning skin

By enabling the Enable **Lightning Runtime for Flows** setting, all Flows launched from a URL or from Setup use the Lightning runtime experience instead of using the Classic runtime experience. For the most part, the only difference between the two runtime experiences is the look and feel. There are some key points that you may consider while enabling it. They are as follows:

| Flow Distribution Method | Lightning Runtime for Flows is not enabled | Lightning Runtime for Flows is enabled |
| --- | --- | --- |
| **Visualforce page** | Classic runtime | Classic runtime |
| **Custom Button** | Classic runtime | Lightning runtime |
| **Custom Link** | Classic runtime | Lightning runtime |
| **Web link** | Classic runtime | Lightning runtime |
| **Direct Link** | Classic runtime | Lightning runtime |
| **Lightning Page** | Lightning runtime | Lightning runtime |
| **Redirect Method** | It will work as designed | It will work as designed. In Lightning Experience, you can redirect a Flow in a web tab only to a Visualforce page. |
| **List buttons** that are set to display an existing window with or without a sidebar | Will work as per the design | Won't appear in Lightning Experience. |
| **Custom Buttons** that are using JavaScript | Will work as per the design | Won't appear in Lightning Experience. |

\*It might be possible some of them change over the time. For more updated Flow runtime experience, you may need to refer to the Salesforce help article.

Currently, the Lightning runtime doesn't support passing values to **Picklist**, **Multi-select picklist**, **sObject**, and **Collection variables** of data types from outside the Flow.

Let's look at a business scenario. Robby Williams is working as a system administrator at Universal Containers. He has received a requirement from the management to enable **Lightning Runtime for Flows** and open the `Real estate commission calculator` Flow created in `Chapter 2`, *Creating Flow through Point and Click*, from Salesorce1 mobile app access.

Let's break the requirements into two parts:

- Enable Lightning runtime for all Flows.
- Then, create App Page through which we can access Flow on Salesforce1 mobile apps.

Th following is the approach that we are going to follow in order to enable Lightning runtime experience for Flows:

1. Navigate to **Setup (Gear Icon)** | **Setup** | **PLATFORM TOOLS** | **Process Automation** | **Process Automation Settings**.

2. Then, select the **Enable Lightning Runtime for Flows** checkbox, as shown in the following screenshot:

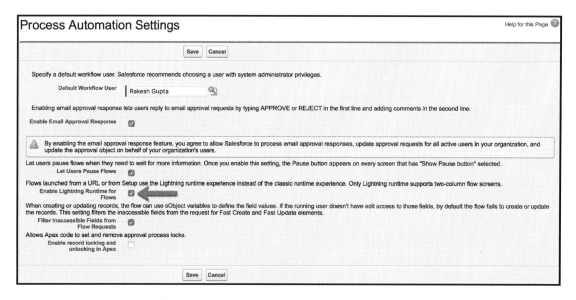

3. Once you are done, click on the **Save** button.

By enabling this setting, you can now control whether a Flow displays in one or two columns if you distribute the Flow via a URL or via a Lightning Page. Now, Flows will use the Lighting runtime experience where applicable, as per the preceding table. Once you have enabled this feature, you will see a new component type in your page, **Flow (Beta)**, as shown in the following screenshot:

If you're not yet familiar with the Lightning Experience, explore Trailhead Lightning modules by visiting the URL `https://trailhead.salesforce.com/en/modules/lex_migr ation_introduction`.

# Hands on 2 - embedding a Flow into a Lightning App Page

The next step is to open a Flow access from the Salesforce1 mobile apps. For this, we will use Lighting App pages. Before going ahead, let's discuss the different types of Lightning Pages that we can create with the Lightning App Builder:

- **App Page**: You can use an app page to create a home page for a third-party app that your users quickly access from the Salesforce1 and Lightning Experience navigation menus.
- **Home Page**: Yes, now it is possible to add your Flows to a home page. You can use Home pages to display with features relevant to specific types of users and assign the customized pages to different user profiles.
- **Record Page**: By using a record page, you can create a customized version of an object's record page, modifying it to your users' needs.

Perform the following steps to create a Lightning App Page and to embed Flow component to it:

1. Navigate to **Setup (Gear Icon)** | **Setup** | **PLATFORM TOOLS** | **User Interface** | **Lightning App Builder** and click on the **New** button.

2. On the next screen, select **App Page** and then click on the **Next** button, as shown in the following screenshot:

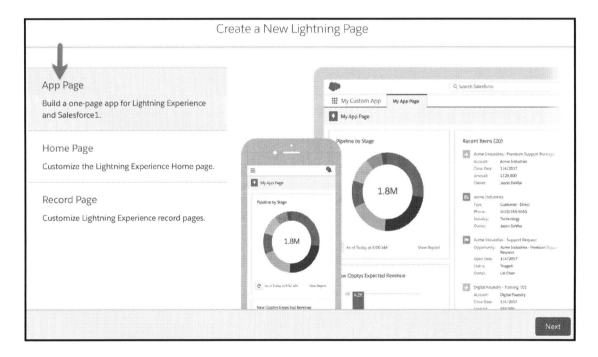

3. The next step is to enter the **Label** to your Lightning App Page for this use `Brokerage Calculator` as the label.

4. Once you are done, click on the **Next** button.

5. The next step is to select the template. Select the **One Column** template, as shown in the following screenshot:

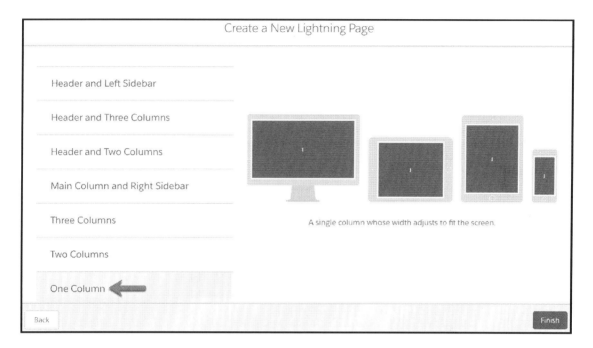

6. Once you are done, click on the **Finish** button.

7.  Now we have to add a few components to the page. In this scenario, drag the
    **Flow (Beta)** component onto the top region. It should look like what is shown in
    the following screenshot:

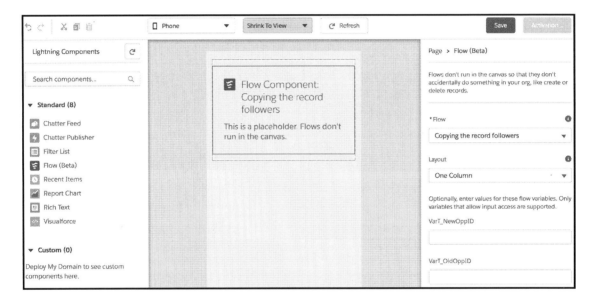

By default, the first active Flow is selected by the component to display. As you
can see, **Copying the record followers** is selected in the preceding screenshot.

8.  To select the **Real estate commission calculator** Flow, we have to change the
    component properties. In the properties pane, select the **Real estate brokerage
    calculator** under **Flow**, and for **Layout**, select **One Column**, as shown in the
    following screenshot:

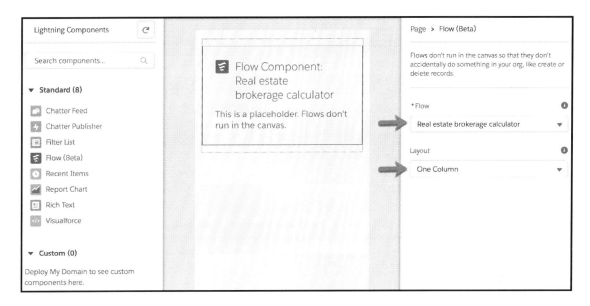

The **Flow (Beta)** component will only display the active Flows of type **Flow** for **Flow (Beta)** component.

> 9. Once you are done, click on the **Save** button and then select the **Not Yet** Button.

## Hands on 3- enabling Lightning App Pages to Salesforce1 and Lightning Experience users

The final step is to activate the page, adjust its visibility, and set its position in the Salesforce1 navigation menu and Lightning Experience app navigation bars. Your users can't access the app page until you activate it. Perform the following steps to activate the Lightning App Page that you have just created:

> 1. Click on the **Activation** button; it is available in the top-right corner of the page.

2. Under **PAGE SETTINGS,** it will allow you to change a few things, as mentioned here:

- The **App Name** will auto-populate from label, which you entered in **step three** of *Hands on two--embedding a Flow into Lightning App Page*. For the current scenario, don't change it. The label that you give the Lightning Page is used as the label for its custom tab.

- The **Icon** will allow you to choose the icon that represents your app in Salesforce1 and Lightning Experience. For the current scenario, select **Castle** as an icon by clicking on the **Change...** link.

- On the **Page Activation** section, when you activate the Lightning App Page, a custom tab (**Lightning Page Tabs**) is created for it. It allows you to manage the tab visibility from the setup. As of now, keep the tab's visibility open to all users, that is, **Activate for all users:**

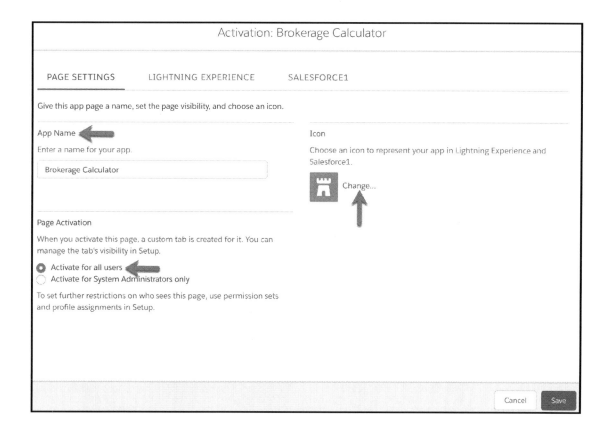

At the end, your page settings should look like what is shown in the preceding screenshot. Wait, don't rush to active the page now; otherwise, your users can't access this page until you add it to Lightning Experience or Salesforce1.

3. The next step is to configure the **LIGHTNING EXPERIENCE** tab. To do that, perform the following instructions:

      1. Click on the **LIGHTNING EXPERIENCE** tab.

      2. Select a Lightning app; for the current scenario, select the **Sales** app, and then click on the A**dd page to app** button, as shown in the following screenshot:

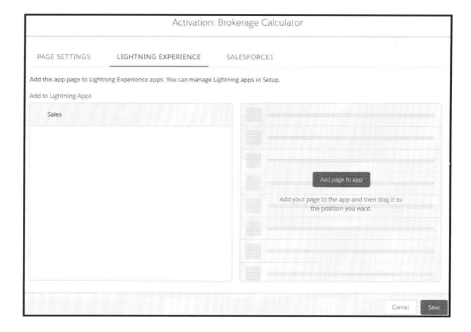

The page you are adding to the Lighting Experience menu bar will appear in the second position by default. If you put it into the top position, it becomes the landing page for all your Lightning Experience users.

4. The final step is to configure the **SALESFORCE1** tab. To do that, perform the following instructions:

    1. Click on the **SALESFORCE1** tab.

    2. For **Salesforce1 Activation**, select the **Salesforce1 Navigation Menu**, and then click on the **Add page to app** button. It should look like what is shown in the following screenshot:

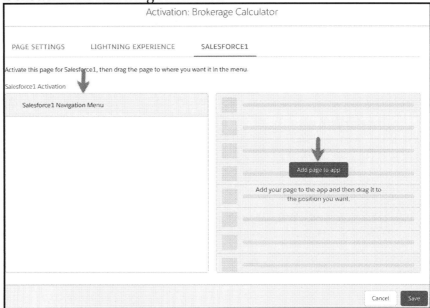

The page you are adding to the Salesforce1 navigation menu will appear below the Smart Search Items menu item. If you leave the **Brokerage Calculator** page there, it will appear in the Apps section of the Salesforce1 menu. Let's leave it there.

5. Once you are done, click on the **Save** button.

Now the **Brokerage Calculator** app page is ready for your Salesforce1 and Lightning Experience users. Your users can access the `Real estate commission calculator` Flow from the Salesforce1 mobile app with the Lightning runtime experience. It should look like what is shown in the following screenshot in the Salesforce1 mobile app:

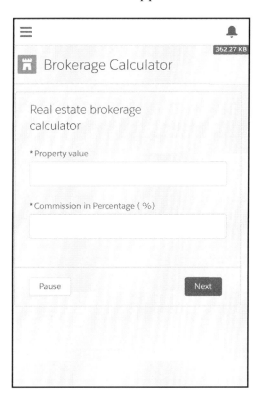

You will also be able to access Brokerage Calculator on Lightning Experience, and it should look like what is shown in the following screenshot:

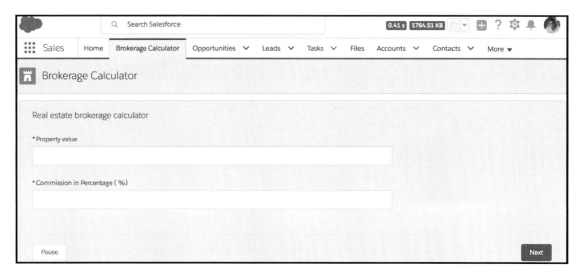

Use App Pages to open up your standalone Flows (Flow that don't require a Record ID to start) access to your users via the Salesforce1 mobile app and Lightning Experience.

# Hands on 4 - embedding a Flow into a Lightning Record Page

Until now, we have learned how to embed Standalone Flows in Lightning App Pages and open them up for Lightning Experience and Salesforce1 mobile app users. But what about the Flows that required Record ID to process user input? For example, suppose you have developed a Flow that allows your users to create an opportunity from an Account and then associate it with the Account from where the Flow gets started. In this scenario, the Flow needs the Account ID. In classic Salesforce, you can use the custom button to pass the Account ID, and you can do the same thing for Lightning Experience too. But the situation is different when you are planning to embed a Flow in Lightning Record Pages, then there is a secret way through which you can pass the origin record ID to your Flow.

Let's look at a business scenario. Helina Jolly is working as a system administrator at Universal Containers. She created the `Create Leads` Flow in `Chapter 3`, *Manipulating Records in Visual Workflow*. Currently, their users are accessing it via a custom button added to the campaign detail page. This is because Universal Containers have already enabled Lightning Experience to their Salesforce organization and also enabled Lightning runtime for Flows. Now they are planning to embed `Create Leads` Flow in Campaign's Lightning Record Page.

Now you can give your users a customized view for each object's records using the Lightning App Builder. Lightning App Builder allows you to add, remove, or reorder components on a Lightning Record Page. The following is the approach that we are going to follow in order to solve the preceding business requirement:

1. Navigate to **Setup (Gear Icon)** | **Setup** | **PLATFORM TOOLS** | **Objects and Fields** | **Object Manager**.

2. To find the **Campaign** object, enter the first few characters of its label or name in the **Find in Page** box.

3. The next step is to click on **Lightning Record Pages** section and click on **New** button, as shown in the following screenshot:

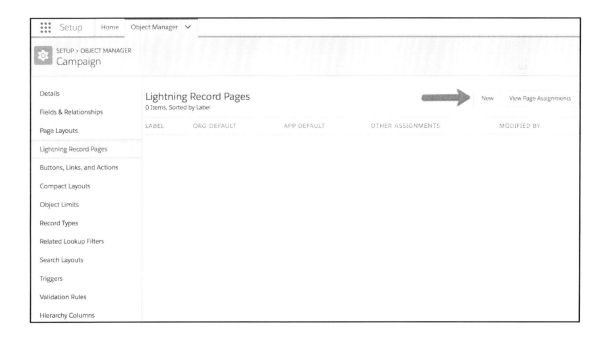

4. It will redirect you to a new page where you have to select the Lightning page type; for the current business scenario, select **Record Page**, as shown in the following screenshot:

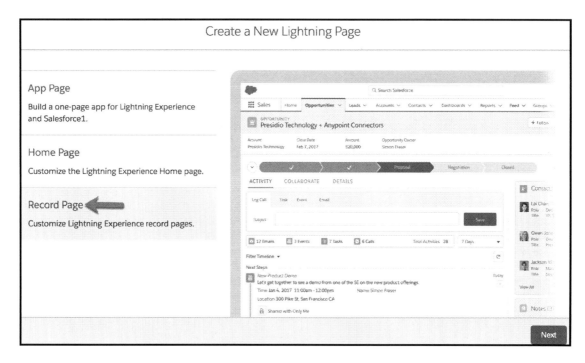

5. Once you are done, click on the **Next** button.

6. The next step is to enter the **Label** to your Lightning Record Page for this use `Campaign with Flows` as the **Label** and **Campaign** as **Object**. It will look like what is shown in the following screenshot:

7. Once you are done, click on the **Next** button.

8. The next step is to select the template; you can select the template that suits your business use case. Select the **Header and Right Sidebar**, as shown in the following screenshot:

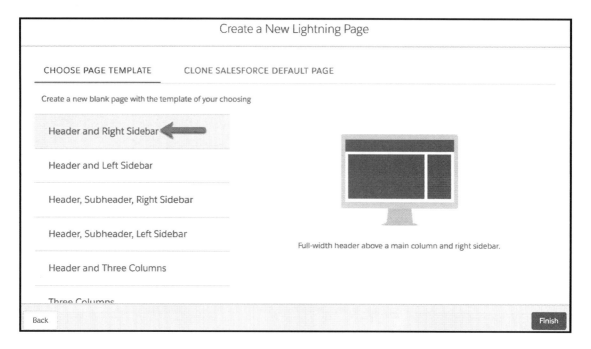

9. Once you are done, click on the **Finish** button.

10. In the Components pane, you see all the standard components available for campaign record pages and any custom components that you've installed in your organization. In the Lightning App Builder, add, edit, or remove components to customize the page's layout. Add these components to your record page:

   1. Drag the **Highlights Panel** component into the top region of the page.

   2. Drag the **Record Detail** component to the lower-right region.

   3. Drag the **Flow (Beta)** component to the lower-left region.

Your record page now looks like what is shown in the following screenshot:

11. Once you are done, click on the **Save** button and then select the **Not Yet** Button.

# Hands on 5 - displaying two columns Flows

If Lightning runtime for Flows is enabled in your Salesforce organization, you can control whether a Flow displays in one column or two columns. Before using this feature, it is important to understand how the Flow layout currently works.

- Currently, it is not possible to control the layout at the screen or field level because the layout setting is applied at the Flow level. If you choose a Flow to use two columns, then every screen in that Flow is displayed in two columns.

- Currently, it is not possible to control which fields go in which columns. If the Flow is set to display two columns, the fields alternate in each column. For example, the odd order fields (first, third, fifth, and so on) are placed in the left-hand side column. The even order fields (second, fourth, sixth, and so on) are placed in the right-hand side column.

- Currently, it is not possible to configure the *Tab* key behavior. This means that if a user navigates screens with the *Tab* key, they will tab through all the fields in the left-hand side column and then all the fields in the right-hand side column.

- Currently, two-column Flow layout is not responsive, so don't enable two columns layout for Flow if users will run it from a phone or small tablet.

Perform the following steps to configure two column Flows:

1. Open the Lightning Record Page **Campaign with Flows** for the campaign object that you have just created.

2. Click on the **Flow (Beta)** component that you have added to the lower-left region. Configure the component, as mentioned here:

   - **Flow**: Select the `Create Leads` Flow. Only active Flows of type Flow are available.

   - **Layout**: Select the **Two Columns** layout. By default, Flows is displayed in one column.

   - **Input Variables**: You may see other properties based on your Flow setup. If a variable is set as an input variable, then you can see those variables here.

   - **Pass record ID into this variable**: This option is available only for Text input variables in Record pages. As per the requirement, we have to pass the Campaign ID to the Flow variable `{!VarTCampaignID}`. To do that, select the **Pass record ID into this variable** for `{!VarTCampaignID}` variable, as shown in the following screenshot:

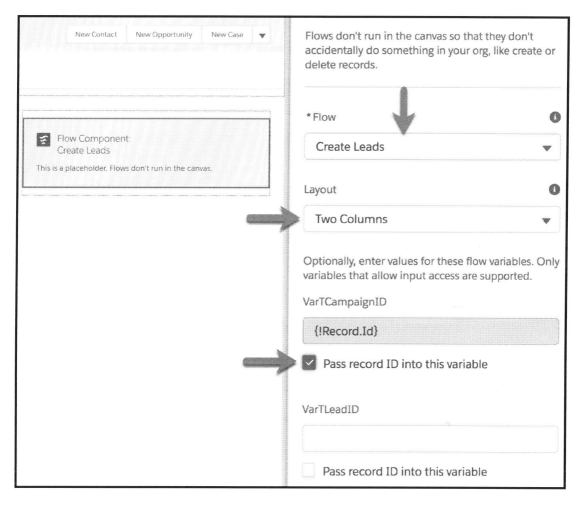

3. Once you are done, click on the **Save** button.

# Enabling custom record page for your Lightning Experience users

The final step is to activate the record page. By activating it, you are are allowing your users to access it. Perform the following steps to activate the Lightning Record Page that you have just created:

1. Click on the **Activation** button; it is available in the top-right corner of the page.

2. Now you have a few options for activating a record page. They are as follows:

- You can make the record page the org default for the object

- You can make the record page the default object record page for specific Lightning Apps

- You can assign the record page to a combination of Lightning Apps, record types, and profiles

For the current business scenario, click on **ORG DEFAULT** and then click on **Assign as Org Default,** as shown in the following screenshot:

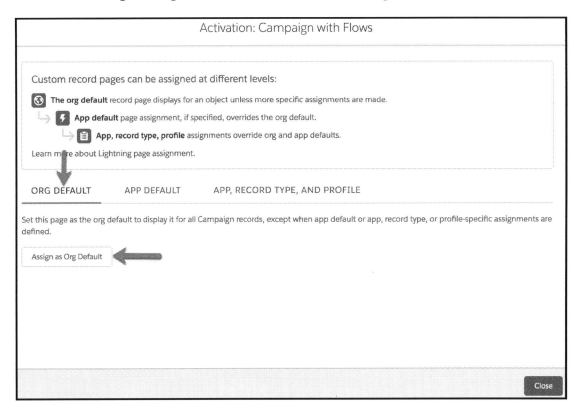

3. Once you are done, click on the **Save** button.

4. To test this, identify a campaign record and go to the campaign details page. Then, try to create a new lead record, as shown in the following screenshot:

5. Click on the **Lead** tab and open the lead you have just created. Lead is auto-associated with a campaign record form where you have created this lead.

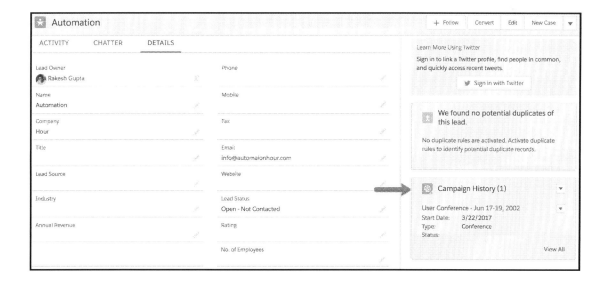

This is another way to access the Flow in Lightning Experience. Remember that in the lightning experience, a redirect URL won't work. Likewise, you can create Lightning Home Page to embed a Flow there.

# Hands on 6 - displaying a two-column Flow through a custom button

When your users are accessing Flows through a URL, it is possible to control whether to show the screens with one column or two columns. Two-column screens are supported only if you have enabled Lightning runtime for Flows.

Let's look at a business scenario. Alice Atwood is working as a system administrator at Universal Containers. She has created `Clone existing Opportunity` Flow in `Chapter 3`, *Manipulating Records in Visual Workflow,* for exercise question six, as shown in the following screenshot:

Currently, they are using a custom button on the opportunity page to access it. The button code should look like what is shown in the following screenshot:

Now she has received a requirement from the Sales users to make it a two-column Flow.

Perform the following steps to make a Flow into two columns when it is accessed via a URL:

1. Navigate to the button code and add the following code at the end of the URL:

```
flowLayout=twoColumn
```

At the end, the new URL should look like what is shown in the following:

```
/flow/RakeshGupta/Clone_existing_Opportunity?VarT_OppName=
{!Opportunity.Name}&flowLayout=twoColumn
```

At the end, the custom button will look like what is shown in the following screenshot:

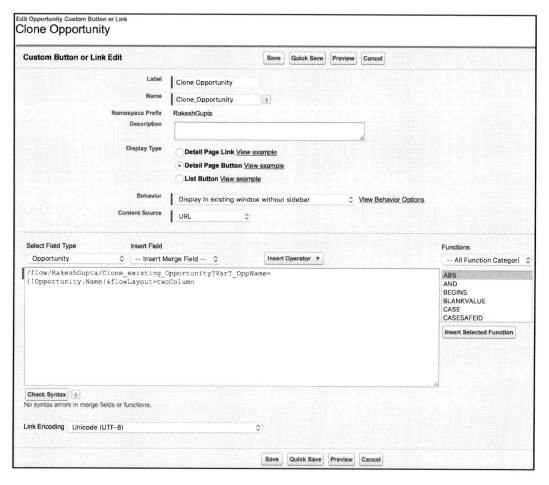

2. Once you are done, click on the **Save** button.

3. To test this, identify an opportunity record and go to the opportunity details page. Then, click on the **Clone Opportunity** button. The Flow screen should look like what is shown in the following screenshot:

Now onward, the preceding Flow will be displayed as a two-column screen to users.

# Hands on 7 - redirect Flows that render in Lightning Runtime

The URL parameter retURL lets you control what happens when a Flow interview finishes. The Lightning runtime also respects the URL parameter retURL.

Let's look at a business scenario. Alice Atwood is very happy now, as she received appreciation from her manager. After a few hours, he receives another requirement, as follows:

- After successful cloning of an opportunity records, business wants to redirect the users to old opportunity record.

# Adding a retURL to custom button

To set the finish location or to redirect a user to a specific page after completing the Flow execution for a custom button/link, navigate to the custom button, **Create Lead**, that we have created in the preceding example and append the `retURL` function to the button URL. For this scenario, append `&retURL={!Opportunity.Id}` at the end of the URL. Finally, the Flow URL will look like this:

```
/flow/RakeshGupta/Clone_existing_Opportunity?VarT_OppName={!Opportunity
.Name}&flowLayout=twoColumn&retURL={!Opportunity.Id}
```

At the end, the custom button will look like what is shown in the following screenshot:

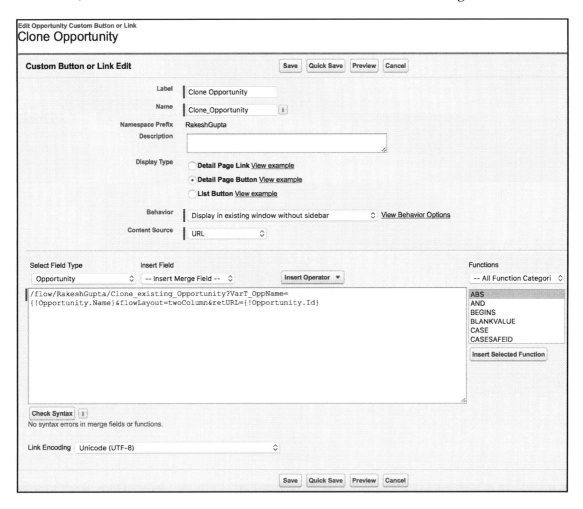

Once you are done, click on the **Save** button. To verify, go the opportunity tab and try to clone an existing opportunity by clicking on the **Clone Opportunity** button. At the end, after entering the data and clicking on the **Next** button, Flow will redirect you to the opportunity detail page, from where you initiated this process.

# A few points to remember

The following are some noteworthy points to remember:

1. When a user opens a Lightning Page that has a Flow component, the Flow also runs on the page load. Make sure that your Flow doesn't perform any DML operations such as creating or deleting records from the first screen.

2. It is not possible to embed an autolaunched Flow into Lightning Pages.

3. Currently, it is not possible to pass the values to input variables **Picklist**, **Multi-select picklist**, **sObject** and **Collection variables.**

4. In the Lightning, runtime Flows Text input variables can accept a maximum length of 4,000 characters.

5. If you delete an sObject variable or sObject collection variable, any variable assignments that use the deleted variable are set to **null**.

6. The Cloud Flow Designer cannot open Flows that are installed from managed packages.

7. When Lightning runtime is enabled for a Salesforce organization, Flows in Salesforce Classic don't load the Web tab and Custom buttons or links that are set to display in an existing window with or without a sidebar.

8. Users can't enter more than 16 digits, including digits before and after a decimal point.

# Exercises

1. Develop a Flow that allows a Sales rep to enter details of a survey about an Opportunity once it is Closed Lost. The fields of the survey are as follows:

   - Customer name (autopopulated from the Account name)
   - Business Lost Reason
   - Please provide more details
   - Name of the competitor who won the opportunity

   Embed this Flow in the Opportunity record page, and a Sales rep can access it only when an opportunity is Closed Lost; else, this message should be displayed: `Survey is not available for Open or Closed Won opportunities.`

2. Create a Flow that allows the Sales reps to raise a case (**Type** = `Admin Bug`, add this value to the type drop-down) with the system administrator so that they can register a Salesforce related bug for further investigation. Use Lightning App Pages to access the Flow in the Salesforce1 mobile app.

3. Create an application that allows your users to record the **Punch In** and **Punch Out** time using the Flow. Read it carefully; I have broken this requirement into multiple parts:

   1. First, create a custom object to store the daily **Punch In/Out** for users, as shown in the following screenshot:

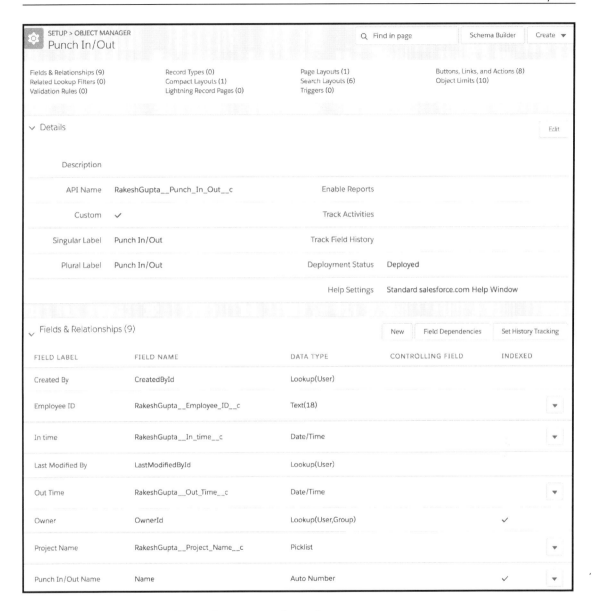

2. For the **Project Name** drop-down, use
   **Apollo**, **Aurora**, **Eagle**, **Excalibur**, and **Firestorm** as values.
3. Now create a screen from where users can select a project but not the
   punch-in time. The **Punch In** time should be auto-populated based on
   the current date/time. Your first screen should look like what is shown
   in the following screenshot:

4. Once users are able to **Punch In**, display the success message as shown in the following screenshot:

5. After a successful **Punch In**, it should display the **Punch Out** screen only, as shown in the following screenshot. Make sure that all the fields are in the read-only mode. Autopopulate the **Punch Out** time based on the current date/time:

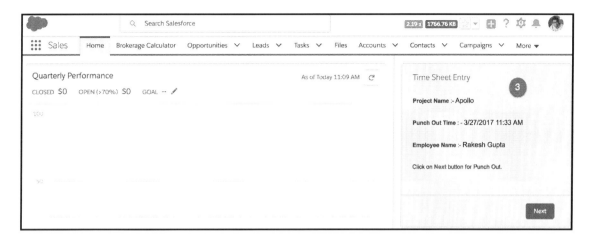

6. Once users are able to **Punch Out**, display the success message as shown in the following screenshot:

7. After a successful **Punch Out**, it should display the generic message for the entire day, as shown in the following screenshot. Make sure that there is no button available on the screen:

8. At the end, the **Punch In/Out** record should look like what is shown in the following screenshot:

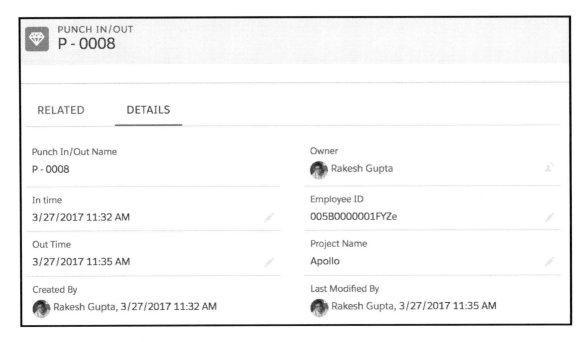

9. Make sure that users are allowed to press **Punch In** and **Punch Out** once in a day.
10. Allows users to access this complete end-to-end application (Flow) from the Salesforce1 mobile app and Lightning Experience.
11. Use the Salesforce automation tool to send a reminder e-mail to users at 11:30 AM if there is no **Punch In/Out** record created for the user on that day.
12. It might be possible that users forget to punch out sometimes. To handle such scenarios use Salesforce Automation tool to make sure that **Punch Out** is set after 4 hrs of **Punch In** time by default. For example, if the punch in time is 10:00 AM, then the default punch out time for such records is 02:00 PM.
13. Create a batch job (but wait, you don't have to write code for this. But if you want, you are free to do that). Send a reminder e-mail to users if their weekly punch in/out time is less than 40 hrs. Refer to Chapter 7, *Building Applications without Code*, to understand how to create schedule jobs using Flow and Process Builder.

14. Sometimes, it might be possible that users forget to punch in for some days. Handling such scenarios allows them to create a case (**Type**: - `Missed Punch In`). The case should capture **In Time** (the date/time field), **Out Time** (date/time field) and **Project Name**. Auto sends this type of case for their manager's approval, and if the case is approved, then auto creates a backdated punch in/out record for that date (it means backdated entry). Also, send an e-mail notification to employees after the punch in/out record creation (only for backdated entries). You might need to create a custom **Backdated_Entry__c checkbox**.

**Assumptions**

- Make sure that only one record is created for punch in/out for a user on a daily basis.

- Make sure that users can't access the punch in/out records on the user interface. It will make sure that they are not manipulating the punch in/out records.

- Make sure that **Employee Id** field is not null while creating the punch in/out record.

If you are able to complete these requirements, then give yourself a pat on the back! You are now a master of Salesforce automation tools. Reach out to me; I would like to see how you have handled the complete end-to-end solution.

# Summary

In this chapter, we went through various concepts to access a Flow in Lightning Experience. We started the chapter with the concept of enabling the Lightning runtime for Flows. Then, we moved on and discussed the way in which you can embed a Flow in Lightning App Pages and Record Pages. We also covered the concepts of enabling two column Flows in the Lightning runtime experience.

After completing this chapter, you will have good knowledge of Salesforce Flow and Process Builder. If you want to explore this further, you may refer to the following blogs:

- `http://www.salesforceweek.ly/`
- `https://automationchampion.com/`
- `http://salesforceyoda.com/`
- `http://jenwlee.wordpress.com`
- `salesforcesidekick.com`

Don't forget to join the official Salesforce Workflow Automation Chatter group in Success Community. You can do that
at `https://success.salesforce.com/_ui/core/chatter/groups/GroupProfilePage?g=0F9`
`300000001rzc&s=workflo&r=1`.

# Index

22641097R00250

Made in the USA
San Bernardino, CA
15 January 2019